D1715431

Metaphysics and Science

MIND ASSOCIATION OCCASIONAL SERIES

This series consists of carefully selected volumes of significant original papers on predefined themes, normally growing out of a conference supported by a Mind Association Major Conference Grant. The Association nominates an editor or editors for each collection, and may cooperate with other bodies in promoting conferences or other scholarly activities in connection with the preparation of particular volumes.

Director, Mind Association: M. Fricker
Publications Officer: M. A. Stewart

FEARS: Misgivings

Metaphysics and Science

IT TRUE /
Nietzsche
NOT REALITY
creation of
Humans

" Man is in error throughout his strife"
Johann Wolfgang von Goethe

" KNOWLEDGE... ACQUIRED under
compulsion obtaining no hold on
the mind. "
— Plato —

EDITED BY
Stephen Mumford
and Matthew Tugby

" Everyone is or more or less mad on one
point. " — Rudyard Kipling —

" I have only one eye
I have a right to be blind sometimes.
— HORATIO NELSON—

" The AGED LOVE what is practical while impetuous
YOUTH LONGS ONLY FOR what is dAZZLING."
— PETRARCH —

" IT is permitted me to take good fortune
where I find it ." — MOLIERE —

" Behold the life At EASE; it drifts,
THE SHARPENED life commands its COURSE."
— GEORGE Meredith —

" What wd life be w/o arithmetic, but
a scene of horrors ?" — Sydney Smith —

OXFORD
UNIVERSITY PRESS

" A trap is only a trap if you do not
know about it. If you know about it, it is
a challenge
— China Mieville—

OXFORD
UNIVERSITY PRESS

Great Clarendon Street, Oxford, OX2 6DP,
United Kingdom

Oxford University Press is a department of the University of Oxford.
It furthers the University's objective of excellence in research, scholarship,
and education by publishing worldwide. Oxford is a registered trade mark of
Oxford University Press in the UK and in certain other countries

First Edition published in 2013

Impression: 1

British Library Cataloguing in Publication Data

Data available

ISBN 978-0-19-967452-7

Printed in Great Britain by
CPI Group (UK) Ltd, Croydon, CR0 4YY

Contents

If you start w/ a tragic view, w/ a "Life is just suffering" then a ... Freeman Dyson

Introduction

Part I. Laws

Part II. Dispositions and Causes

Part III. Natural Kinds

Part IV. Emergence

Notes on Contributors

HELEN BEEBEE is Samuel Hall Professor of Philosophy at the University of Manchester. She has published extensively on topics relating to the metaphysics of science, including *The Semantics and Metaphysics of Natural Kinds* (Routledge, 2010, co-edited with Nigel Sabbarton-Leary) and *The Oxford Handbook of Causation* (Oxford University Press, 2009, co-edited with Christopher Hitchcock and Peter Menzies), as well as articles in journals such as *The Journal of Philosophy*, *Philosophy and Phenomenological Research*, *Analysis*, and *Nous*.

ANDREAS HÜTTEMANN is Professor of Philosophy at the University of Cologne. He is author of *What's Wrong with Microphysicalism?* (Routledge, 2004) and co-editor (with Gerhard Ernst) of *Time, Chance and Reduction* (Cambridge University Press, 2010). His current research interest is the philosophy of causation and reduction.

MARC LANGE is the Theda Perdue Distinguished Professor of Philosophy and Chair of the Philosophy Department at the University of North Carolina at Chapel Hill. His books include *Laws and Lawmakers: Science, Metaphysics, and the Laws of Nature* (Oxford University Press, 2009) and *An Introduction to the Philosophy of Physics: Locality, Fields, Energy and Mass* (Blackwell, 2002).

JENNIFER MCKITRICK is an Associate Professor of Philosophy at the University of Nebraska–Lincoln. She specializes in metaphysics. She is the author of several papers on dispositions, including 'The Bare Metaphysical Possibility of Bare Dispositions' (*Philosophy and Phenomenological Research*, 2003) and 'A Case for Extrinsic Dispositions' (*Australasian Journal of Philosophy*, 2003). She is currently working on a book on dispositions.

STEPHEN MUMFORD is Professor of Metaphysics in the Department of Philosophy at the University of Nottingham, UK, and Professor II at the Norwegian University of Life Science (UMB). He is the author of *Dispositions* (Oxford University Press, 1998), *Russell on Metaphysics* (Routledge, 2003), *Laws in Nature* (Routledge, 2004), *David Armstrong* (Acumen, 2007), *Watching Sport: Aesthetics, Ethics and Emotions* (Routledge, 2011), *Getting Causes from Powers* (Oxford University Press, 2011 with Rani Lill Anjum) and *Metaphysics: a very Short Introduction* (OUP, 2012). He was editor of George Molnar's posthumous *Powers: a Study in Metaphysics* (Oxford University Press, 2003).

L. A. PAUL is Professor of Philosophy at the University of North Carolina at Chapel Hill. Her main areas of interest are in metaphysics, with special attention paid to causation, time, mereology, properties, and ontological categories, and in philosophy of mind, with special attention paid to temporal experience and the nature of subjectivity. Her book, *Causation: A User's Guide*, co-authored with Ned Hall, will be published by Oxford University Press in 2013.

JOHN T. ROBERTS is Professor of Philosophy at the University of North Carolina at Chapel Hill. He is the author of *The Law-Governed Universe* (Oxford University Press, 2008) and many articles concerning laws of nature, chance, and related topics.

EMMA TOBIN is lecturer in the Philosophy of Science at University College London. Previously, she was a core researcher on the AHRC Metaphysics of Science project based at the University of Bristol. She is the author of a number of papers on topics in the philosophy of science, primarily on natural kinds and laws of nature.

MATTHEW TUGBY is Teaching Fellow in Philosophy at the University of Birmingham. Previously, he was a core researcher on the AHRC Metaphysics of Science project based at the University of Nottingham. He has published on the topic of dispositions and is interested in a range of topics at the intersection of metaphysics and the philosophy of science.

JESSICA WILSON is Associate Professor of Philosophy at the University of Toronto. Her primary research interests are in general metaphysics (especially modality and indeterminacy) and the metaphysics of science (especially inter-theoretic relations). Recent publications include 'What is Hume's Dictum, and Why Believe It?' (*Philosophy and Phenomenological Research*, 2010) and 'Fundamental Determinables' (*Philosopher's Imprint*, 2011). She is working on a book titled *Metaphysical Emergence*.

JIM WOODWARD is Distinguished Professor in the Department of History and Philosophy of Science at the University of Pittsburgh. From 1983 to 2010 he taught at the California Institute of Technology, where he was the J. O. and Juliette Koepfli Professor of Humanities. He was the President of the Philosophy of Science Association (2010–2012) and the author of *Making Things Happen: A Theory of Causal Explanation*, which won the 2005 Lakatos award.

Acknowledgements

The origin of these papers is to be found in the AHRC-funded Metaphysics of Science project and its final international conference hosted at the University of Nottingham.

The editors would like to thank Eleanor Collins of Oxford University Press and Professor M. A. Stewart, editor of the Mind Association Occasional Series, for support and advice in the compilation of this volume. We would like to thank all our authors and referees for their helpful assistance.

Introduction

1

What is the metaphysics of science?

Stephen Mumford and Matthew Tugby

1 The emergence of modern metaphysics of science

The label 'metaphysics of science' is one that has come to be used for a philosophical sub-discipline that has been gaining momentum for roughly forty years. The emergence of this sub-discipline has been made possible by the (perhaps partial) recovery of metaphysics from the blow dealt to it by the Neo-Humean empiricist movements of the first half of the 20th century. Without this recovery, not only would the metaphysics of science be non-existent as a discipline, the term 'metaphysics of science' would come close to being an oxymoron. The reason for this is that according to the aforementioned empiricist views (for example, Carnap 1935, Ayer 1936, and Schlick 1938), metaphysical statements have little meaning because, unlike the statements of natural science, they are typically neither analytic nor suitably a posteriori. On this view, the metaphysics of science becomes a discipline in which philosophers ultimately say meaningless things about natural science, which is itself characterized (in part) by the fact that it is meaningful above all other disciplines. Clearly, this would make the metaphysics of science pointless in a way that is ironic.

Fortunately, many of the concepts and debates which were cast into the bonfire by these radical empiricist movements have regained currency, and even if there is much disagreement between metaphysicians of science on the issues they debate, there is at least an assumption that philosophers can have meaningful debates about such issues. The main aim of this chapter is to try to identify in general terms what those issues are. More precisely, we will address the following two questions, among others. First, what do the various debates falling within the metaphysics of science have in common, if anything? Second, what distinguishes a question within the metaphysics of science from questions in other areas of metaphysics?

Answering the above questions is no easy task, but as a way of beginning to illustrate the sorts of debates that take place within the metaphysics of science, let us say a little about the debate on whether science supports the view that there are necessities in nature. This is an appropriate starting point for two reasons. First, the concept of necessity in nature is the kind of metaphysical concept that the Neo-Humean empiricists were arguably sceptical of above all others. Second, the point at which philosophers began to take a renewed interest in the debate concerning necessity in nature arguably marked the point at which the modern discipline of metaphysics of science began.

The main reason empiricists had been so hostile towards metaphysical concepts, such as that of natural necessity, is that these concepts were not thought to be sufficiently grounded in experience. If a concept is not grounded in some aspect of experience, then it was thought to be rendered utterly mysterious and insignificant. If notions of natural necessity have any meaning at all, the Humean empiricists say, this is only because we have an internal (observable) feeling of inevitability which attends our observations of the regularities in the world. But such a feeling, existing as it does in the mind, is not what the notion of natural necessity was initially intended to capture.

Now, one way of questioning these empiricist conclusions is to question the strict separation between metaphysical a priori statements on the one hand, and scientific a posteriori statements on the other. If one can successfully argue there to be a more subtle and complex relationship between metaphysical and scientific statements, one which allows there to be an interplay between the two, then perhaps the empiricists' anti-metaphysical conclusions can be avoided. In the 1970s, these kinds of arguments did indeed start to emerge. At this time, there was a general feeling that science itself might support certain metaphysical claims, and in the other direction it was thought that scientific statements might themselves rest in some way on various metaphysical assumptions. The former point was strikingly made by Kripke (1972) and Putnam (1973) in the aforementioned debate about necessities in nature. Not only did they argue there to be metaphysical necessities concerning natural kinds, such as that water is necessarily the compound H_2O, they also argued this to be a form of a posteriori necessity; a kind of necessity that is revealed at least in part through scientific observation.

Kripke and Putnam's work arguably provided the springboard for debates about natural necessities in other aspects of nature. In 1975 Harré and Madden published a now too-little-discussed book in which they argued for a thoroughly anti-Humean metaphysical outlook, in the light of science, on which nature is seen to be full of causal powers bringing causal necessities to the world. This has since led to the development of many other causal power ontologies, such as those of Shoemaker (1980), Cartwright (1999), Martin (1993), Ellis (2001), Molnar (2003), Mumford (2004), and Bird (2007a). Interest in the causal variety of metaphysical necessity also led, in part, to new work on the related concept of lawhood, a concept already employed pervasively in natural science. Metaphysicians of science began to wonder whether, if we can have justified beliefs in other kinds of metaphysical necessities, there might be reasons also for taking scientific laws to be necessary. If so, then what grounds this necessity? If the laws are merely contingent, then what, if anything, explains why they continue to hold? These questions were attracting new interest from metaphysicians of science, and one of the first full-length studies on the issue of lawhood came in 1983 with the publication of Armstrong's *What is a Law of Nature?*. Since then, the topic of lawhood has been at the heart of the discipline, along with those relating to the aforementioned notions of kindhood and causation.

We do not wish to give the impression from what has been said thus far that all metaphysicians of science agree that scientific discoveries (or the very existence of science itself) support beliefs in metaphysical necessities of various kinds. On the contrary, there are many metaphysicians of science who can be said justifiably to be Humean in spirit. Such philosophers tend to claim that science is neither underpinned by, nor lends support to, metaphysical necessities relating to kindhood, lawhood, and causation. What is clear, however, is that their engagement in these very issues shows that they think there are meaningful debates to be had in the area of metaphysics of science. This in itself, as we have tried to suggest, has marked a significant development in philosophy.

We also do not wish to give the impression from what has been said so far that debates surrounding the issue of metaphysical necessity are the only debates within the metaphysics of science. But this general debate does provide a good illustration of how the feeling has emerged in some quarters that there is a mutual dependence between metaphysics and natural science. As we have suggested, the strong empiricism of the early 20th century is typically now thought to be too radical and naive in its treatment of metaphysics. Likewise, an extreme rationalistic 'armchair' form of metaphysics, which does not engage with the current discoveries of science, is also thought to be misguided. There is an increasing feeling that the best scientists and metaphysicians are those who talk to each other. NEW

Before beginning our search for a more detailed definition of the metaphysics of science, it is worth mentioning a more recent trend within modern metaphysics of science, one which has emerged during the past decade or so. This is the project of system building. As has been briefly indicated already (and as will be shown further as the chapter proceeds), the core scientific concepts of kindhood, lawhood, and causation are interrelated, and this has led some philosophers to attempt to build ontological systems which can simultaneously account for them all. These systems can even be seen as attempts to underpin the entire body of scientific statements, bearing in mind that scientific statements typically relate in some way to kinds, laws, or causal facts. This 'underpinning' is often described in the now popular terminology of truthmaking. The modern system builders have been concerned with what it is that makes scientific statements true. What is it, for example, that makes it the case that a scientific law either does or does not hold? Various answers seem possible, or at least imaginable, which indeed explains why there are debates to be had within the discipline of metaphysics of science. This also indicates, in part, what was wrong with the radical empiricism of the first half of the 20th century. Whilst these empiricists rightly took scientific statements seriously, they typically did not ask in virtue of what these statements might be true, overlooking important philosophical issues as a result.

Answers that current system builders have given concerning the metaphysical underpinnings of science have varied considerably. Ellis (2001), for example, has argued that our total body of scientific statements can only be accounted for if we accept a metaphysical system containing six fundamental ontological categories. E. J. Lowe (2006), in contrast, argues that only his four-category ontology provides an adequate metaphysical foundation for natural science. Heil (2003) is more parsimonious still, arguing for a two-category ontology. The debates between the system builders within the metaphysics of science are ongoing. But again, the very existence of these debates shows that the presuppositions which have led to the emergence of the metaphysics of science remain, and that the discipline is in a state of health.

2 The beginnings of a definition

We have identified some of the metaphysical-cum-scientific concepts with which metaphysicians of science are concerned: natural kinds, laws, causation, and causal power. This immediately gives us a sense of what the metaphysics of science, as the term is now commonly used, *is not*. One obvious interpretation of the metaphysics of science could be that it is the study of specific metaphysical debates as they arise within specific scientific sub-disciplines. A notorious example is the debate concerning absolute versus relative conceptions of space, which was contested for example by the Newtonians and Einsteinians. While this is a metaphysical debate which has been scientifically informed, this is not the kind of debate with which contemporary metaphysicians of science are typically concerned.[1] They are rather concerned with debating the more *general* scientific-cum-metaphysical concepts, concepts which are deployed in *all* the natural sciences, including the special sciences. Chemists, for example, speak of chemical kinds and properties, and chemical laws concerning those kinds and properties. Biologists speak of *their* own biological kinds and laws. Psychologists identify psychological laws, and so on. In contrast, the concepts of, say, absolute and relational space, are not common to all the sciences: they are specifically concepts developed within the discipline of physics. This point shows again how the system builders within the metaphysics of science are extremely ambitious: they claim to offer a metaphysical system which can underpin *all* branches of natural science.

There are also other ways in which the term 'metaphysics of science' could be taken by someone not familiar with the history of the discipline. One could think, for example, that the term 'metaphysics of science' refers to metaphysics in general, whilst conveying a sense that metaphysics should not depart too far from the concerns and discoveries of current science. Several current philosophers hold this kind of view, showing hostility to what we might call the 'armchair metaphysicians' who do not make an effort to engage with current science (see for example Ladyman and Ross 2007). It is clear, however, that this agenda is orthogonal to the concerns of those within the discipline of metaphysics of science. Those interested in studying the central metaphysical concepts

---

[1] This is not to say that papers on metaphysical issues within specific branches of science do not sometimes fall under the heading of 'metaphysics of science' in conferences, for example. Our point is just that such papers are not at the core of the discipline as we understand it.

within natural science *may or may not* disapprove of more abstract metaphysicians who think about issues which are less obviously connected with the subject-matter of current science.

It is fairly clear, then, what the discipline of metaphysics of science *is not*. But can we say anything more insightful than merely identifying the kinds of concepts which metaphysicians of science investigate? Is there a common theme or aim running through each of the debates within the metaphysics of science? If the answer is yes, then a general definition of the discipline should be achievable, and such a definition may well be philosophically illuminating. It may, for example, reveal something about the essential nature of science itself.

We believe that there is a common theme and aim running through each debate within the metaphysics of science, and the aim of the remainder of this chapter will be to begin to uncover it. However, the definition we will arrive at will have to be vague in some respects. To aim for an exact definition would be unrealistic for a chapter-length piece, for reasons we will shortly explain. But regardless of how the precise details of the definition are to be spelled out, we hope that the general insights we offer will be clear and justified.

One of the problems regarding the delineation of the metaphysics of science is that the definition of science is itself a matter of philosophical controversy. Some are even sceptical as to whether a sharp criterion for distinguishing science from non-science is possible (see for example Feyerabend 1975). The fact that there is an ever-increasing range of aims and methods within the various scientific disciplines lends weight to this scepticism. Philosophers cannot even agree on what kind of general entity science should be classified as. It has been taken at one time or another to be a set of statements, a set of propositions, a tool, a method, a research activity, an ideology, a research network, a research institution, and even a philosophy, to name but a few proposals.

There is however some agreement on what science is not. The radical empiricist view of science, mentioned earlier, now has few adherents. According to that view, science is distinguished by the fact that it is the only respectable discipline, as it is constituted by a set of statements which, unlike metaphysical statements, are genuinely meaningful. More precisely, scientific statements are said on this view to be meaningful insofar as they are either analytic (as are, for example, logical truths), or synthetic, which is to say they are verifiable in some way through empirical observation. However, formulating a synthetic principle of verifiability in a satisfactory way proved extremely difficult, not to mention the fact that the very distinction between the analytic and synthetic was shown to be questionable (see Quine 1951). Each formulation of the proposed principle was subject to counterexamples, modified versions were subject to further counterexamples, and so on. *etc.*

These complaints led to a move away from trying to capture the nature of science using the notion of verifiability. Famously, for example, Popper claimed that what is important and unique to science is not verifiability, but *falsifiability*. What distinguishes a genuine science from, say, astrology or Freudian analysis, according to Popper, is that its

theories can be *falsified* by experiential anomalies. Science is risky. But this characterization also came with problems. As Lakatos (1978) and Thagard (1978) point out, scientists
do not automatically abandon their core theories when an evidential anomaly occurs,
nor should they. Rather than accepting that their theories are false in light of recalcitrant
observations, scientists look for alternative explanations for the anomalies, by questioning the reliability of their testing methods or questioning the auxiliary hypotheses
which, in conjunction with the core theory, entail that the data in question is indeed
anomalous. Furthermore, argues Lakatos, it is a good thing that scientists proceed in
this way, for falsification stratagems lead to overhasty rejections of sound theories
(1978: 112).

The above line of argument suggests that science involves, in part, finding ways of
explaining new facts and 'anomalies' that arise (see also Thagard 1978). Criticisms of
previous demarcation criteria also led Lakatos and others to propose a further plausible
distinguishing feature of genuine science. What genuine, progressive sciences have in
common is that they predict facts, many of which are *novel* (1978). Popper appears to
agree on this point also. (Popper's view merely differs on the issue of what scientists
should do when the novel predictions *go wrong*.) For example, Popper presents Einstein's
gravitational theory as a paradigm case of a genuine scientific theory yielding novel and
strikingly precise predictions (as opposed to non-scientific theories which, according to
Popper, are typically compatible with any outcome, such as Adlerian psychology and the
Marxist theory of history (1957)). Einstein's theory implies, for example, that light is
attracted to very heavy bodies. This idea had not occurred to physicists before, nor did it
seem to have any *prima facie* plausibility. Now, a consequence of this idea was that the
light from a star whose apparent position is actually quite close to the sun would travel in
such a direction that, to us, the star would appear to be slightly shifted away from the sun.
Using data taken during a daytime eclipse, which allowed the stars close to the sun to be
visible, it was discovered that Einstein's prediction was indeed correct (Popper 1957). As
Popper points out, this prediction was highly novel and also risky: had the star appeared
not to have moved, or to have moved to a lesser or greater extent than expected, the
theory would have been embarrassed. But given this highly novel prediction was accurate, Einstein's theory was shown to be an instance of genuine, impressive science.[2]

We take it that for all the disagreements over the details of the correct definition of
science, there are some general distinguishing features of science which most in the
demarcation debate can agree on. Regardless of whether science is best understood as a
set of statements or propositions, or say a research activity, what distinguishes a genuine

[2] Note that although Einstein's theory superseded Newtonianism, this does not detract from Newtonianism's status as a genuine science, for it too made outstanding novel predictions, as Lakatos explains (1978).
For example, contrary to the dominant views of comet motion, Newton's theory entailed that some comets
moved in hyperbolas, and others in parabolas. Using Newton's theory, Halley predicted that a certain comet
(now called 'Halley's Comet', of course) moved in the former way, and that it would return in seventy-two
years. Seventy-two years later the comet did indeed return, and this took the credibility of Newton's theory
to yet further levels.

science from mere pseudo-science, at least in part, is that it makes predictions (many of which are novel), and provides explanations for new facts and anomalies. It is these main features that we will take into account in formulating our definition of the metaphysics of science. There is, of course, much more to be said about the demarcation of science, but the kind of demarcation criteria identified, rough as they are, will be sufficient to allow us to get across our main points concerning the metaphysics of science.[3]

Taking into account the features of science we have identified thus far, and taking into account earlier comments, we may propose the following definition of the metaphysics of science, which we can then proceed to build upon:

> **MOS def****: The philosophical study of the general metaphysical notions that are applied in all our scientific disciplines, disciplines which offer novel predictions and provide explanations of new facts and anomalies within their given domain.

Now, a question one might ask about the presence of these metaphysical notions in all scientific disciplines—such as those of kindhood, lawhood, causation, and causal power—concerns whether it is an *accident* that these concepts are central to all of science. Our view is that it is not, and an exploration of why this is so will further our understanding of the nature of the metaphysics of science.

The claim that it is not accidental that the notions of kindhood, lawhood, and causation are at the heart of all the sciences suggests that without kinds, laws, and causation, science as we know it would not even be possible. Given our partial definition of science, this is to say that without kindhood, lawhood, and causation, *neither systematic scientific predictions nor explanations would be possible*. This is a thought we find plausible, as will be explained in the following sections. This thought also indicates why the metaphysics of science has developed in precisely the way it has, i.e. as primarily an investigation into the nature of kinds, laws, and causation.

This modal suggestion, that the metaphysics of science is an investigation of the metaphysical preconditions of science, has rather a Kantian flavour. But arguably, the idea that certain metaphysical phenomena are necessary for science was present in ancient thinking, as we will now see.

3 Ancient metaphysics of science and the modal claim

The well-known Platonic theory of forms (or 'ideas') is an early example of an ontological theory of kinds. As well as the physical realm of mutable particulars, there is, according to Plato, a non-physical transcendent realm of immutable kinds, which the

---

[3] Classificatory work, for example, might also be said to be at the heart of natural science. It could be argued, however, that even this activity is not independent of that of providing predictions and explanations, since, for example, certain natural kind classifications have to be made before many laws can be formulated. In any case, as stated above, in order to make the main points of this chapter we do not require a more precise demarcation of science than that offered here.

physical particulars instantiate. Since Plato proposed his theory, a significant number of metaphysicians have continued to advocate kind ontologies of various sorts (see for example Ellis 2001 and Lowe 2006), although most modern metaphysicians tend to avoid the claim that kinds exist in a transcendent realm.

Now, in his *Metaphysics*, Aristotle refers to a number of arguments in support of the ontology of forms that he was aware of from the Platonic schools. Interestingly for our purposes, one of these was an argument from science, and this perhaps constituted one of the first exercises within the metaphysics of science. As Melling writes, the argument is described by Alexander as being, roughly, that: '[I]f the sciences have any validity, if they can attain knowledge, then there must be a realm of immutable, intelligible realities which are the true objects of knowledge' (1987, p. 117). The argument thus takes us from the existence of science, and in particular the generalizations it gives rise to, to the thought that there must be objects of a kind which makes the activity of science, and specifically scientific knowledge, possible. Alexander articulates this thought in connection with medicine and the rational science of geometry:

> ...if medicine is not a science of this particular health but of health simply, there will be a certain health-itself; and if geometry is not a science of this particular equal and this particular commensurate, but of equal simply and the commensurate simply, there will be a certain equal-itself and a commensurate-itself; and these are the Ideas (Alexander, *Metaphysics Commentary*, 79.3–88.2)

The key insight here is clearly that science typically deals not with facts about particulars, but rather facts of a more general character, or as Alexander puts it, of a simple character. This is to say that science typically tells us about the nature of *kinds* of individuals rather than specific individuals. To use examples from Alexander's themes of medicine and geometry, the scientists might say for example that 'penicillin cures Lyme disease' or that the 'square of the hypotenuse equals the square of the opposite plus the square of the adjacent'. These statements are about Lyme disease *in general* and right-angled triangles *in general*.

Now, importantly for our purposes, the Platonic argument from science has a modal force to it: given the nature of scientific knowledge, specifically its general character, the world needs to be such-and-such a way metaphysically. We may of course think that the Platonists overstep the mark in thinking that the nature of science leads us directly to the theory of Forms. Whether irreducible kinds (not to mention transcendent kinds) provide the most plausible truthmakers for kind generalizations is a matter of ongoing controversy. Nevertheless, the general question of what the world needs to be like metaphysically in order for science to be possible and scientific claims to be true, is one that we take to be insightful, and one that actually lies at the heart of the metaphysics of science, if only implicitly.[4] One reason for thinking this latter point holds is that it provides

---

[4] We accept that many will find this to be quite a strong claim, and so it is worth pointing out that most of the points to follow stand even if one takes the metaphysics of science to have the more modest aim of investigating what the world *could* be like in order for science as we know it to arise. (Thanks go to an anonymous referee for this point.)

an explanation as to why the specific subject-matter of the metaphysics of science is as it is. Let us explain.

We have already highlighted that the key debates within current metaphysics of science concern the natures of kindhood, lawhood, causation, and causal powers,[5] but as mentioned in the last section, there remains a question about *why* these are the core topics of the discipline, aside from the fact that they are concepts which are found in all branches of science. Our discussion of Platonic metaphysics of science has suggested a possible explanation, and one which we find plausible: kinds, laws, causation, and causal powers (whatever their metaphysical natures may turn out to be) are precisely what make scientific enquiry as we know it possible. Bearing in mind our earlier comments about the nature of science, this is to say that the aforementioned phenomena are those which, for example, make scientific predictions and explanations possible. In the next section, we will explore the main reasons for accepting this modal aspect of the metaphysics of science.

4 Order in the world

A world in which there are kinds, laws, and causal powers is a world in which there is *order*. In such worlds, certain causal dispositions or powers are associated with certain natural kinds, a relationship which may be expressed by some of the natural laws. An example of such a relationship is that expressed by the law 'electrons are negatively charged' or 'salt dissolves in water'. Because of the general character of such laws, they tell us what causal dispositions we can expect from any *instance* of the kind in question. When we encounter a new electron or a new piece of salt, we do not have to perform tests to determine whether that particular electron is negatively charged or that particular salt is soluble. The law alone tells us what to expect, and the law is made possible by the natural-kind structure of the world and its relationship with the causal dispositions.[6] In a chaotic, disorderly world in which there are no natural kind structures, and in which events occur entirely randomly, there would not be the patterns in nature that are required for there to be natural laws.[7]

Now, it also seems plausible that within this chaotic, disorderly world, it would not be possible to make the kinds of predictions (not to mention *novel* predictions) or construct

---

[5] Talk of causal powers has an anti-Humean flavour, but we do not intend the term 'power' to be metaphysically loaded (i.e. we are not ruling out here that powers are to be understood in some reductionist sense).

[6] The precise nature of this relationship is itself a matter of ongoing debate in the metaphysics of science (see for example Bird (2001), who argues that salt dissolves in water as a matter of metaphysical necessity. See also replies by Beebee (2002) and Psillos (2002), who argue the relationship between salt and solubility is contingent (yet regular)).

[7] One may doubt whether this kind of world is *physically* possible. This question does not matter for our purposes. We can at least say that such a world is metaphysically possible.

the kinds of explanations that we find in natural science.[8] Scientific predictions concern what will happen to certain entities, and in order to begin formulating a scientific prediction, we typically ask what kinds of things those entities are. We then consider which causal dispositions things of those kinds have. Once we have established this, we can then identify the causal laws (typically functional laws) relevant to those causal dispositions. Finally, we can feed the specific data we have about the relevant entities into those relevant causal law(s), thereby generating data about what will happen to those individuals at certain points in time. In short, then, the facts about kinds and causal powers, facts which the laws can capture, enable scientists to deliver the systematic predictions and to do so in a strikingly efficient way.

This is not to say that, in our world, determinate predictions will always be possible (or even possible at all). For example, there are reasons for thinking that the causal powers at the level of quantum mechanics are indeterministic or 'chancy', which is reflected in the fact that the best laws we have in that domain are probabilistic. As such, any predictions based on those laws can only deliver probabilities about the outcomes. But such predictions are nevertheless useful, and certainly better than anything we could hope for in the disorderly world described earlier. A world involving probabilistic laws is one in which the future possibilities are narrowed down to quite a considerable degree. In contrast, a disorderly world is one in which anything goes: the future possibilities are not constrained in any way. A disorderly world should not therefore be confused with a 'chancy' world. A chancy world, unlike a disorderly one, is a scientific world.

The modal point holds equally for the process of explanation. Let us consider the most common form of explanation: causal explanation.[9] To say that an event or fact, call it X, is explained by Y is to say that Y is responsible for X, the paradigm case being where X is caused by Y. Notice, however, that in the chaotic world described above, which is void of kindhood and causation, nothing could be held responsible for anything else. Things would just happen, randomly, for no reason at all. For any given event that occurred in that world, all we could say about it is simply that 'it just happened'. But it is doubtful that this constitutes an explanation at all, and it is certainly not a scientific explanation.

The precise nature of the phenomena that impose order on the world and allow science to be possible is a matter of ongoing debate, and our intention has not been to

[8] Perhaps in some minimal sense we could try to make predictions in a chaotic world, if, say, a certain particular happened to behave in a regular way over a given period. It seems clear, though, that in such a world we would not be able to construct the kinds of stable and systematic predictions which natural science delivers.

[9] Etymology suggests a very close relationship between explanation and causation. When we say Y explains X, we say X because Y: notice the *cause* in be*cause*. However, whether causal explanation is the *only* respectable kind of explanation is a matter of controversy. For example, according to one influential account of explanation—the deductive-nomological view (see Hempel 1965)—it is the laws which play an essential role in scientific explanation. But there is no need to address the details here, for that view too is consistent with our general thesis that world-order is a precondition of explanation (laws being an essential aspect of world-order).

address any of the specific debates concerning the metaphysics of these phenomena. What we have tried to indicate, however, is how and why the study of kindhood, lawhood, causation, and causal power is at the heart of the metaphysics of science. The reason is that it is precisely these phenomena which bring order to the world, and it is therefore the job of the metaphysician of science to find out just what kinds, laws, causal powers, and causation amount to ontologically. In short, then, the metaphysics of science is the metaphysics of *order*.

Taking into account the insights of the last two sections, we are now in a position to adjust our definition as follows:

> **MOS def*:** The metaphysical study of the aspects of reality, such as kindhood, lawhood, causal power, and causation, which impose order on the world and make our scientific disciplines possible (that is, disciplines which are able to provide predictions—often novel ones—and offer explanations for new facts and anomalies within their given domain).

5 The relationship between scientific disciplines

Finally, there is one important aspect of the metaphysics of science which we have not yet addressed, and one which we must now build into our definition. Earlier we saw how the various branches of science—physics, chemistry, and biology, for instance—are similar in that they all trade on the notions of kinds, laws, and causation. But there are clearly considerable dissimilarities between the various branches of science. Physicists posit very different kinds of entities to, say, the chemists or the biologists, and as a result their laws look very different to those of the chemist or biologist. The differences are more striking still in the case of the 'higher-level' sciences such as psychology. What are we to make of these differences? What does the existence of a multitude of scientific disciplines, and their diversity, teach us metaphysically? Some have suspected that the differences are ultimately superficial, and that in principle the physicists could explain all of the entities and laws of the other sciences using the language of physics. This is the reductionist stance. It is, however, far from obvious that attempts to reduce all scientific claims to physics can ever be successful. For one thing, physicists who have previously attempted such reductions have encountered immediate hurdles. Take chemistry, for example. While the laws of chemistry can in principle be derived from the laws of quantum electrodynamics, it seems this can only be achieved if certain information describing suitable *chemical* conditions is first fed into the equations (for further discussion see Gell-Mann 1994). The prospects for explaining away chemical facts using only the concepts found in physics are not as bright as some had assumed.

Might it be, then, that the existence of the diverse branches of science tells us that reality is layered, with each distinct level containing unique kinds of entities and laws? To think in this way pushes us towards a view known as emergentism. But this view has also been shown to face difficulties, and so it may be that we ultimately need a middle position, one that allows scientific disciplines other than physics to be legitimate in their own right, but without completely cutting them off from each other, and particularly not from physics. Needless to say, this issue is a matter of ongoing debate. What is important from our perspective is merely that the domain of the metaphysics of science seems to be the best arena for this debate. Scientists tend to specialize in their own branches of science, each with their own concerns. Even if scientists are interested in these broader questions about how the branches of science relate, which surely the most curious scientists are, it is beyond their remit to spend large amounts of time thinking about them. Their primary job as scientists, we have suggested, is to develop theories which have great systematic predictive and explanatory power. In order to tackle the broader philosophical questions, it is necessary to take a step back from any specific scientific practice, and as philosophers, metaphysicians of science are well positioned to do this.

There is also perhaps a deeper reason why investigating the relationship between different branches of science falls naturally within the remit of metaphysics of science. We have claimed that the metaphysics of science is the metaphysics of order. And it seems clear that in investigating the relationship between the different sciences, we are likely to learn something about the order of the world (in terms of how it is fundamentally layered) Or if, for example, a strong form of reductionism is true, we may find that the natural world has just one layer, and that the order found in the special sciences is derived from the order found in physics (assuming physics is the reduction base).

Taking into account this aspect of the metaphysics of science, we may now propose our final definition:

> **MOS def:** The metaphysical study of the aspects of reality, such as kindhood, lawhood, causal power, and causation, which impose order on the world and make our scientific disciplines possible (that is, disciplines which are able to provide predictions—often novel—and offer explanations for new facts and anomalies within their given domain), and also the study of the metaphysical relationship between the various scientific disciplines.

6 The acid test

As a way of testing the adequacy of the definition proposed, we should consider whether it successfully marks off questions falling within the metaphysics of science from other metaphysical questions. The metaphysics of science, we have claimed, is the metaphysics of world-order. We must therefore consider whether the metaphysical issues falling outside of the metaphysics of science are independent of questions relating to the existence and nature of world-order. We suggest that they are.

There are many branches of metaphysics, each of which concerns different aspects of reality. It would be unrealistic for us to try to survey all the branches of metaphysics and the questions they involve. We can, however, provide a partial list of the core sub-disciplines of metaphysics, and briefly consider whether the debates in those sub-disciplines are largely independent of issues relating to what we have called world-order. Here are some of the main sub-disciplines: the metaphysics of particulars; the metaphysics of properties; the metaphysics of time; the metaphysics of space; the metaphysics of composition; the metaphysics of identity; the metaphysics of parthood; the metaphysics of persistence; the metaphysics of numbers; the metaphysics of propositions.

We do not think it takes a large amount of reflection to see that the core questions within these sub-disciplines are indeed independent of questions relating to the metaphysical nature of world-order. We take this to show that even though our definition may be vague in some respects, it is along the right lines.

Let us briefly consider the first few items on the list. First, let's take the metaphysics of particulars, which is a classical metaphysical topic. Are particulars made up of substances, which properties hook onto, or are particulars merely bundles of properties? This question is, we suggest, independent of the metaphysics of world-order. Consider the chaotic, disorderly world discussed earlier. Particulars could exist in this world, as well as a scientific world, and so questions concerning the metaphysics of order do not have much, if any, bearing on this sub-discipline.

Take another core topic in classical metaphysics: the metaphysics of properties. Are properties best thought of as universals, tropes, or otherwise? Again, answers to this question do not seem to be constrained by facts concerning world-order. There seems no reason why entities such as tropes and universals should only exist in an ordered world. Furthermore, the trope versus universals debate can be had independently of the various debates concerning the metaphysics of order. Both realists and reductionists about causal dispositions can, for example, be either trope or universals theorists (see for example Molnar (2003) who is a trope realist about powers and Ellis (2001) who is also a powers realist, but prefers a universals view). This is not to say, of course, that metaphysicians of science are not also interested in the metaphysics of properties. And we should concede that at least one metaphysician has claimed that there is a link between the metaphysics of properties and world-order. Armstrong (1983) argues, for instance, that a credible theory of laws requires realism about universals. Obviously, if it is right that laws are relations between universals then for that reason the metaphysics of properties would be part of the metaphysics of science.

Let us now briefly consider the metaphysics of time. The core question within this discipline concerns whether time is best conceived as the A-series or B-series. Again, this question is independent of issues of world-order. Time could exist in an order-less world, and the various views about the metaphysics of ordered worlds appear to be compatible with both the 'A' and 'B' theory of time.

Finally, let us briefly consider the metaphysics of space, the central question of which is: is space absolute or relative? As we saw earlier in the chapter, this metaphysical question is one which scientists have debated, but it is not a primary concern of metaphysicians of science. This is because the outcome of this debate is independent of the metaphysical questions about world-order. The existence of kinds and laws, for example, is conceivable on either the absolutist or relationalist conceptions.

Due to space constraints, we will not continue to go though each item on the list. We hope, however, that we have said enough to indicate that the prospects for passing the acid test are good, and that, upon reflection, debates outside of the metaphysics of science can be seen to lie outside of the metaphysics of world-order. Such reflections lend weight to our definition, for our key claim has been, to repeat, that the metaphysics of science is the metaphysics of order.

7 Summary

We began with the observation that, historically, debates within modern metaphysics of science have been centred primarily on issues relating to the natures of kindhood, lawhood, causal power, and causation. We went on to suggest an explanation for this, which is that kinds, laws, and causation are all what bring order to the world, and as such are needed for the very existence of science as we know it. The metaphysics of science is thus concerned with the preconditions of science: the metaphysics of science is the metaphysics of order. In the course of arguing for this understanding of the metaphysics of science, we also briefly considered what might demarcate scientific disciplines from non-scientific disciplines. This issue has long been a controversial one, and so for the purposes of this chapter we settled upon a rather minimal demarcation criterion, which says scientific disciplines are those which are able to deliver systematic predictions (many of which are novel), and explain facts (many of which are new or previously unexplained). With this understanding of science in play, the necessity of kindhood, lawhood, and causation for science was highlighted by the point that in a disorderly world (i.e. one void of kindhood, lawhood, and causation), it would not be possible to make systematic predictions and provide explanations—that is, to do natural science.

We then added to the definition proposed by identifying a further key debate within modern metaphysics of science: that concerning the relationship between the various scientific disciplines. We argued that the discipline of metaphysics of science provides the best arena for this debate, because scientists themselves work within, and are therefore constrained by, their own specific scientific disciplines. Moreover, investigating the relationship between the various branches of science is itself part of the project of investigating the nature of the world's order. After adding to our definition in light of this observation, we finally tested the plausibility of our definition by considering whether it clearly marks off debates within the metaphysics of science from other metaphysical debates. After considering some of the core metaphysical debates outside of the metaphysics of science, we suggested that our definition is indeed along the right lines on the basis that these debates are largely independent of the existence and nature of world-order.

8 The articles in this volume

The aim of this volume is to provide a snapshot of current important research on each of the core topics within the metaphysics of science identified above: the topics of laws, causation and dispositions (or 'powers'), natural kinds, and emergence. Accordingly, the volume is divided into four distinct parts, with each devoted to one of these topics. We will conclude this introductory chapter by briefly introducing the main questions and arguments in each chapter, and indicating where appropriate how the chapters within each part relate to one another.

Part 1: Laws

This part begins with Roberts' 'Measurement, Laws, and Counterfactuals'. The core issue addressed concerns how a certain feature of laws is to be explained. Roberts offers a new answer to this question, and one which will potentially shed light on how it is that scientists are able to draw inferences about laws. Indeed, these two broad themes—that of explaining laws and their features, and that of showing how law-based inferences are possible—are also main concerns of the other two chapters in this part of the volume. Woodward is concerned to shed light on the nature of law (and also causal) inferences, while Lange is concerned with explaining a specific kind of law. As Roberts' chapter shows, these two broad themes are not unrelated.

Roberts begins by noting a striking fact about the modal nature of both laws and legitimate measurement methods. The feature in question is that both laws and legitimate measurement methods are *counterfactually resilient*. What does this mean? Well, to say that a law is counterfactually resilient is to say, roughly, that a genuine law (as opposed, say, to an accidental regularity) is one which holds across a variety of counterfactual suppositions. To say that a legitimate measurement method is counterfactually resilient (as opposed, say, to a method which delivers accurate measurements largely through luck) is to say that such methods deliver accurate measurements across a variety of counterfactual suppositions. But precisely which range of counterfactual suppositions are taken to be the relevant ones? Roberts suggests different people will disagree on this issue. Roberts is not concerned to settle this issue, but claims merely that whatever reasons one has for taking certain counterfactual suppositions to be relevant in the case of laws, those same reasons will also lead one to view the counterfactual resilience of measurement methods in the same way.

What Roberts attempts to establish, then, is that laws and measurement methods are closely connected insofar as they are both counterfactually resilient in the same sorts of ways. Is there an underlying explanation for this connection? Roberts suggests there is, and spends the rest of chapter arguing for a novel explanation for this connection.

Roberts' proposal is that the counterfactual resilience of measurement methods is what explains the counterfactual resilience of laws. The pay-off for accepting that the explanation runs in this direction is as follows. The counterfactual resilience of legitimate measurement methods can itself be explained, independently, by facts about epistemic norms concerning the nature of evidence, argues Roberts. Thus the picture Roberts presents is explanatorily rich in that the counterfactual resilience of both laws and (legitimate) measurement methods are explained. But on the alternative picture whereby the counterfactual resilience of laws is taken to be more basic than that of legitimate measurement methods, it is far less clear, according to Roberts, that the counterfactual resilience of the laws will itself be susceptible to a further explanation.

In the second chapter in the laws section, 'Laws, Causes and Invariance', Woodward is concerned with the kinds of evidential reasoning scientists use to infer laws and causal claims. It is extremely important for metaphysicians to understand how scientific methodology works, Woodward suggests. For this ensures that philosophers do not end up trying to provide metaphysical foundations for non-existent features of science.

The view of laws which is Woodward's starting point is the Lewis-style Best Systems Analysis. As is well known, Lewis develops this theory in the context of his Humean Supervenience thesis, which states that all facts (which will include those concerning laws) supervene on the spatiotemporal distribution of particular matters of fact, each of which is itself entirely non-modal in nature. On the Best Systems picture, laws consist in the axioms or theorems that occur in the strongest and simplest systemization of the four-dimensional distribution of non-modal facts. In short, the laws capture the most general regularities that occur in a world. Now, according to Woodward, part of the justification for the Best Systems view is that it is supposed to provide a framework which coheres with how law inferences and theory choice in science operate (though in a rather idealized form). But the picture the Best Systems Analysis presents does not sit well with how science does in fact work, Woodward claims. Woodward concedes, however, that if it is not the case that laws supervene on something like a Humean Supervenience base, it becomes difficult to see how scientists are able to establish laws through empirical testing.

In order to overcome this dilemma, Woodward suggests we must look at how scientists *actually* draw causal and law inferences in a range of scenarios, and use these insights to help develop the metaphysics. This is precisely what Woodward sets about doing in this chapter. By studying a range of examples from science, Woodward argues that the Lewisian Best Systems picture (and also the view of causation it lends itself to) is shown to be too simplified. In Woodward's view, inferring laws is not simply a matter of applying criteria like simplicity and strength, nor is the evidential base for law inferences entirely non-modal in character, as Lewis's systems suggest. For example, when investigating causal relations and laws, scientists implement intervention and invariance principles. But implementing these principles requires a background of further modal beliefs. We cannot identify a suitable intervention method, for example, unless we already have beliefs about how that intervention will *causally* interact with the experimental elements. More generally, the empirical assumptions which help us to draw causal and law inferences do themselves have causal or nomic import, which suggests that drawing causal and nomic inferences is more complex than the Best Systems Analysis suggests.

In the final chapter of the laws section, Lange returns to a general theme, present in the Roberts chapter, of explaining laws. Because laws form such a central part of any

Since Laws form a general part
of such any

scientific theory, it is perhaps natural to think that laws—particularly physical laws—are explanatorily fundamental. But we should not be too hasty. We have already seen how Roberts, in the first chapter of the volume, suggests that the counterfactual resilience of laws can be explained by further facts. But are physical laws in general ever susceptible to a deeper explanation?

In 'How to Explain the Lorentz Transformations', Lange provides us with a case study, and asks whether a certain type of law might have a deeper explanation. The laws in question are those concerning Lorentz transformations. These laws emerged as a result of Einstein's special theory of relativity and, roughly speaking, Lorentz transformations specify how a point-like event's spacetime co-ordinates in one inertial-frame maps onto its co-ordinates in another frame. Lorentz transformations play a fundamental role in the special theory of relativity, since it is essentially facts about these transformations which give rise to some of the most well-known and surprising consequences of the special theory, such as the relativity of simultaneity.

Given the fundamental role of Lorentz transformation laws in Einstein's theory, it is perhaps natural to think that they are not themselves susceptible to further explanation. Lange's aim is to question this assumption, though, by exploring what various explanations of Lorentz transformations might look like. Perhaps the nature of Lorentz transformations can be explained in terms of what the fundamental force laws happen to be, for example. Or, more interestingly from a metaphysical perspective, perhaps an explanation might be available in terms of the very nature of relativity and the geometry of spacetime itself.

This latter explanation would be deep indeed, but we cannot expect such an explanation to come easily. For one thing, it will require us to get a grip on how facts about relativity and spacetime geometry (and so the Lorentz transformations themselves) can transcend the various force laws. Lange attempts to do just this by showing what such an explanation would be like, with the help of some modal metaphysics. If successful, Lange's proposal has the striking consequence that physical laws—the Lorentz transformations in this case—can, in a certain sense, be explained in a non-dynamic way. Finally, Lange shows how his explanatory strategy might be applied to laws in classical physics, specifically Newton's law.

Part 2: Dispositions and causes

In recent decades, disposition-based ontologies have become more and more popular in the metaphysics of science. On such views, at least some of the natural properties of the world are said to be irreducibly dispositional in character, which is to say they are, by their very nature, properties for certain behavioural manifestations. Because of this feature of dispositions, there is clearly a close connection between dispositions and causation. Indeed, Shoemaker, who was one of the first to propose a dispositional view of natural properties, called it the 'causal theory of properties' (1980). More recently, irreducible dispositions are often called causal powers, as is the case in the McKitrick chapter in this volume.

But what, precisely, is the relationship between dispositions and causation? How does realism about dispositions impact on our understanding of causal talk and of the behavioural mechanisms in the world? Both of the chapters in this part of the volume are concerned with these broad questions.

In Hüttemann's 'A Disposition-based Process-theory of Causation', he argues that the dispositional view of properties can help us to find a place for causation in physics. Since Russell's infamous 1912 paper, 'On the Notion of Cause', the concept of causation has been viewed with suspicion, particularly in the philosophy of physics. Russell argued that the concept of causation is too imprecise to be useful in physics, and that the main aims of physics can be carried out perfectly well without invoking causal concepts.

Yet, in spite of Russell's claims, and similar sceptical conclusions from others such as Mach, the notion of causation has continued to be employed pervasively in science—particularly in the special sciences. Clearly, then, we need some account of why, at least in some cases, it is natural to frame scientific claims in causal terms. This is essentially Hüttemann's aim: to find a place for causation in our scientific world-view, despite Russell's scepticism.

Hüttemann begins by motivating the claim that dispositional properties are needed in physics. Rather than employing purely metaphysical arguments, as some dispositional theorists do, Hüttemann motivates the dispositional view by looking at specific examples from physics involving compound systems. We should accept dispositional properties, Hüttemann argues, because they provide the best explanation for the interactions between parts of compound physical systems. These dispositional properties, in turn, serve to ground the very laws governing those physical systems. The main example Hüttemann appeals to concerns the interaction between Hamiltonian rotators and oscillators in quantum mechanics.

After outlining his theory of dispositions, Hüttemann then suggests how causation might be understood. Notably, the view Hüttemann advocates is not the view that simply sees dispositions as the causes of their manifestations. Although this is perhaps the most obvious way of understanding causation in the context of dispositionalism, Hüttemann argues that this simplistic view does not sit well with the examples discussed from physics.

Instead, Hüttemann's theory is based on the following central claim: a cause is a disturbing factor which diverts a system away from the behaviour it is naturally disposed to display (what he calls the 'default behaviour'). Since this theory is based on the temporal evolution of systems, it may be classed as a process-theory of causation. After developing the details of his view, Hüttemann identifies some favourable consequences of the view, compares the theory with other versions of the process-theory, and finally discusses some modal implications.

In McKitrick's 'How to Activate a Power' the focus is again realism about dispositions (or what she calls 'powers'). McKitrick's main aim is to explore the relationship between a power, its manifestation, and the 'triggering' circumstances which lead to its manifestation. This relationship has typically been thought to be relatively unproblematic, but

McKitrick's new work suggests that dispositonalists may not have understood this relationship as well as they might have assumed.

In her discussion of dispositions and their triggers, McKitrick avoids using causal language. But like Hütteman's view of dispositions, the theories McKitrick discusses have potential implications for a theory of causation. If one takes it that the cause–effect relationship is just the relationship between a power and its manifestation, understanding the precise nature of triggering conditions promises to reveal something important about the nature of causal mechanisms.

McKitrick's starting point is the strongest version of dispositionalism: the view that *all* natural properties are powers (what McKitrick calls 'pan-dispositionalism'). How, McKitrick asks, are we to understand a triggering event if all properties are powers? If events consist in things gaining different properties, as seems plausible, triggering events seem to invite a number mysteries. For a start, when one considers concrete examples of power manifestation, it is not always clear that a new distinctive power has been brought about during a triggering event. And even in cases where plausible candidates can be found, it is noticeable that those 'triggering' powers can in many cases exist without the manifestation event taking place. This means we then need a further story about what takes us from the instantiation of the 'triggering' power to the final manifestation event. In short, it seems we need a further triggering factor which serves to explain why the initial triggering power is activated. But this, McKitrick highlights, is a regress in the making.

After exploring the precise nature of this regress worry, McKitrick explores a number of possible solutions and draws out their implications. These solutions include the idea that triggering powers do not themselves require further triggers but are, rather, constantly manifesting powers. This solution can also be supplemented with the suggestion that each of these constantly manifesting 'triggering' powers are typically one amongst many other triggering powers, all of which must work in conjunction in order to give rise to the final manifestation. After considering some problems facing these proposals, another solution that McKitrick considers involves dropping the assumption that manifestations are always the manifestation of a *single* power only. In the final section, McKitrick summarizes the lessons that can be learned from her discussion of these various proposals.

Part 3: Natural kinds

As we saw earlier in this chapter, one of the main aims of science is to categorize nature: that is, to find out what kinds of things there are. This categorization project is revealed most clearly by the periodic table in chemistry, but natural kind terms are used pervasively in all domains of science. But what precisely are natural kinds? If we were to take scientific talk seriously, it would be natural to suppose that what scientists are doing when they identify kinds is discovering objective divisions that exist in the world: they are 'carving nature at its joints'. This realist construal of natural kinds also lends itself to the view that each natural kind has its own essence, something in virtue of which it is clearly marked off from other kinds.

But need we take natural kinds as metaphysically seriously as the above remarks suggest? In order to accommodate natural kind talk and the role of natural kinds in science, must we view natural kinds as entities which form an ineliminable ontological category of their own—and as entities with their own distinctive essences? The three chapters in this part of the volume all help to address these general questions. Although each of the three chapters approaches the metaphysics of kinds debate in a quite different way, their conclusions all have something in common: they express scepticism about the necessity and feasibility of a strong realism about kind structure.

As we saw earlier in this chapter, it was arguably Kripke and Putnam who were the catalysts for the modern debate on natural kinds. They famously argued that theoretical identifications of natural kinds, such as 'water is H_2O', are necessary a posteriori, and for this reason their view about the semantics of natural kind terms was taken by many to go hand in hand with an essentialist view about natural kinds. In Beebee's 'How to Carve across the Joints in Nature Without Abandoning Kripke–Putnam Semantics', she questions whether acceptance of the Kripke–Putnam view really does, by itself, have these natural kind essentialist implications. Beebee argues that it does not.

Beebee's starting point is Salmon's view about the relationship between the Kripke–Putnam thesis and realist natural kind essentialism. In Salmon's view, a non-trivial essentialist claim has to be presupposed in order to get to the necessary a posteriori claim about theoretical identities, and it is this that explains why the Kripke–Putnam thesis and essentialism go hand in hand. Crucially, however, this non-trivial essentialist claim is not one that has any of the strong metaphysical implications that natural kind essentialists typically endorse, argues Beebee. The non-trivial essentialism which Salmon speaks of is, argues Beebee, relatively trivial by most metaphysical lights. And so one can happily accept the Kripke–Putnam view without accepting the stronger essentialist view that natural kind classifications objectively carve nature at its fundamental joints.

Beebee's central argument is that the 'non-trivial' essentialist claim which, according to Salmon, is involved in the Kripke–Putnam thesis, is not one which rules out there being cross-cutting kinds. In particular, she argues that the Kripke–Putnam view is compatible both with species pluralism and Kuhnian relativism. The basic line of argument is that, assuming the range of natural kinds goes beyond those kinds for which we have vernacular names (a claim which all natural kind essentialists endorse), deference to scientific theories is required in fixing the reference of natural kind terms. But that those theories describe a mind- and theory-independent reality, and that they do not admit a non-hierarchical structure for the categories they deploy, are theses that are independent of anything that can be derived from Kripke–Putnam semantics. And because those are the kinds of theses at the heart of natural kind essentialism, the view is not one that can be derived from Kripke–Putnam semantics itself. Beebee concludes her chapter by summarizing the general implications these results have for the wider essentialist debate.

In Tobin's paper 'Are Natural Kinds and Natural Properties Distinct?', she asks what it could mean for a set of objects to belong to a certain kind, beyond mere facts about which natural properties those objects share. The reason this is an important question is that thoroughgoing realists about natural kinds take it that a distinct category of substantial kinds is needed in our ontology, in addition to the category of properties. Yet, if it were possible to account for talk about natural kinds purely in terms of shared properties, what need would there be for a separate ontological category of kinds? Tobin argues that natural kinds can indeed be understood purely in terms of natural properties, and that views suggesting otherwise are unpersuasive. The upshot is that the robust realist views about natural kinds discussed earlier are undermined.

Tobin begins by exploring the three main ways in which natural kind divisions might be accounted for in terms of natural properties. The first proposal, which is Lewisian, is one which relies on there being a fundamental distinction between properties which are perfectly natural, and those which are less natural. On this view, two objects are of the same kind insofar as they share the same perfectly natural properties. The second proposal is one which is available to those who take natural properties to be universals, such as Armstrong. On this view, objects are said to be members of the same kind insofar as they instantiate the same conjunctive property universal. The third proposal is Quinean in spirit and trades on the set-theoretic understanding of properties. On this view, two objects are of the same natural kind insofar as they belong to a set whose members share a natural property. Again, this approach trades on the Lewisian distinction between properties which are natural and those which are not. It is this distinction which prevents any set whatsoever from corresponding to a genuine natural kind.

Given the availability of the above strategies, all of which suggest a distinctive ontological category of natural kinds is superfluous, why is it that some metaphysicians of science have nevertheless maintained that a distinct category of natural kinds is needed? It is to this question that Tobin now turns, with the aim of showing that these views about the distinctness of natural kinds face problems.

The main argument in favour of robust natural kind realism which Tobin addresses is the one discussed earlier: the essentialist argument. There are different ways in which essentialists explain the essences of natural kinds, and Tobin examines the main strategies in turn. The first account is one which takes natural kind essences to be substantival universals, the second account takes it that natural kinds possess a sortal essence, and the third account takes it that natural kinds possess a causal essence. Tobin argues that each of these strategies faces problems. This, together with the claim that natural kinds can be accounted for in terms of natural properties, leads Tobin to conclude that classification into natural kinds can reflect real differences between natural groups, without the supplementary ontological distinction between properties and kinds.

In Paul's 'Realism about Structure and Kinds', she addresses the natural kinds debate (now commonly framed in terms of the notion of joint carving *structure*) from the perspective of theories of reference. One thing that has been shown in modern meta-physics of science, in some areas at least, is that metaphysics and the philosophy of language are not unrelated. Let us assume, for example, that metaphysical realism is correct: there is a mind-independent reality and our best scientific theories carve it at its joints. What precisely does this mean, say, in the case of scientific claims about the natural kinds of the world? Well, for one thing, in order for metaphysical realism to hold, it looks like the terms in our theories—natural kind terms in this case—must have a *determinate* reference. For if this were not the case, it would no longer be clear how our natural kind theories could trace out the objective natural kind structure of the world. More generally, it would be difficult to see how any aspect of our theories latches onto a mind-independent world, if reference is indeterminate. Therefore, one way of assessing the feasibility of natural kind realism—and metaphysical realism in general—is to evaluate the claim that reference is determinate.

Paul begins her assessment by outlining the two main theories of determinate reference: the causal theory and the descriptive theory (the causal version of descriptivism being the most promising, according to Paul). Paul suggests that the best overall theory of reference is likely to be one which combines both of these approaches. In the case of fundamental physics, causal descriptivism is most appropriate, according to Paul, though this may not be true of all areas. Since Paul's primary interest is in fundamental physics, she focuses mainly on causal descriptivism for the purposes of this paper.

Paul then moves to a discussion of one of the most influential worries concerning realist theories of reference: Putnam's model-theoretic argument. The argument says, roughly, that an (ideal) scientific theory can always be modelled in a way which maps it onto the world in multiple, equally legitimate ways (i.e. ways in which the theory comes out true). On each of these mappings, the terms in the theory will denote different things, and since according to Putnam there is no question of saying which mapping is the correct one, we must accept that reference is radically indeterminate.

After discussing the key assumptions lying behind this objection, Paul discusses the Lewisian response, which trades on the objective ('natural') samenesses and differences in nature. Paul argues that while this response avoids the conclusion that nearly any interpretation of a scientific theory will make it come out as true, it may still be the case that *more than one* interpretation would make it come out as true. This argument is based on the possibility of what Paul calls the 'permutability' of structure. Thus, even if structure is postulated, reference may still be indeterminate to some extent if permutability is possible.

The obvious realist answer, Paul suggests, is to deny that the actual kind-structure of the world happens to be such that it is indeed permutable. But this, Paul argues, may weaken the realist's position, since it makes the success of realism hostage to what look like contingent properties of the world's structure. Thus, a surprising and counterintuitive result has been identified for the realist view.

Part 4: Emergence

Some complex natural systems which are the target of scientific investigation are said to be *nonlinear*. To say that a system is nonlinear is to say, broadly speaking, that the overall features and/or behaviours of the system cannot be seen as arising purely out of the additive combinations of the features and/or behaviours of the elements composing the system. For obvious reasons, the discovery of such systems has traditionally been taken to show that a version of the emergentist view of nature (outlined earlier in the chapter) must be correct, at least in the case of some scientific areas.

But precisely what bearing does nonlinearity have on questions concerning emergence? Is nonlinearity always a mark of robust metaphysical emergence, rather than mere epistemological emergence? If so, precisely what kind of metaphysical emergence do cases of nonlinearity suggest? In particular, does such emergence imply the falsity of physicalism, the view that all facts about the world are reducible to physical facts? These are some of the questions Wilson addresses in her chapter 'Nonlinearity and Metaphysical Emergence'.

Wilson begins with a historical discussion about how, in the British Emergentist tradition particularly, nonlinearity was taken to be sufficient for strong metaphysical emergence. Strong metaphysical emergence in the British Emergentists' sense was taken to occur when complex entities or systems could be said to be subject to new laws, laws over-and-above the physical laws governing the components of those entities or systems. Strong emergence in this sense implies the rejection of physicalism, and strikingly, it was thought that the apparent existence of nonlinear systems showed precisely that physicalism is false. As Wilson explains, however, cases of nonlinearity were since discovered which did not plausibly involve new laws (such as population growth, for example), suggesting that the traditional account of metaphysical emergence was too strong. Wilson does suggest, though, that it would be beneficial if a more plausible, nuanced definition of strong metaphysical emergence could be formulated, to help us to distinguish between physically acceptable cases of nonlinearity and cases of nonlinearity which violate physicalism. Wilson concludes the opening section by offering just this.

Wilson then moves on to the contemporary debate about nonlinearity, in particular views which say there are cases of nonlinearity involving properly emergent features or behaviours, but emergence of a kind which is compatible with physicalism (i.e. 'weak' emergence). Wilson argues, however, that none of these views (e.g. those of Newman, Bedau, and Batterman) succeed in providing a notion of emergence which is genuinely metaphysical. These accounts of emergence, Wilson argues, are either obviously epistemic from the start, or appeal to cases in which the alleged 'emergent' features could in principle be ontologically reduced, thereby generating a merely representational form of emergence.

Does this mean that we should give up altogether on the prospect of establishing genuine (weak) metaphysical emergence in some cases of nonlinearity? Wilson suggests not, and sets about formulating a new definition of weak emergence which is genuinely metaphysical in nature and yet is compatible with physicalism. The formulation in question is based on the thought that metaphysical emergence involves the elimination of degrees of freedom, which set the parameters needed to describe an entity or system as being in a characteristic state. More precisely, Wilson claims that an entity is weakly emergent if the system out of which it arises has degrees of freedom some of which are eliminated relative to the composing entities. After establishing this formulation, Wilson argues that the emergence involved here is genuinely metaphysical and that, strikingly, there are actual cases of nonlinearity which plausibly have precisely this feature.

degrees / freedom set the parameters —
needed to describe (an entity or
system) as being in a characteristic
state.

PART I

Laws

→ of a given system whose subjects
are prisoners w/o which there
would be no need for the
system. [of the subjects]
The system goog is about managing
their lives, in a one design fits
all manner, the purpose / which
[other than providing food, hygiene,
+ some exercise — the basics needed
to stay alive] is to RESTRICT OR
CONTROL THEIR MOVEMENTS — their
freedom, no ∆'t than PENNED
CATTLE.

   CATTLE ~~which~~ when compared
to those GRAZING ON the RANGE,
provide a STARK CONTRAST

Roles + RELATIONS IN EACH SCENE. AS significant
it unfolds.

DECISIONS made + their effects in these
MEANINGful or significant scenes (immediately
or later)

LAWS' COUNTERFACTUAL robustness is " REAL " +
"objectv" (NOT AN ARTEFACT) w/o relying ON ASSPTNS
ABOUT ___ ___ (ontology + metaphysics)

*[handwritten top margin: CNCPT / MSMNT — its NORM √ — Epistemic
role that it ("") PLAYS IN the practice / sci]*

2

Measurements, laws, and counterfactuals

[handwritten: " BOTH real + objv " (LAWS)]

John T. Roberts

[handwritten right margin: (shower up)]

1 Introduction

In this chapter I ~~will~~ sketch and motivate a new philosophical approach to laws of nature.[1] This approach is not easily classified as either 'Humean' or 'non-Humean', though it does appear to be consistent with a Humean ontology. It seeks to explain the special status of laws, and their counterfactual robustness, in terms of their relation to the concept of measurement and the normative–epistemic role that measurement plays in the practice of science. What is most novel about it (I think) is that it aims to vindicate the idea that the laws' counterfactual robustness is both real and objective—not an artefact of our decisions about what to 'hold constant' in counterfactual reasoning—without relying on any particular assumptions about ontology or metaphysics. ~~So inso-far as~~ this theory is plausible, it suggests that there are important limits to what we can learn about metaphysics and ontology from the fact that science seems to portray the universe as law-governed.

[handwritten: U presented as law-governed]

2 Two great truths about counterfactuals

To motivate my account, I will begin with two plausible and familiar claims. In the interest of space, I won't spend much time defending them; I trust that neither will be very controversial. The first is the familiar thought that:

LCR: The laws of nature are distinguished from other true regularities ~~by the fact that~~ they ~~would still have~~ hold under a very broad range of counterfactual suppositions.

[handwritten left margin: b | c]

[handwritten right margin: LCR]

I will call this claim 'LCR', which stands for 'the laws are counterfactually resilient'.

---

[1] The view is described and defended in more detail in my 2008. However, the discussion here goes beyond what I said there in several ways.

The second claim concerns what I will call *legitimate measurement methods.* These are the procedures that can be used to reach judgments about the values of empirical variables—distances, temperatures, pH values, etc.—which can play the role of basic items of evidence in science. I assume that in order for a procedure to be a legitimate measurement method, it must be *reliable,* in the sense that whenever the procedure is carried out correctly, there is some kind of positive correlation between the result of the measurement and the value of the variable being measured.[2] But mere reliability is not enough to make a procedure a legitimate measurement procedure. To take just one sort of example: The procedure of finding out the height of a mountain by looking it up in the *Encyclopaedia Britannica* is, as a matter of fact, very reliable. And since it involves using the senses, it is in the most general sense an *empirical* procedure as well. But nobody would call it a way of *measuring* the height of a mountain. Instead, it is simply a way of finding out about the results of previous evidence gathering, to which the person consulting the reference book is prepared to defer. This raises an important question: What more does an empirical procedure have to have—over and above mere *de facto* reliability—in order to count as a legitimate measurement procedure?

The second of the two claims I want to start with is an incomplete answer to this question. It is that:

> MCR: The legitimate measurement methods are distinguished from other *de facto* reliable empirical procedures by their counterfactual reliability—the fact that when correctly carried out, their results counterfactually track the value of the variable getting measured.

('MCR' stands for 'measurements are counterfactually reliable'.) For example, when we use sophisticated surveyors' methods to determine the height of a mountain, the result we get will counterfactually track the height we are measuring: Had the height of the mountain been different from what it actually is, while we were still using our methods correctly, we would still have gotten an accurate result. Similarly, had other conditions been different in a wide variety of ways, correct applications of the method would still have given accurate results. By contrast, what the method of looking up the height of the mountain in the *Britannica* counterfactually tracks is not the height of the mountain, but instead what is said about the height of the mountain in the *Britannica.* In the actual world, of course, this means that this procedure is extremely accurate—maybe even a lot more accurate than the method of getting surveyors' tools and performing a fresh measurement would be. But the surveyors' method is more counterfactually reliable. And it is greater counterfactual reliability, rather than greater *de facto* accuracy, that sets apart the legitimate measurement methods.

It might be worth lingering over this point a moment. The reason the method of looking up the height in the *Britannica* is not counterfactually reliable is that what it takes for you to correctly carry out the method is just for you to do your part right—to

---

[2] Thus, the sense of 'reliable' at issue here is not modal or counterfactual; it simply involves a correlation. To flag this, I will usually call it '*de facto*' reliability'.

FOR A Procedure to be A Legitimate MM it must be RELIABLE

identify a copy of the *Britannica*, open the right volume to the right page, look to the right row and column in the right table, and correctly process the numeral printed there. You could have done all of this perfectly correctly even if, say, the publishers of the *Britannica* had employed an incompetent typesetter to work on the volume in question—but we do not want to say with much confidence that in that case, you would still have arrived at a correct judgment about the height of the mountain. By contrast, what it takes for you to correctly carry out a legitimate surveyors' technique involves making sure you have the right equipment, making sure that it is constructed and set up correctly, making sure that atmospheric conditions are good for making a measurement, and then carrying out the technique in the right way. Had you done all of that correctly, you would have got a good result; this just doesn't allow leeway for something to have wrecked your measurement so long as you carried the method out correctly. For example, if your tools had a defect you were unaware of, then you would not have got the right answer, but then (unbeknownst to you) you would not have carried out the method correctly either. Of course, there is always the logical possibility of your having got the wrong answer, even if you had carried out the method correctly. Had the laws of optics been totally different from what they are, so that light travelled in serpentine lines rather than straight ones, then the surveyors' method you are employing would not have been reliable at all. That is merely a *logical* point: Such a difference in the laws of optics is inconsistent with the *de facto* reliability of actual surveyors' methods, which are based on the assumption that light travels in straight lines. But so long as we are considering counterfactual scenarios that are *logically* consistent with your method's reliability, it is not easy to find one under which your method would not still have been *de facto* reliable. By contrast, it is very easy to think of counterfactual scenarios that are logically consistent with the reliability of the *Britannica* method, but are such that it isn't true that that method would still have been reliable (even when carried out perfectly correctly) had one of those scenarios obtained. (For example, the scenario of the incompetent typesetter.)

The crucial difference between the two kinds of method is this: When you carry out a method that is relevantly like the *Britannica* method, you make your success dependent on luck in a certain way: *It isn't enough for you to do your part exactly right; you need other people to have done their part right in order for your method to be successful.* If they have done their part right, that's in a certain sense good luck for you. By contrast, if you correctly carry out a legitimate measurement procedure, you thereby eliminate the need to depend on this sort of luck. Of course, there are many other ways in which you might still be lucky: It is lucky for you that you were able to discover this method of measuring mountain heights; you are lucky you were able to afford the equipment, and lucky it didn't break during shipping; you are lucky to have been at the mountain on a day when atmospheric conditions were sufficiently clear to carry out the method; perhaps you are even lucky not to be a brain in a vat. But, *given that you did in fact successfully carry out the method correctly*, no further luck-dependence seems necessary for you to get the right result. This, I suggest, is what sets legitimate measurement methods apart from other methods such as the *Britannica* method, which are in fact perfectly reliable but do not count as real measurement methods: The latter, even when carried out perfectly correctly, still depend on an extra bit of luck for their reliability. For this reason, the legitimate measurement methods are distinguished by their counterfactual reliability, as MCR says.

As I formulated them above, LCR and MCR are both somewhat vague. Their vagueness concerns the range of counterfactual suppositions in question: LCR tells us that the laws would still have held under a great many counterfactual suppositions, but which ones? MCR tells us that the legitimate measurement methods would still have tracked the variables being measured, but across what range of counterfactual scenarios would they have done so? There are many ways in which we might answer these questions. For example:

LCR': The laws of nature are distinguished from other true regularities by the fact that they form a *stable set*: that is, they would all still have been true under any counterfactual supposition that is metaphysically compossible with them all.

MCR': The legitimate measurement methods are distinguished from the other *de facto* reliable empirical methods by the fact that they would still have been *de facto* reliable under any counterfactual supposition that is metaphysically compossible with the *de facto* reliability of all of them; in other words, the propositions expressing their *de facto* reliability form a stable set.

(This concept of a *stable set* is borrowed from Marc Lange.[3] LCR' and MCR' precisify LCR and MCR by specifying that the range of counterfactual invariance involved in them is as great as it could possibly be: No set of truths could possibly be such that they would all still have been true even under a counterfactual supposition that is *not* compossible with the whole set.[4] So the most resilient a set could possibly be under counterfactual suppositions is for it to be such that all of its members would still have been true under any counterfactual supposition compossible with the set—that is, for it to be *stable*.)

Some philosophers hold that the laws are just as counterfactually resilient as LCR' says they are (e.g. Lange 2009; Carroll 1994). Others hold that they are not quite that resilient: Lewis 1979 and Bennett 2003, for example, hold that the nearest possible world where some physically possible counterfactual suppositions hold are worlds where a small miracle occurs, allowing history to violate the actual laws just enough to bring about the truth of the supposition while leaving almost all of the actual past history intact. (For example, the nearest possible world at which Nixon pushed the button at time *t* is a world in which history is exactly the same as in the actual world up to some

---

[3] See for example Lange 2005.

[4] A quick way to see this, using the Stalnaker/Lewis possible-worlds framework: If A is not compossible with the set S, then there is no possible world where A is true and all members of S are, too. So trivially, the nearest possible worlds where A is true are worlds where at least one member of S is false. That is, not all members of S would still have been true had it been the case that A.

time slightly before t, when a small violation of the actual laws allows a fateful event to occur in Nixon's brain, and all of the actual laws are obeyed thereafter.) If their view is right, then LCR is true, but LCR' isn't: The right way to make LCR precise is something else. The principal motivation for this small-miracle view is the thought that we must adopt it in order to uphold the principle that counterfactuals typically do not backtrack: Had things been different at time t, then perhaps they would also have been different at times later than t, but they would not have been different at times earlier than t. This is hard to reconcile with LCR; the problem is especially acute if Laplacian determinism is true, since then the actual laws together with a difference at one time would seem to entail a difference at every other time.

This is not the place to try to settle whether it is true that counterfactuals typically do not backtrack, or whether it is true that the small-miracle view is the only way to uphold this principle.[5] The important point here is that someone who is motivated to reject LCR' on these grounds will have equally good grounds for rejecting MCR': For MCR' leads to backtracking counterfactuals too. For example, if the outcome of a legitimate measurement of the brightness of a star ten light-years from Earth that was in fact carried out completely correctly had been different from what it actually was, then it seems that either that star would have had a different brightness ten years ago (which would be a case of backtracking), or else the measurement would have been carried out incorrectly (which is again a case of backtracking) or else that method would not have been reliable after all. So if we want to insist on rejecting backtracking, in this case we'll have to allow that the *de facto* reliability of the legitimate measurement methods is not quite as counterfactually resilient as MCR' implies.

In the rest of this chapter, I won't need to make any assumptions about how LCR and MCR should be made precise. But I will need to assume that they should be made precise in similar ways: If the laws are maximally counterfactually resilient, so that LCR' is true, then the legitimate measurement methods are also maximally counterfactually reliable, so that MCR' is true. If there must be limitations on the resilience of the laws in order to keep out backtracking, then there must be the very same limitations on the counterfactual reliability of the measurement methods. The general point is that whatever the range of counterfactual scenarios over which LCR holds, MCR holds over the same range of counterfactual scenarios. For present purposes, we don't need to make LCR and MCR any more precise than they are, but we do need to recognize that if they are to be made more precise, they must both be made more precise in the same way.

So, we have these two great truths, LCR and MCR. Because of their similarity, it is hard to believe that they are not related in some important way. Is there some explanatory connection between them?

---

[5] I criticize these reasons for rejecting LCR' in my 2008, pp. 228–42.

3 The obvious explanation

The obvious answer seems to be that there is—that LCR helps to explain MCR. But in order for this to be so there needs to be a certain kind of connection between the property of lawhood and the property of legitimate-measurement-method-hood. That connection is:

> NAM: What it is to be a legitimate measurement method is to be an empirical procedure for finding out the value of an empirical variable whose reliability is guaranteed by the laws of nature.

('NAM' stands for 'nomological analysis of measurement'.) If this is true, then the fact that laws of nature are counterfactually resilient explains why the legitimate measurement methods are counterfactually reliable.

This seems to provide an explanation of why good measurements counterfactually track the things they are measurements of. This explanation rests on NAM and LCR. But what explains these two principles? NAM is a putative analysis of what a legitimate measurement method is. If correct, it's plausibly an explanatory starting point: Being a legitimate measurement method *just is* being nomologically reliable; there's nothing further to be said. What about LCR? It expresses what is widely regarded as one of the most important and most puzzling of the features that characterize laws of nature. Not many philosophers would be willing to accept it as a basic, unexplained explainer. It is a fact that cries out for some kind of explanation. One job for a philosophical theory of lawhood is to provide that explanation. We want an account of what it is for something to be a law of nature that explains why lawhood should confer counterfactual resilience on those truths that have it. It has turned out to be very hard to do that.

4 A less obvious explanation

But once we recognize the similarity between LCR and MCR, a new possibility presents itself: Perhaps the obvious answer gets things backwards. Perhaps it is not that LCR helps to explain why MCR is true. Maybe it is the other way around: MCR helps to explain LCR.

This requires there to be a certain connection between the property of lawhood and the property of legitimate-measurement-hood, but now the needed connection is the reverse of what we needed before: Instead of a nomological analysis of measurement, we have a measurement-based analysis of lawhood:

> MAL: What it is to be a law of nature is to be one of the general truths that follow from the reliability of the legitimate measurement methods.[6]

---

[6] This is a simplified version of the account defended in my 2008. This simplified version implies that the laws are closed under entailment, which many find implausible. To avoid this consequence, we can modify this version of the MAL so that it is an analysis of nomological necessity rather than lawhood. Or, we can add further conditions (e.g. logical contingency) for something to count as a law. Neither modification would affect the argument of this paper.

('MAL' stands for 'measurability account of laws'.) Given the MAL, we have an explanation of why the laws are counterfactually resilient: First of all, the legitimate measurement methods would all still have been reliable, even under a wide range of counterfactual suppositions, and second, what it is to be a law is just to be one of the general truths that would still have been true so long as the legitimate measurement methods were all still reliable—which they would have been, under a wide range of counterfactual suppositions.[7]

Thus, we have an explanation of LCR that rests on two principles: MAL and MCR. It is natural to ask what explains these principles. MAL is a putative analysis of one property in terms of another; if true, it is plausibly explanatorily basic. MCR is the principle that measurement methods are counterfactually reliable. It is not very plausible to suggest that this principle is explanatory bedrock: It cries out for explanation in terms of something more basic. We might try to answer this cry by simply saying that unless some method were counterfactually reliable, we wouldn't count it as a legitimate measurement method, and so MCR must be true. But this response brings little satisfaction, if any: Now we just want to know what makes some empirical procedures counterfactually reliable. In order for any procedure to be counterfactually reliable, a whole bunch of counterfactuals have to be true—what we really want to know is, what makes all those counterfactuals true?

So we stand in need of some explanation of why all the counterfactuals that have to be true in order for MCR to be true should be true. And we need this explanation to refrain from appealing to the counterfactual resilience of the laws of nature, on pain of circularity. Where should we look for the explanation we seek?

5 Why measurements are counterfactually reliable

I think we should look to the role played by legitimate measurement methods in scientific practice. Legitimate measurement methods play a very special epistemic role: They are the ultimate sources of basic evidence in scientific inquiry. By *basic* evidence, I mean evidence that is 'fresh from the source': It is not obtained by consulting records of previously gathered evidence, but by having a new empirical interaction with the world. And the character of this new empirical interaction is what determines the content of the evidence, in such a way that the content of the evidence is sensitive to the value of the variable that the evidence is about. What does this sensitivity amount to? The obvious answer is that it amounts to counterfactual covariance: The content of the evidence

---

[7] An obvious objection arises here: A non-negotiable requirement for any philosophical theory of lawhood is that it get the extension of lawhood right, and it is not at all obvious that the MAL does get it right. In fact, there are some pretty obvious reasons for suspecting that it doesn't get it right—for example, the MAL seems to imply that all laws of nature concern measurement methods, but there seem to be plenty of laws that have nothing to do with measurement. I beg the reader's patience: This worry will be addressed in section 6 below.

delivered by a legitimate source of basic evidence must counterfactually track the variable that the evidence is about. In short, the legitimate sources of basic evidence are sources of information that are not only *de facto* reliable, but also counterfactually reliable.

This suggests the following argument, which might explain why MCR is true:

(1) Legitimate measurement methods are legitimate sources of basic evidence;
(2) A method is a legitimate source of basic evidence only if it is counterfactually reliable.

So, (MCR) legitimate measurement methods are counterfactually reliable.

Premises (1) and (2) are each plausible, and the conclusion MCR does validly follow from them. But even if this argument suffices to establish the truth of MCR, you might still have your doubts about whether it really explains why MCR is true.

The obvious objection to raise here is that this argument seems to get the explanation backwards: The reason why a method gets to count as a legitimate measurement method is that it is counterfactually reliable. On this view, counterfactual reliability is a virtue that a method must have in order to qualify for the status of legitimate source of basic evidence. But that means that the fact that a certain method is a legitimate source of basic evidence cannot be the reason why it is counterfactually reliable; that puts the cart before the horse. (Maybe this is a better metaphor: It puts the Oscar before the movie.)

The view that this objection is based on is attractive. But we can resist it; there is an alternative. On the alternative view, the counterfactual stability of a legitimate measurement method is a by-product of its normative–epistemic status, rather than a qualification it must have antecedently in order to merit that status. On this alternative picture, it is a mistake to think that claims about the epistemic roles of certain methods are grounded in the truths of various counterfactuals; instead, the epistemic norms are what ground the counterfactuals.

This is an unusual proposal, so let me try to motivate it a bit more. Note that the counterfactuals in question are non-trivial counterfactuals; that is, their antecedents do not logically entail their consequents. Non-trivial counterfactuals are notoriously context-dependent. So there is something about a context of discourse that helps to make some non-trivial counterfactuals true there, and others false there. In the possible-worlds framework, that comes to this: There is something about each context of discourse that somehow picks out a similarity metric over possible worlds to be employed in evaluating counterfactuals in this context. But what is it, exactly, about a given context that singles out one similarity metric rather than another?

One familiar answer is that what determines the similarity metric is which features of the actual world are most salient to us: The worlds that match the actual world on more of the more salient aspects are closer in. But there are well-known problems for this answer. For example, there is the Nixon example: It seems clear that a world in which Nixon pushed the button but then history continued pretty much as it actually did is more similar, in more salient ways, to the actual world than is a world in which there was a nuclear war in the early 1970s. This seems obviously true—even in a context where it is equally obviously true that there would have been a nuclear war if Nixon had pressed the button. So it seems that whatever it is that picks out a similarity metric for a given context, it must be something other than what counts as a salient feature of the actual world in that context.[8]

Lewis 1979 famously responds to the problem posed by cases like the Nixon case by specifying the criteria to be used in evaluating the similarity of possible worlds: The most important criterion is the absence of numerous, large-scale violations of the laws of one world in the other; the second most important criterion is maximizing the spatiotemporal range of complete qualitative agreement between the worlds; the third most important criterion is the absence of even small, localized violations of the laws of one world in the other. Lewis argues convincingly that if counterfactuals are evaluated using a similarity metric based on these criteria, then we avoid the problem posed by the Nixon example.

The question Lewis is answering is not our question, though. He does not provide an explanation of why his similarity metric is the one we should use for evaluating counterfactuals. His justification of this metric is simply that it seems to give answers about the truth-values of particular counterfactuals that match our intuitions in ordinary contexts. There are of course many other similarity metrics we could use, and in some non-standard contexts we use one of these other metrics. Our question is: What is it about a given context (whether ordinary or not) that makes one out of the many similarity metrics the right one to use for that context? The fact that Lewis's metric gets it right about so many particular counterfactuals might be excellent *evidence that it is* in fact the metric that is appropriate to standard contexts. But it does nothing to *explain what makes* it the right metric to use in standard contexts.

Here's a possible answer to our question (or at least, a possible partial answer): In a given context, some but not all empirical methods count as legitimate sources of basic evidence. What determines which ones do? Well, they've got to be reliable, as a matter of actual fact. But not all the *de facto* reliable ones will count as legitimate sources of basic evidence. What makes some so count? Something about the beliefs, presuppositions, epistemic projects, and epistemic practices in play in that context. For short: The *epistemic context* somehow picks out a special subset of the *de facto* reliable methods, and those methods enjoy the elevated normative status of *sources of basic evidence*. The selection of these methods in turn fixes the truth-values of many non-trivial counterfactuals—it makes-true all the ones that have to be true in order for those methods to be counterfactually reliable. This places many constraints on which counterfactuals are true in that context, though it presumably won't settle all the counterfactuals. Thus, it places many constraints on the similarity metric, though it presumably won't fix it uniquely. But it does settle it that those counterfactuals that must be true in order for the basic sources of

---

[8] Fine 1975 makes this point.

evidence to be counterfactually reliable are true. And this is why those sources are counterfactually reliable. This gives us our explanation of MCR.

But how do the facts about which methods are legitimate sources of basic evidence in a given context place any constraints on which counterfactuals are true in that context? There may be many possible answers here; the one I would like to suggest is this: Counterfactuals (or some of them, anyway) are devices we use to express judgments about which things are due to luck (or its lack) and which things are due to virtue (or its lack).[9] If someone or some thing is successful by some measure, then this success might be due to its virtues or to good luck; when we judge that the success is due to virtues, we can express this by asserting the counterfactual robustness of the success—even if circumstances had been less favourable, there would still have been success; by contrast, when we judge that the success is due to luck, we can express this by asserting the counterfactual fragility of the success—had circumstances not been so favourable, there would have been no success. This is just the leading idea of an account of the semantics of (at least some) counterfactuals; much more work would need to be done in order to show how to make this into a proper theory of counterfactuals. But if something along these lines is right, then it is clear why we must treat legitimate sources of basic evidence as counterfactually reliable: *What it is* to regard a method as a legitimate source of basic evidence is to regard it as reliable due to its own virtues and not due to luck. So if counterfactuals are (at least in part) a device for expressing judgments about luck-dependence and luck-independence, then our commitments concerning which methods are legitimate sources of basic evidence directly commit us to affirming a broad class of counterfactuals.

So we have an alternative view that lets us hold on to the idea that the deduction presented at the beginning of this section is explanatory. Should we accept this alternative view? The issue that is now before us concerns the relation between, on the one hand, the special normative epistemological status that legitimate measurement methods have, and on the other, the counterfactual conditionals whose truth is required by the counterfactual reliability of those methods. The issue is about which way the direction of explanation runs here—which thing is in the driver's seat and which is in the passenger's seat, so to speak. The objection that I considered earlier in this section took it for granted that the counterfactuals are in the driver's seat, and the reason why certain methods deserve the special status of legitimate measurement methods is that certain counterfactuals are true. The alternative view that I am proposing says that the normative epistemic role of the legitimate measurement methods is in the driver's seat; the reason why certain counterfactuals are true is that their truth is a consequence of the fact that certain methods have the special epistemic status of legitimate measurement methods. It's a

---

[9] Having this device might be useful for many reasons; for example, the logic of counterfactuals might serve as a useful means of enforcing certain consistency constraints on our judgments about luck and virtue.

question of whether the epistemic norms are at the mercy of the counterfactuals, or whether they are what drive the counterfactuals.

Which view should we accept? That's a very big question. I reckon that in order to settle it, we would have to think long and hard about the nature of counterfactuals in general.[10] Here I just want to point out one important virtue of the view that the epistemic norms are in charge: It enables us to articulate a theory of what laws of nature are that affords a very neat and elegant explanation of why laws of nature support counterfactuals. That theory is the MAL; it says that in any given context, the laws of nature in that context just are the generalizations that follow from the reliability of the procedures that count as legitimate measurement methods in that context.

MAL

6 Objections and replies

According to the MAL, the laws of nature are the general truths that follow from the reliability of all of the legitimate measurement methods. But it is far from clear that this gets the extension of lawhood right. For it is far from clear that every law of nature really does follow from reliability of the legitimate measurement methods. Measurement, after all, is a very special kind of phenomenon; what reason is there to think that all laws of nature will have anything in particular to do with it? I will consider a few different, more specific forms of this objection, and try to show that they can all be overcome.

First form of the objection: If the MAL is right, then every law of nature should be a consequence of facts of the form 'Whenever somebody measures quantity Q using method M,...' and it is just isn't plausible that every law of nature does follow from such facts. For one thing, none of those facts can imply anything about what is going on when nobody is measuring anything. And surely, the laws of nature govern things that happen when nobody is measuring anything!

The right response to this objection is to clarify just what is meant by a *measurement procedure*. I propose that we understand this as a kind of event or process that could be exploited by some agent as a way of measuring something, though it might also occur without being used as a measurement—and it might even occur without the participation of any agent at all. So for example, the method of using a mercury thermometer to measure temperature is rightly understood as a process involving a sealed glass tube containing a mercury column that comes to rest in an environment whose temperature remains constant for long enough for the mercury column to reach thermal

---

[10] If we accept the view I am recommending, then we must eventually face the question of what grounds the epistemic norms that ground the counterfactuals. It would be circular, of course, to appeal to laws of nature or to counterfactuals in our account of this grounding. One option would be to say the epistemic norms are where it stops: They are not themselves grounded in anything more basic. (It is true that the epistemic norms are constrained by actual regularities—a source of evidence that is factually unreliable cannot have the normative status of a legitimate source of basic evidence. But this does not imply that the norms are grounded in the regularities, but only that the regularities constrain the norms.) Another option would be to adopt a projectivist or quasi-realist view of epistemic norms.

equilibrium with the surroundings. What we call the 'result' of this method is a certain function of the height of the mercury column after it reaches equilibrium. This process might be employed by somebody for the purpose of measuring a temperature. But the process itself is not *essentially* one in which any agents are doing anything.

On this way of thinking about measurements, it is useful to think of a measurement method as individuated by three things: A variable Q, which I will call *the object variable* (this is what is being measured); a second variable P, which I will call *the pointer variable* (its value is the result of the measurement); and a condition C, which may be very complex, which I will call *the set-up condition* (this is the condition that must be satisfied in order for the method to have been correctly carried out). When somebody carries out this method as a measurement, they see to it that C obtains, or else they somehow check and make sure that C obtains, and then they check the value of P and read off the value of Q from it. But C might obtain even if nobody is trying to employ this method as method of measuring Q. What it takes for the method to be reliable is for a condition of this form to be true:

R   Whenever condition C obtains, K(P, Q)

where K is some sort of positive correlation relation—it might simply be equality, or it might be some kind of objective probabilistic correlation. If the condition R obtains, then the method of seeing to it that C, or making sure that C, and then reading off the value of Q from that of P will be *de facto* reliable. (In fact, R just is the statement that this method is *de facto* reliable.) But the truth of R will have implications for what is going on whenever conditions C obtain, even when nobody is measuring anything.

There are a couple of conditions that have to be met in order for the method determined by Q, P, and C to be usable as a measurement method. For one thing, the value of P must itself be observable or measurable, by means independent of the method <Q, P, C>. Also, it must be possible at least in principle to be empirically justified in thinking that conditions C hold, again by means independent of the method under discussion. If either of these conditions failed to hold, then it would not be possible to employ this method as a source of empirical information.[11] But so long as both are satisfied, the method determined by Q, P, and C is a candidate for measurement-method-hood. A further requirement is that R must be logically contingent; so, for example, the set-up condition C cannot specify that K(P, Q) holds. (If we did not impose this requirement, we would have to count endless trivial procedures as legitimate measurement methods— e.g. the procedure of detecting the mass of the sun in kilograms by examining any digital readout that matches that mass.)

---

[11] This might seem to make the notion of a legitimate measurement method circular, since whether <Q, P, C> is a legitimate measurement method depends on what other legitimate measurement methods are available. But in fact there is recursion rather than circularity here: In any context, certain methods are presupposed to be basic legitimate methods; their legitimacy together with other facts make other methods legitimate, and so forth. See my 2008, section 8.6 for more details.

It is important to note how flexible the form R is. Any logically contingent proposition that asserts a correlation between two variables at least one of which is measurable, under conditions that can be known empirically to obtain, can be written in the form R. And whenever a proposition of the form of R holds, the MAL allows that it is possible for it to be a law of nature. Conversely, whenever a proposition of the form R is a law of nature, it seems that the corresponding method should count as a legitimate measurement procedure: After all, it will be a usable empirical procedure for finding out the value of Q, which is not only reliable, but also counterfactually reliable, since its reliability is a matter of natural law. So every law of nature that takes the form of R should count as a law of nature according to the MAL, and it is plausible that a very wide variety of laws take the form of R.[12] So the MAL will be able to count a wide variety of putative laws as laws of nature—including many putative laws that appear to have nothing to do with measurement as such.

I have met the follow-up objection[13] that the move I have just made trivializes the MAL by stretching the notion of a legitimate measurement method so far that any law of nature would count as providing one. The thought seems to be that if a 'legitimate measurement method' is just any old method whose reliability is vouchsafed by some law, then we lack the independent grip on the concept of a *legitimate measurement method* that we would need in order to be able to use that concept in an informative analysis of lawhood. It would be as if we proposed to analyse knowledge as justified true belief and then said that 'justification' just meant whatever a true belief has to have in order to be a case of knowledge.

I do indeed hold that there is a conceptual connection between lawhood and measurement that is strong enough that we can simply 'read off' facts about what is and is not a good measurement method from the facts about the laws; in particular, any empirical finding-out procedure whose reliability is vouchsafed by laws is a legitimate measurement procedure. But it does not follow from this that the concept of a legitimate measurement method is not sufficiently independent of that of a law for there to be an informative reduction of laws to measurement. All that follows is that there is a close connection between the two; this is perfectly consistent with the hypothesis that it is lawhood that is reducible to legitimate measurement, rather than the other way around. It is also consistent with (what I claim is) the fact that a perfectly good way of finding out whether something is a good measurement method is by drawing inferences from what we know about the laws. (The order of metaphysical constitution doesn't have to coincide with the order of epistemic discovery; for example, the hypothesis that macro-properties are metaphysically reducible to micro-properties is perfectly consistent with

---

[12] Objection: But perhaps not every such law really does correspond to a legitimate method; after all, mere *de facto* reliability is not sufficient for legitimacy! Reply: But if a method's *de facto* reliability is a matter of nomological necessity, then the method evidently has what it takes to play the role of a measurement in science; so if R is really a law, it does count as a law according to the MAL. See the discussion of the follow-up objection, immediately below. (Thanks to an anonymous referee.)

[13] Thanks to an anonymous referee.

the fact that the usual way of finding out about micro-properties is by drawing inferences from what we know about macro-properties. Ditto for laws and legitimate measurement methods.) So it is perfectly coherent to hold that we have an independent grip on what a legitimate measurement method is, which allows us to use it in an informative analysis of lawhood, even though we should be prepared to count any empirical finding-out procedure whose reliability is secured by the laws as a legitimate measurement method.

But do we really have such an independent grip on legitimate measurement? I think we do. The concept of a legitimate measurement method is irreducibly epistemic and normative: A legitimate measurement method is a *de facto* reliable procedure for finding out the value of one natural variable, by bringing about a correlation between it and a second natural variable, *that is capable of playing the role of a source of ultimate evidence in science*—i.e. (roughly speaking) a method such that were someone to use it, they would be epistemically licensed to employ their result as an item of basic scientific evidence (i.e. evidence that depends for its authority as evidence neither on inference nor on deference to testimony or records).[14] This concept is indispensible to science: No one could practise science without making use of it, at least implicitly. I doubt that it can be analysed in terms of anything more basic—in particular, I doubt that it can be analysed in terms of regularities, laws, or counterfactuals. But that is not to say that, in order to find out whether some procedure is a legitimate measurement method, we cannot rely on inferences drawn from what we already know about which regularities, laws, and counterfactuals hold. On the contrary: That is probably the most useful way we have of finding out whether something is a good measurement method.[15] In the practice of science (and empirical inquiry more generally) we always already believe some procedures to be legitimate measurement methods, and we can use these beliefs together with what we know and what we come to learn about such things as laws and counterfactuals to learn that other procedures are legitimate measurement methods (and sometimes to correct our earlier judgments). For example, when we find out that our nomological beliefs imply that a certain empirical finding-out procedure is nomologically reliable, this gives us a compelling reason to allow that procedure to play the epistemic role of a measurement method in science. Again, these useful inferential linkages show only that there is a tight connection between laws and measurements; they do not imply that the concept of a measurement is dependent on that of lawhood in a way that makes it inappropriate to reduce lawhood to measurement.

[14] But what if they didn't know it was a legitimate measurement method? In that case, they might not be epistemically justified (in an internalist sense) in believing their result. The notion of legitimate measurement method, and that of the kind of 'epistemic license' just used in the text, is an externalist one; you can have it without having the kind of justification internalism is concerned with (just as in some contexts, your senses might license you to form certain beliefs without your knowing that they do).

[15] There is no inconsistency here, since the order of epistemic discovery need not coincide with the order of metaphysical constitution.

(2)

Second form of the objection: There might be laws of nature that govern only relations among unobservable quantities. But the MAL implies that there are no such laws, since it says that all laws are consequences of propositions of the form R, in which the pointer variable P is observable.

In reply to this form of the objection, the first thing to point out is that the sense of 'observability' in which P must be observable is very weak. All that is required is that it is possible to make an empirical determination of the value of P: P must be in principle *measurable*. All kinds of variables that would have been considered unobservable theoretical quantities during the heyday of logical empiricism will make this cut, including electric charge, the masses of celestial bodies, and pH values.

Still, the MAL does imply that there cannot be any laws governing quantities that are not in principle measurable, even in this very broad sense. The move for a defender of the MAL to make here is simply to acknowledge the consequence that there could be no such laws of nature. This need not be a very painful concession to make. Most of the principles that we take to be laws of nature relate quantities that are in principle measurable. There are exceptions: For example, in classical electrodynamics there are laws governing the values of the scalar and vector potentials, whose values are in principle undetectable. But for that very reason, these potentials are usually considered ontologically suspect in the context of classical physics: The fact that the potentials are in principle undetectable is one standard justification for regarding them as 'surplus structure' that lacks genuine physical content. So it is not implausible to suppose that the putative laws in which the potentials figure are not true laws of nature, though they might play an important role within a useful formalism.

(3)

Third form of the objection: There may be conditions under which nothing that could remotely be called a measurement process could take place—for example, the conditions deep in the interior of a star, or very near a black hole where the tidal forces would very quickly rip us and our equipment apart. To coin a technical term, let's call conditions like these 'horrible conditions'. According to the MAL, every law of nature has to be derivable from facts about which measurement procedures are reliable. Those facts obviously imply nothing at all about what goes on in horrible conditions, since there can be no measurements made under horrible conditions. So the MAL implies that what goes on under horrible conditions is completely outside the scope of the laws. But this seems wrong: We think that what goes on under horrible conditions is governed by the laws of nature.[16]

Reply: Why should we think that the MAL can't allow laws that govern what happens under horrible conditions? According to the MAL, every law has to be a principle of the following form, or else derivable from principles of the following form:

R   Whenever condition C obtains, K(P, Q)

---

[16] I am grateful to Wayne Myrvold for pressing this objection forcefully.

every law / nature has to be derivable
from facts / about which most procedures are
reliable

R, whenever words C obtain, K(P,Q)

R will have implications for what goes on under horrible conditions, so long as C is compatible with horrible conditions. Why can't C be compatible with horrible conditions? The objector will answer: 'Because C is supposed to be the condition that is satisfied whenever somebody correctly carries out a certain measurement method—but nobody can measure anything under horrible conditions! So, C can't be satisfied under horrible conditions.' But that isn't quite right: Remember that a measurement method is a kind of event or process that might be exploited by an agent in order to measure something, but might also occur when no measurement is taking place. The objection takes for granted that this means something like this:

(a) If M is a legitimate measurement method, then M must be a type of occurrence such that wherever it is nomologically possible for a token of M to occur, it is nomologically possible for a token occurrence of M to be employed as a measurement of Q by some agent.

And (a) does seem to imply that a legitimate measurement method cannot have any token occurrences in horrible conditions. But why should we accept (a)? Why not instead suppose something weaker:

(b) If M is a legitimate measurement method, then M must be a type of occurrence such that for each token occurrence of M: *If* some agent *had* exploited that occurrence as a way of finding out about the value of Q, then that agent *would have* legitimately measured Q.

Unlike (a), (b) allows that a legitimate measurement method might be a kind of occurrence some tokens of which occur under horrible conditions. It isn't necessary for it to be nomologically possible for an agent actually to exploit each and every one of its token instances as a measurement; all that is required is that for each one of those tokens, a certain subjunctive conditional is true: If some agent were to use that token as a way of finding out about the value of Q, then she would thereby legitimately measure Q. And this seems to be enough to capture the idea that a measurement procedure is a kind of process that would be legitimate to exploit as a way of gaining information—if only you could get yourself in a position to do so. In the usual case, not all token occurrences of M will actually be used by some agent as a measurement, so many of these subjunctive conditionals will be counterfactuals. In a case where some of the token occurrences occur under horrible conditions, the subjunctive will not only be a counterfactual—it will be a counterlegal. But this doesn't mean it wouldn't be true.

You might ask: But what makes it true? Here I want to give the same answer I gave before: In any given context, features of the epistemic practices in play will single out some but not all of the *de facto* reliable methods as the ones that are legitimate measurement methods. This places certain constraints on which counterfactuals are true in that context. In particular, every counterfactual that has to be true in order for the legitimate measurement methods to be legitimate measurement methods must be true. And this includes the counterlegals that tell us that the legitimate measurement methods would still have been legitimate measurement methods even if (what is physically impossible) they had been employed under horrible conditions.

Notice that *that* counterlegal is one with an explicitly normative consequent—and counterlegals of that type are perhaps the easiest ones to see to the truth of (when they are true). For example, if I were to drive a knife through your heart at a speed greater than c, I would thereby do something morally wrong; if I were to draw an inference according to modus ponens while riding on a perpetual motion machine, I would be epistemically justified in drawing this inference; etc. Such counterlegals seem clearly true because the norms that ground their consequents are counterfactually robust enough to extend even into nomologically impossible realms, so to speak. The moral norms can classify an action as either morally justified or morally unjustified without regard to whether it is nomologically possible for someone to carry out that action, and just so, the epistemic norms can classify the use of a method as a legitimate or an illegitimate act of measurement without regard to whether it is nomologically possible for anyone to employ that method. In either case, when the norms classify a nomologically impossible action as legitimate (in whichever sense), this shows itself in the truth of a counterlegal about what someone's status would be if they did carry out that action.

This answers the objection: The MAL can allow that there are laws of nature governing what happens even under horrible conditions because it can allow that some legitimate measurement methods can be instantiated even under horrible conditions.

7 Some examples

It might be worth looking at an example or two to get a feel for how the MAL works.[17] Suppose for the sake of simplicity that we are living in a Newtonian world. It is true, then, that for any body, the total impressed force F on that body is equal to its mass m multiplied by its acceleration a. So one empirical method for determining the total impressed force on a body is to find out both what its mass is and what its acceleration is, and multiply the two. This is a method in which the pointer variable is the product ma and the object variable is F. (And the set-up condition is one that is vacuously satisfied, since this correlation between the object and pointer variables holds under all conditions in a

---

[17] In these examples, it might appear that I am proceeding backwards from the standpoint of the MAL: I begin with an assumption about what the laws are—they are Newtonian—and then work out which methods are counterfactually reliable and which are legitimate. According to the MAL, though, the counterfactuals as well as the laws are grounded in the legitimate measurement methods, so shouldn't I start with them? Recall, though, that the MAL does not imply that we cannot figure out whether a method is legitimate by drawing an inference from premises about laws (see the preceding section). Moreover, my aim here is to illustrate the extensional adequacy of the MAL, by showing that the relation it claims to hold between the laws and the legitimate measurement methods agrees with our independent judgments about what counts as a law and what as a legitimate measurement method. To do that, I need to rely on our ordinary ways of figuring out what is a good measurement method; it would be question-begging to rely on the MAL itself to generate the answers.

Newtonian world.) It is possible to exploit this as an empirical method, because both the mass m and the acceleration **a** are themselves measurable by other methods. And clearly, someone who correctly carries out this method may legitimately be said to have measured the impressed force on the body in question. Thus, F = ma counts as a law according to the MAL. (It's just that simple.)

By contrast, suppose that it just happens to be the case that for every planet in the universe, its mass m is related to its mean orbital speed by the function Φ; so, m = Φ(s). (So long as no two planets have exactly the same mean orbital speed, this is bound to be true for some function Φ.) So here is a method for finding out the mass of a planet: Measure its mean orbital speed, plug the result into Φ, and do the calculation. *Ex hypothesi*, that method is *de facto* reliable. But it does not qualify as a legitimate measurement method; its *de facto* reliability is a large-scale accident or fluke, and this flukiness is not consistent with the legitimacy of this method as a source of basic evidence. Thus, the equation m = Φ(s) is not a law of nature in a Newtonian world—which is obviously the right answer, since in Newtonian physics there is no reason to expect there to be any particular nomic correlation between a planet's mass and its mean orbital speed.

8 Broader issues

Is the MAL a Humean account of laws or a non-Humean account? (Here and in what follows, let's understand 'Humean' to mean consistent with the thesis of Humean Supervenience.[18]) The question is not straightforward. The MAL analyses lawhood in terms of legitimate measurement methods, but it does not offer a theory of what a legitimate measurement method is—except to say that such a method is the kind of thing that has the epistemic–normative status of a source of basic evidence in scientific practice. It is possible to combine the MAL, as defined above, with different theories of the epistemic norms relating to measurement methods, resulting in different overall positions. Combining the MAL with a view of measurement methods that is consistent with Humeanism would result in a Humean view, whereas combining it with a view of measurement incompatible with Humeanism will result in a non-Humean view.

However, it is hard to see what the appeal of combining it with a non-Humean view of measurement would be. For example, one possible non-Humean view of measurement holds that a method counts as a legitimate measurement only if there is a non-logical necessary connection between the value of the pointer variable and that of the object variable. But if we have such non-logical necessary connections in the picture anyway, it's hard to see why we shouldn't just appeal to them directly in giving our account of lawhood, and skip the detour through measurement.

---

[18] I argue that this is not the unique best way to understand the label 'Humean' in this context in my 2008, Chapter 10.

A more interesting question is whether we should adopt a realist or a pragmatist view of legitimate measurement methods, where a *realist* view is one that holds that being a legitimate measurement method is an intrinsic feature of a type of process which that type possesses independently of its use by members of any epistemic community, and a *pragmatist* view is one that holds that what it is for a process type to be a legitimate measurement method is for it to play a certain role within a family of epistemic practices. A pragmatist view might further imply that legitimate-measurement-method-hood is relative to a community or a context, and perhaps also that statements about what is a legitimate measurement method have a contextualist semantics. (It would follow from this that if the MAL is right, then law-statements have a contextualist semantics as well.[19])

On any version of the MAL, lawhood, together with the special counterfactual status associated with the laws, is grounded in something normative, namely the epistemic norms concerning which process-types count as legitimate measurement methods. These epistemic norms are the grounds for the elevated modal status of the laws; they are not themselves reducible to the natural or nomological necessities. Thus, on this view, the true explanation for the peculiar features of laws of nature is found in epistemology rather than in the metaphysical territory of universals, essences, powers, and so forth. It is of course a further question, and a much deeper one, where these epistemic norms come from and how they are grounded.[20]

[19] In my 2008 I develop and defend a pragmatist view that has all of the features just mentioned. There I identify 'the MAL' as that whole pragmatist/contextualist package. It seems to me now, though, that it is worth distinguishing the core of the MAL (which is the view of lawhood defended in this paper) from the pragmatism and contextualism about legitimate measurement methods; these two things don't necessarily stand or fall together.

[20] For helpful feedback on earlier versions of this material I am grateful to audiences at the University of Western Ontario, King's College London, and the Metaphysics of Science '09 Conference in Nottingham, and to Antony Eagle, Heather Gert, William Harper, Matt Kotzen, Marc Lange, Wayne Myrvold, Daniel Nolan, David Papineau, Chris Smeenk, and two anonymous referees.

3

Laws, causes, and invariance[*]

Jim Woodward

1 Introduction: supervenience and underdetermination

My aim in this essay is to explore some issues concerning the structure of our thinking about the concepts of law and cause, as these figure in scientific contexts. I will be particularly concerned with the evidential reasoning we use to infer to causal claims and laws and the way in which we use such claims in explanations. My interests will be primarily epistemic and methodological, rather than metaphysical. My discussion is based on the assumption (and I hope illustrates) that it is possible to say interesting things about how 'cause' and 'law' figure in scientific practice without providing a full-blown metaphysics of science. Despite this, I believe that my discussion is relevant to the claims of metaphysicians in (at least) the following way: providing a plausible metaphysical account of important scientific notions requires that one avoid mistaken views about the structure and interrelations of those notions. Otherwise one may end up attempting to provide metaphysical foundations for non-existent features of science or failing to take account of resources present in actual science used to address some of the problems with which metaphysicians are concerned. I illustrate these points below.

To set the stage for what follows, I begin by recalling a familiar dialectic. Suppose we have a catalogue of all of the non-modal particular facts true of our world—the Humean Supervenience Base (HSB). These facts are 'non-modal' in the sense that their characterization does not require reference to notions like 'law', 'cause', 'physical possibility', 'disposition', and so on. (Further details will not matter for our purposes.) We then ask whether laws and causal claims respect Humean supervenience in the sense of Lewis (1986b)—that is, whether they supervene on this HSB. (Here we may distinguish two possibilities—(i) the supervenience claim might be true of our world, as a matter of contingent fact, or (ii) it might be true in all metaphysically possible worlds. Lewis's official position endorses only (i), although the usual arguments for supervenience, if cogent at all, seem to also support (ii).) The most plausible version of the view that the laws do so

[*] Thanks to John Norton for very helpful comments on an earlier draft.

Empirical test &
Examination

supervene, either in sense (i) or (ii), appeals to a conception of laws advocated by Lewis (and attributed by him to both Mill and Ramsey): the Best Systems Analysis (BSA). On this conception, one considers alternative systemizations that capture features of the HSB. The 'best' systemization (or systemizations) is (are) those that achieve(s) the best balance of 'simplicity' and 'strength'. Laws are those claims (axioms or theorems) that occur in all such best systems and that describe regularities. Simplicity and strength in turn are taken to be characterizable in a domain-independent way, not requiring reference to any particular subject-matter or to unreduced modal assumptions. A substantial part of the appeal of the BSA is that it is supposed to correspond (in a very idealized form) to how abductive inference and theory choice in science work—the HSB represents the most extensive body of inductive evidence we could possibly possess, and (it is contended) simplicity and strength are the criteria scientists actually employ in choosing theories and laws on the basis of this evidence.

Now a familiar puzzle looms. On the one hand, as discussed in more detail below, the generalizations identified as laws in the BSA seem to coincide rather imperfectly (at best) with the generalizations regarded as laws in scientific practice. On the other hand, if we reject the claim that laws supervene on the HSB, we seem (or so it is argued) faced with a massive underdetermination problem in which claims about laws are placed beyond the possibility of empirical test or confirmation. For example, we seem committed to the possibility that there might be two different worlds, in one of which the Schrödinger equation is a law and in the other of which this equation describes a mere regularity, but which are otherwise identical, with the result that no empirical evidence could possibly tell us which of these worlds we inhabit. The upshot is that *both* the claim that the laws supervene on the HSB and the denial of this claim appear to have unattractive consequences. A parallel dilemma holds for causal claims.

When both horns of a dilemma appear to lead to unacceptable results, a good strategy is to re-examine the assumptions leading to the dilemma, rather than opting for impalement on one horn on the grounds that this is less bad than impalement on the other. This re-examination is (part of) what I propose in this chapter. I will focus on the epistemological/methodological motivations for the BSA (and Humean supervenience) and will argue that these are misguided—at least if our goal is to understand how the notions of law and cause figure in actual science. In particular, I will argue that examination of actual cases of inference to conclusions about laws and causal relationships do not take the form of applying criteria like simplicity and strength (as these are understood within the BSA) to an evidential basis that is entirely non-modal in character. Instead, (i) the evidential base in real-life science itself embodies modal commitments (having to do, for example, with the causal structure of the processes that have generated that evidence). Moreover, (ii) even apart from this, in order to reach conclusions about causal and nomological relationships, additional assumptions must be conjoined with this evidential base. These additional assumptions typically do *not* reflect the domain-independent criteria for simplicity and strength on which the BSA focuses. Instead they are domain-specific empirical assumptions that have causal or nomological content. Put very schematically, the typical pattern of inference to laws and to causal claims does not take the BSA-style form:

(1) Non-modal claims (about correlations, spatio-temporal relationships, etc.) + application of criteria involving a best balance of simplicity and strength → conclusions about causal claims and laws.

Instead, such inferences have the following structure:

(2) Non-modal claims + domain specific empirical assumptions having causal or nomological content (including but not limited to assumptions about the structures that generate observed correlations) → conclusions about other causal claims or laws.

Two consequences of (2) are that the underdetermination problems about laws and causal claims are often resolved in very different ways than standard philosophical discussions suggest and that certain possibilities on which philosophers have focused rarely or never arise in actual practice.

The remainder of this essay is organized as follows. Section 2 reprises the BSA account of laws. Section 3 then discusses inference to causal claims, showing how these conform to the inference pattern described under (2) rather than the considerations having to do with simplicity and strength emphasized in the BSA. Section 4 discusses parallel issues about the content and epistemology of laws and the implications of these for the BSA account of laws. A key feature of laws—the fact that they are invariant under changes in initial conditions—is shown to be in considerable tension with the BSA treatment of laws.

2 The best system account of laws

David Lewis gives the following canonical formulation of the BSA:

A contingent generalization is a *law of nature* if and only if it appears as a theorem (or axiom) in each of the true deductive systems that achieves a best combination of simplicity and strength (1986a: 73)

Strength is understood as informativeness—a theory is stronger the more possibilities it excludes. Simplicity is understood as having to do with very general considerations that are domain-independent in the sense of not resting on subject-matter-specific empirical considerations. Often these considerations are taken to be broadly formal or syntactic in character. Lewis's examples include the claim that 'a linear function is simpler than a quartic or step function' and that a 'shorter alteration of prenex quantifiers is simpler than a longer one'. Other simplicity-based considerations that are invoked in discussions of the BSA rest on domain-general 'counting' intuitions—e.g. theories postulating fewer different kinds of entities are simpler. Although the details of how simplicity and strength are to be understood may not seem crucial to the BSA project, it *is* crucial that both simplicity and strength be specifiable in a way that does not presuppose or rely on assumptions that themselves have causal or nomological content, since this would undermine the reductive goals of the project.

As Hall (forthcoming) remarks, there are at least two different strands to Lewis's statement of the BSA. The 'official' doctrine is a metaphysical claim, according to which laws supervene on the HSB and the BSA shows us how this is the case. However, there is also an accompanying epistemological back-story. This is that the BSA describes, in an abstract or idealized way, the considerations that guide real scientists in identifying laws. In particular, the idea is that we should think in terms of an idealized, super-intelligent scientific investigator who has access to all of the information in the HSB and who then constructs systemizations of this information which aim at achieving a best balance of simplicity and strength. The theorems/axioms describing regularities common to these systemizations will at least approximately or largely coincide with generalizations we presently regard as laws because the procedure employed is just an idealization or extension of the procedure actual scientists employ in discovering laws.

Lewis is quite explicit about this aspect of the BSA, writing:

… I take a suitable system to be one that has the virtues we aspire to in our own theory-building, and that has them to the greatest extent possible given the way the world is.

This feature of the BSA is not readily dispensable. I have already suggested it is far from obvious that the application of the BSA to the HSB leads to a notion of law that picks out just those generalizations regarded as laws in contemporary science. Much of the appeal of the BSA rests on the assumption that, not withstanding this, the BSA is a reasonable description of how theory-choice in science actually proceeds, so that even if the details may be murky and the fit with scientific practice less than exact, something like the BSA must capture the criteria by which scientists identify laws, thus validating the conclusion that laws just *are* whatever satisfy these criteria. If this assumption is not correct—if scientists do not in fact identify laws by constructing systemizations that achieve a best balance of simplicity and strength, as these virtues are understood in the BSA—then it is hard to see why we should accept the BSA.

3 Causal inference, supervenience, and the BSA

To explore these issues, I begin with some very simple and schematic problems involving causal inference. These problems are in some respects different from corresponding issues surrounding laws of nature, but I believe a number of the considerations which surface in connection with the former also transfer to the latter.

Suppose that in a small corner of *our* world (not some merely logically or metaphysically possible world), two variables X and Y are (or at least appear to be) correlated or non-independent. Standard treatments of causal inference tell us that there are a number of different ways this correlation may arise. Confining ourselves to some of the simplest possibilities, the correlation might be due to (or reflect that) (i) X causes Y, (ii) Y causes X, or (iii) might be due to some third factor Z, which we have not yet observed, but which acts as a common cause of both X and Y, with there being no causal connection from X to Y or from Y to X.

$X \rightarrow Y$	$Y \rightarrow X$	$X \leftarrow Z \rightarrow Y$
(i)	*(ii)*	*(iii)*

Another apparent possibility is that (iv) the correlation between X and Y arises by chance or coincidence, without being the result of some underlying causal structure like (i), (ii), and (iii). There are standard statistical procedures that allow us to test for this possibility in the following sense: If we have information about how the values of X and Y we observe are generated from the underlying population from which they come (e.g. if the values of X and Y are a random sample from a single underling population), then, relative to this information, we can test the hypothesis that X and Y are independent in this underlying population, but because of chance variation appear to be correlated in the sample we draw. Assumptions like random sampling (or any other assumption that might allow us to address the possibility that the sample is misleading about the underlying population) are most naturally understood as assumptions about the *causal* structure of the procedure or mechanism by which the sample is generated. Without such additional assumptions the sample correlation in itself has no interpretable evidential significance for what is going on in the underlying population. Thus even in this case it is the conjunction of the sample correlation and additional assumptions that have causal or modal content (rather than just the sample correlation itself) that warrants any conclusion about the underlying population and about whether the sample correlation is merely accidental. Note also that in this context the claim that the sample correlation is 'accidental' means simply that the sample is misleading about the underlying population. This notion of 'accidental' does not allow us to attach any sense to the possibility that the correlation holds in the underlying population but only 'accidentally'.

Suppose the hypothesis that X and Y are non-independent in the underlying population survives whatever tests we employ and we accordingly focus on (i), (ii), and (iii), which we are willing to regard as the only remaining possibilities. Confining ourselves to these, we see that without further information or additional assumptions, we (still) face an underdetermination problem: on any plausible conception of evidential support, the information that X and Y are correlated does not in itself differentially support any one of these alternatives over the others. Indeed, this is so even if we manage to identify some third variable Z which is correlated with X and Y—this by itself does not show that Z is a common cause of X and Y, since, for example, X may instead cause Z which causes Y, the X–Z correlation may be due to yet another variable W, and so on.

My view is that in real-life science this underdetermination problem is rarely solved just by appeal to the sorts of abstract, domain-independent simplicity considerations that figure in the BSA. In particular, researchers do not proceed by arguing that one of (i)–(iii) is 'simpler' than the others and should be preferred for that reason. To begin with, it is hard to see how simplicity considerations could be used to discriminate between (i) and (ii). And even if (iii) is judged less simple either than (i) or (ii) on the grounds that it involves three variables rather than two and two causal connections rather than just one, there is general agreement that this would be very poor grounds for dismissing (iii)—correlations between two variables that arise because of the confounding influence of a third are extremely common in nature, and it would be terrible methodology to simply dismiss this possibility, on the grounds that it is not 'simple'. Nor is it plausible that one of the above three alternatives is 'stronger' than the others.

Another move which is not seriously considered in real science is that of insisting that this apparent underdetermination problem is illusory; that (i)–(iii) are not really alternatives at all; and that instead are merely equivalent ways of encoding the same correlational facts. The kind of local, small-world problem of casual underdetermination described above is ubiquitous in many areas of science, and scientists work to solve these problems, rather than denying that they can arise. Instead, solutions to the sort of underdetermination problem under discussion appeal to two interrelated considerations, often employed together: additional empirical assumptions (which may be modal or causal in character[1]) and additional evidence.

Here is a simple illustration involving a form of scientific inference that is undeniably central to science—inference from the results of an appropriately designed experiment. Suppose it is possible to experimentally manipulate the value of X via some process that affects Y (and is known to affect Y), if at all only through X, in the sense that all causal routes (if any) from the experimenter's manipulations I to Y, go through X as an intermediary, and there is no cause of the manipulation I itself that affects Y via a causal route that does not go through X.[2] Following a now established usage, I will call such a manipulation an *intervention* on X with respect to Y. If and only if, under such interventions on X, Y consistently changes value, we may conclude that X causes Y. Similarly, if interventions on Y are correlated with changes in the value of X, we conclude that Y causes X. Finally, if X and Y are correlated but neither interventions on X are correlated with Y nor interventions on Y with X, then we conclude that X does not cause Y and Y does not cause X. Thus, if (i)–(iii) are the only possibilities, the correlation between X and Y must be the result of some third factor Z, even if we are unable to identify that factor.

Let us consider the structure of these inductive inferences (since that is what they are) in a bit more detail. First, they take the general form of an *eliminative induction*, in which one argues for one of the alternatives (i)–(iii) by ruling out the others. Second, the

---

[1] The idea that getting causal conclusions from statistical data requires causal assumptions of some kind as input is a major theme of Cartwright 1979 and is widely recognized in the statistics and econometrics literature.

[2] Randomized experiments furnish one important class of cases of experimental manipulations that exhibit the characteristics just described and in which information about what would happen under such manipulations can be used to address underdetermination problems. For details see Woodward 2003, chapter 2.

inferences rely on a principle connecting what happens under interventions to the existence of causal relationships: very roughly a principle like:

(M) X causes Y if and only if X and Y would be correlated under interventions on X.

This principle is fairly general but still a good deal more specific, in terms of its content, than a completely domain-independent simplicity constraint like the advice to always choose linear relationships over quadratics. For example, M doesn't apply to domains where the notion of an intervention doesn't make sense or where the relationships of interest are not causal relationships (e.g. formal theories of syntax). M does some of the work some philosophers suppose is accomplished by appeals to domain-general simplicity constraints but looks different from such constraints.

In fact, this way of putting matters understates what is distinctive about appeal to M, for this doesn't just involve combining M with the original evidential base represented by the correlation between X and Y—call this C—to solve the underdetermination problem. Rather, the intervention itself creates (or if you don't like that word, at least makes use of information in) a different, and in some respects richer evidential base than that represented by C. To explain this, we need to consider in more detail what an intervention does. On one widely accepted understanding, an intervention on X alters the structure of the causal relationships in which X is embedded, putting the variable intervened on, X, entirely under the control of the intervention variable I so that the values of X are fixed by the intervention and not by whatever causal factors previously determined the value of that variable. Graphically, this has a simple representation: the intervention I on X, breaks all arrows directed into X in the original system, replacing these with a single arrow from I to X, and preserves all other arrows, including those directed out of X. Thus if X causes Y $(X \rightarrow Y)$, an intervention on X yields the following structure: $I \rightarrow X \rightarrow Y$.

By contrast, if the correlation between X and Y arises because Z is a common cause of both X and Y, then the effect of an intervention on X is to replace the structure (iii) above with the structure:

$$I \rightarrow X \quad Z \rightarrow Y$$

It is because, in this second case, interventions on X will 'break' the arrows directed into X, that we expect that X and Y will not remain correlated under these interventions, telling us that, in these cases, X does not cause Y. Thus the result of an intervention on X in (iii) is to generate a *new* set of regularities in which X and Y are independent and which are distinct from the original correlation C. It is the combination of this new evidence with M, which allows us to resolve the original underdetermination problem.

Next a word about reduction: causal notions occur on both sides of M since the notion of an intervention is characterized causally. This makes M unsuitable as a principle that might figure in a reductive analysis of causation. However, it does not follow that M, when used for methodological or epistemic purposes, is viciously circular or unilluminating. The reason is that the causal information required to recognize whether one has carried out an intervention on *X* with respect to *Y* is not information about the existence or not of a causal link between *X* and *Y*. Instead, it is information about *other* causal relationships—about, for example, the existence of a causal relationship between *I* and *X*, between *I* and certain other causes of *Y* (besides *X*), and so on. If we call the assumptions about these already known causal relationships A and the new causal conclusions to which we are inferring B, then the general pattern exemplified by the role of M in causal inference is something like:

Known causal assumptions A + correlational information→ 'New' Causal conclusions B (where A is different from B)

Put slightly differently, at least in this particular case, the solution to the puzzle of how one gets conclusions about causal relationships from purely correlational, non-modal premises is that one *doesn't*—the modal content in the conclusions derives from the combination of correlational information with additional premises that are already causal or modal in character.

Of course, one can go on to ask about the status of the causal assumptions A on which we rely as premises—where do they come from and what justifies our believing them? Don't such premises have to ultimately emerge from or be grounded in information that is entirely non-causal in character? Here it is natural to invoke the anti-foundationalist picture associated with Neurath's raft. As an empirical matter, there is no reason to suppose that we ever engage in causal inference in situations in which we have no causal background information[3] at all and must rely instead only on purely correlational information. Instead, we begin in *media res*, in a context in which we already have some causal information which we then use in combination with non-causal information to reach new causal conclusions. We can test particular causal background assumptions by making use of still other causal assumptions, but there is no reason to suppose that this process bottoms out in some procedure that allows us to reach causal conclusions by relying on non-causal information alone. Of course it can always be contended that the causal assumptions employed in the above inferences 'must in principle' be fully replaceable by non-causal information, but those making this claim need to show in detail how this can be accomplished. It is not enough to merely assert that this 'must' be possible.

So far I have been focusing on cases in which we learn about causal relationships by experiments. Although I lack the space to provide details, I would argue that a broadly similar pattern also holds in connection with causal inference from purely observational (that is non-experimental data). As a brief example, work by Spirtes et al. (2001) shows that if we are willing to assume two principles (labelled by them Causal Markov (**CM**) and Faithfulness (**F**) conditions) connecting causal structure to correlational relationships, we may sometimes (but by no means always) 'identify' that causal structure, in the

---

[3] Causal background knowledge in this context includes predispositions to take certain correlational relations as causal. Arguably such predispositions play an important role in cognitive development.

sense that a unique structure is picked out by the correlational information, given the connecting principles. (To give the reader a hint of what is involved, causal relationships are represented by directed graphs, correlational relations by an accompanying probability distribution, and a graph **G** with vertices **V** and accompanying probability distribution **P** satisfies the Causal Markov condition if for any two variables X and Y in **V**, X and Y are independent of all other variables in **V** except possibly for their descendants, conditional on their parents. Condition **F** is a kind of converse.) The overall structure of these inferences is similar to the pattern when **M** is employed. Causal conclusions are not inferred from correlational data alone or just from the application of completely domain-general criteria like simplicity and strength to correlational data. Instead, the principles employed to get us from correlational information to causal conclusions are much more domain-specific and whether they hold in any particular case is an empirical question, the answer to which is very much dependent on background knowledge. (Both **CM** and **F** are principles that apply distinctively to *causal* inference, rather than to inductive inference in general, and there is a long list of conditions under which **CM** fails to hold—see Hausman and Woodward 1999.) Moreover, while **CM** and **F** allow us to infer from correlational information to causal conclusions, they certainly don't provide the basis for a reduction of the latter to the former. In addition, application of these principles to correlational information will *sometimes* allow us to resolve underdetermination problems, but not always—this depends on the details of correlational information in question.

As an illustration, suppose X and Y are correlated, and we wish to know whether causal structure (i)–(iii) from above lies behind this correlation. Suppose also X and Y are embedded in a larger structure which has the following features: First, there are variables. W and Z which are not correlated with one another but are correlated with X and which furthermore are dependent conditional on X—in other words, $W \perp Z, W/\!\!\perp X, Z /\!\!\perp X$ and $W/\!\!\perp Z \mid X$ (where $X\perp Y$ means X and Y are independent and $X/\!\!\perp Y$ means X and Y are dependent). Second, there are variables U and V which bear a parallel relationship to Y, so that one has the following structure:

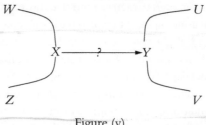

Figure (v)

where an undirected edge between two variables means they are correlated, but implies nothing about the causal relationships which generate this correlation, and the arrow from X to Y which is punctuated by a question mark indicates that we wish to determine whether X causes Y or whether instead they are related in some other way. Given **CM** and **F**, further correlations (or their absence) among these variables, $W, Z, U, V, X,$ and Y will allow us to identify which of (i), (ii), and (iii) is the correct causal structure. Put somewhat more 'metaphysically', the correlational facts described above, combined with the principles **CM** and **F**, are sufficient to 'fix' which of the causal structures (i)–(iii) holds.

However, this result is limited in the following respects. First, nothing guarantees that, in the situation under investigation, the additional variables $W, Z, U,$ and V will be present with the right correlational relationships—it is presumably a 'contingent' matter whether these are present—and if they are not, whatever correlations are present may not fix what the causal structure is, at least relative to **CM** and **F**. Second, there are many cases in which the same correlations are consistent with a number of different causal structures, even given **CM** and **F**. For example, the correlations generated by the common cause structure (iii) will also be generated by the structures $X{\to}Z{\to}Y$ and $Y{\to}Z{\to}X$, so that which of these structures holds is underdetermined by these correlations, even given **CM** and **F**. As these examples illustrate, the partial solution to underdetermination problems provided by **CM** and **F** does not in any way show or require that causal claims must always be 'reducible' to or even 'supervene on' correlational claims.

CM and **F** prompt a general observation about appeals to 'simplicity' in science. It would not be unreasonable to interpret these principles as embodying a particular conception of simplicity which is being used to guide causal inference.[4] However, 'simplicity' in this context means something very different from what it means in the BSA. The conception of simplicity embodied in **CM** and **F** rests on domain-specific empirical assumptions about the subject-matter to which they are applied, rather than on formal or trans-empirical assumptions applicable to all of science. Studies of inductive inference elsewhere in science reveal a similar pattern. For example, Sober (1988) argues that while appeals to simplicity considerations play a role in phylogenetic inference, the considerations in question rest on domain-specific empirical assumptions about the processes underlying speciation rather than on purely formal considerations or on considerations that apply globally to all domains. Thus while it is not wrong to suppose that simplicity, properly understood, plays a role in inductive inference and theory-choice in science, it is wrong to suppose that simplicity in the sense in which it is understood in the BSA plays this role.

The examples above are cases in which the causal relationships and the associated correlations involve 'small' or 'local' structures which we think of as embedded in a much larger world. The question that is implicit in discussions of Humean supervenience is how we should think about matters when the structures and correlations in question are 'scaled up' to encompass the entire universe. Suppose that we consider 'all'

---

[4] For example, **F** rules out causal structures that are non-simple in the sense of postulating certain kinds of complex coincidences in which e.g. X affects Y via two different routes which just happen to cancel.

the correlations that will ever occur anywhere in our universe and 'all' other non-modal facts—in other words, the entire HSB. Now we no longer face the problem that the correlation in some sample that we are able to observe may be misleading about an underlying population correlation, since the HSB contains all information about population correlations. Similarly, since the HSB contains all correlations that ever hold, there is no issue about experimentation or other naturally occurring processes revealing new, previously unrealized correlations (as real-life experimentation does). Next consider the following line of thought: Even if, as we have argued, local correlational information by itself underdetermines local causal structure and to the extent we can infer to a unique causal structure, domain-specific connecting principles are required, might it not be the case that matters are completely different when we consider the entire HSB, with this sufficing by itself to fix the causal structure of the entire universe (given the assumptions of the BSA)?

One reason for scepticism about this suggestion is simply that there seems to be nothing in our actual practices of causal inference (which largely have to do with local inferential problems) that warrants this conclusion or even makes it seem plausible. In such local problems, causal claims fail to supervene on or reduce to local Humean facts, and additional appeals to domain-independent considerations of simplicity and strength also don't seem sufficient to yield supervenience. The defender of Humean supervenience (understood as the thesis that the causal structure of the whole universe supervenes on the full HSB) must hold that when we scale up to the entire universe, matters become fundamentally different, but what positive grounds are there for supposing that this sort of discontinuity exists? In addition, as we have seen, one reason why causal structure may fail to be fixed by local non-modal facts, even given connecting principles like **M**, **CM**, and **F**, is that, as a contingent matter, nature may fail to cooperate in producing enough of the right non-modal facts—there may be correlations such that if they were to occur, these would be consistent with (would 'fix') one unique causal structure, but initial conditions may be such that these correlations remain unrealized. For example, if the right pattern of correlations occurs among variables in Figure (v), this will be enough to fix that X causes Y (rather than Y causing X or some other possibility), but (locally at least) nothing guarantees that such correlations will occur. It appears that only if we have such a guarantee at the global level (that is, a guarantee that the HSB includes enough correlations to disambiguate all possible candidates for the global causal structure), supervenience will be plausible. Where does this guarantee come from?

Does that mean we should conclude instead that global causal structure does *not* supervene on the HSB? Although I was once prepared to draw this conclusion (cf. *MTH*, Chapter 6), I now think a different response is preferable. I suggest we should conclude instead that the entire exercise of asking whether or not causal structure supervenes on the HSB is unilluminating and irrelevant to understanding *our* conception of causation and how it relates to evidence. (I will argue below that a similar conclusion follows for the relationship between laws and the HSB.) Our conception of causation is formulated for situations in which we don't have access to anything like the full HSB but rather to much more limited and local forms of evidence. Our conception is also such that it fits with (and its application is guided by) the availability of principles like **M**, **CM**, and **F**—principles that have causal and nomological content built into them. These aspects of the situations in which we infer to and reason about causal conclusions help to structure our concept of causation and to endow it with the features it possesses. It is unclear why we should suppose that we can cast light on this concept and how it relates to evidence by ignoring the features just described and by focusing attention instead on entirely imaginary scenarios in which we suppose we have access to a set of facts (the HSB) we will never know about and in which we are also asked to imagine that we are guided by ill-defined principles (achieving a best balance of simplicity and strength) that do not in fact characterize our best inferential practices. Why suppose that the 'intuitions' that result from such exercises (either pro or con supervenience) track anything objective?

4 Laws and invariance

I turn now to laws. First, some terminology. 'Laws' can be used to refer either to generalizations representing relationships in nature, or to those relationships themselves. Since some regimentation is necessary, I will use the word in the former sense. I assume, however, that if a generalization is a law, then it must accurately represent (at least up to some level of approximation or within a certain range or regime of circumstances) how matters stand in nature, even though the law itself is not 'in' nature. This fits with some aspects of ordinary scientific usage, according to which, e.g., Maxwell's equations, the Schrödinger equation, and so on are described as laws of nature.

Turning to more substantive issues, begin with the idea that we can construct successful theories about nature that involve a distinction between laws and initial (or boundary) conditions (hereafter ICs) and that, moreover, this distinction plays a central role in many familiar physical theories. Here is a familiar quotation from Wigner (1979) expressing the idea:

The regularities in the phenomena which physical science endeavors to uncover are called the laws of nature. The name is actually very appropriate. Just as legal laws regulate actions and behavior (under certain conditions) but do not try to regulate all actions and behavior, the laws of physics also determine the behavior of its objects of interest only under certain well-defined conditions but leave much freedom otherwise. The elements of the behavior which are not specified by the laws of nature are called initial conditions. (1979: 39)

Elsewhere, Wigner writes:

The world is very complicated and it is clearly impossible for the human mind to understand it completely. Man has therefore devised an artifice which permits the complicated nature of the world to be blamed on something which is called accidental and thus permits him to abstract a domain in which simple laws can be found. The complications are called initial conditions; the domain of regularities, laws of nature. Unnatural as such a division of the world's structure may appear from a very detached point of view, and probable though it is that the possibility of such a division has its own limits, the underlying abstraction is probably one of the most fruitful ones the human mind has made. (1979: 3)

Wigner's remarks suggest several points. The first is that laws and ICs are not characterized independently, but rather with reference to one another—so that when a theorist adopts a particular 'split' between laws and initial conditions, she makes a decision about what goes into both categories at the same time. The second is that although the law/IC distinction is useful in many contexts, this is consistent with the distinction turning out not to be a clear or useful one in other (e.g. some cosmological) contexts. It is an empirical question whether a given part of nature (or all of it) admits of an illuminating split between laws and initial conditions.

As Wigner and others also emphasize, one important way in which the law/IC distinction manifests itself is in the very different way in which various specific symmetry and invariance conditions interact with or constrain laws, on the one hand, and initial conditions on the other. For example, genuine laws are expected to remain invariant under changes in, e.g., absolute position or absolute velocity in the sense that the relationships described by the laws will continue to hold under such changes. By contrast, although there may be patterns or regularities in initial conditions, there is no such expectation that these will satisfy similar symmetry/invariance conditions. Thus, among other considerations, we require a distinction between laws and initial conditions if we are to make sense of the role of invariance principles. John Earman, no friend of metaphysically extravagant, non-Humean notions of law, expresses this point as follows:

... [I]nvariance principles can be formulated only if one admits the existence of two types of information which correspond in present-day physics to initial [and boundary] conditions and laws of nature. It would be very difficult to find a meaning for invariance principles if the two categories of our knowledge of the physical world [laws vs. initial/boundary conditions] could no longer be sharply drawn.

In thinking about the role of laws and initial conditions in science, I favour taking these notions and the contrast between them (as well as related notions that are also part of the same nomically committed circle of concepts: invariance, physical independence, and so on) as primitive. By this I mean merely that I will not attempt to provide an account that explains these notions in terms of notions that are not already part of this circle of concepts.[5] I believe, however, that it is possible to say something about how these two notions are *connected*. It is at this point that notions like *invariance* (now understood in a generalized sense explained below) enter the picture. The idea I want to defend is that a central feature of laws is that they describe relationships that will (or would) continue to hold over some substantial range of different ICs, as well as other conditions. A generalization having this feature is stable or invariant under those

[5] In particular I make no claim that these notions are metaphysically primitive or brute—I have no idea what this might mean.

conditions. If we think of initial conditions as specifications of the values taken by variables figuring in a law when it is applied to particular systems, then the conditions over which laws are invariant will include different ICs, including values of ICs brought about by intervention-like changes, of which more below. For example, the Newtonian inverse square law describing the gravitational force between two masses will continue to hold under changes in the distance between the masses, and the magnitudes of the masses themselves, both variables that figure in this law. Usually or always laws will also be invariant under changes in many other sorts of conditions as well, including conditions that one doesn't naturally think of as ICs, and that do not correspond to variables that explicitly figure in the law. (I will call these *background conditions*.) For example, the Newtonian inverse square law will/would continue to hold under changes in such background conditions as the colour or shape of the masses that attract one another gravitationally. Note that on this understanding of invariance, the notion has counterfactual commitments built into it.

One way in which this stability feature of laws manifests itself in scientific practice is in scientists' willingness to combine the same law with many different ICs and to then use the law to calculate what would happen under these different conditions, a procedure that obviously presupposes that the law will continue to hold under this range of ICs (and typically a range of background conditions as well). Thus, one can take Coulomb's law and combine it with a range of different assumptions about the charge distribution on a conductor, the geometry of the conductor, etc. (whether it is a long, straight wire, a solenoid, etc.) and use this law in combination with these initial conditions to determine in each case what the resulting electrical field would be. Or, to put the point in a more material mode: If one has a long, straight current carrying wire and changes the current through the wire or alters the geometry of the conductor (say by coiling the wire up into a solenoid) the field will change in ways predictable from Coulomb's law, but the relationship between charge, distance, and field described by that law will continue to hold under these changes—it is in this sense that the law describes a relationship that is invariant. We may thus think of the law as describing a physical dependency relationship connecting changes in the charge distribution, etc. to changes in the field.

Laws contrast in this respect with non-lawful, accidental relationships like:

(W) All the wires on L's desk at time t are copper

Special circumstances aside, one may readily empirically verify (e.g. by experiment) that it is possible to introduce a wire onto L's desk that at times before t is not copper and that the upshot of this operation will not be to change the wire into copper and that, moreover, the desk will not repel the wire from its surface. This shows that the generalization (W) and the relationship described by it are not stable or invariant under this sort of change. I believe it is often this feature of (W) that we have in mind when we describe it as paradigmatically 'accidental'.[6] Note that this difference between, on the one hand,

---

[6] There are other ways of understanding the notion of 'accidental'. See Section 2 and discussion below.

(W) and, on the other, the Newtonian inverse square law or Coulomb's law seems to be an objective, empirically ascertainable difference—for example, it doesn't just have to do with a difference in our epistemic attitudes towards (W) and Newton's law. Moreover, it is far from obvious that this difference *merely* has to do with a differences in the ways in which these generalizations fit into some much larger systemization involving many other regularities, as on the BSA picture. Of course the empirical differences in question may influence how we think the different sorts of generalizations fit into such a larger systemization, but this may be a *consequence* of our recognition of the empirical differences just described, rather than the *source* of those differences. Certainly, if one asks how one might go about determining whether W is non-invariant in the way described, it doesn't look as though one needs to proceed by considering alternative large-scale systemizations of all the regularities obtaining in the universe and W's place in these. The empirical considerations that lead us to regard W as non-invariant seem much more local and direct than this.

This pair of examples is meant to motivate the general idea that there is a relationship between lawfulness and invariance. However, in formulating this relationship more precisely we face a number of different issues. First, there are many changes in initial and background conditions over which even paradigmatically accidental generalizations will continue to hold: The generalization (W) will (one supposes) continue to hold if the price of tea in China were to change, if I were wearing a blue shirt rather than a green shirt at time t, and so on. It would also continue to hold if I introduce a new *copper* wire onto L's desk. The fact that even accidental generalizations continue to hold over some changes in initial and background conditions would not create problems for our claims about a law/invariance link if we were prepared to argue that a genuine law must continue to hold under *all* possible ICs and background conditions, since we could then argue that (W) fails to be a law because there are some such conditions (introducing a non-copper wire onto the desk) under which (W) does not hold.

This last line of thought will appeal to those who think that genuine laws are exceptionless, but it comes with substantial costs. One is that many generalizations described as 'laws' in the scientific literature break down (or are believed to break down) under some conditions. For example, Maxwell's equations break down under conditions under which quantum mechanical effects become important, general relativity is widely believed to require correction at very small length scales (the Planck length), and so on. By 'break down' I mean that under these conditions, the generalizations are not even approximately true. As I propose to think about invariance, a generalization like the Newtonian inverse square law that holds to a high level of approximation under a range of classical conditions (e.g. weak gravitational fields) is stable under those conditions, even if, because of General Relativistic corrections, it is not exactly true under those conditions. Again, I think this corresponds to the way in which physicists deploy the concept of law.

Of course, it is open to the defender of the claim that laws must be exceptionless to respond that to the extent such breakdowns occur, the generalizations in question are not really laws. However, if we adopt this stipulation, it remains the case that—call them what you wish—Maxwell's equations and the field equations of GR play a central role in current science, that we appeal to them to explain and predict, and that their discovery is regarded as an important scientific achievement. It thus remains an important project to try to capture the characteristics of such generalizations and to better understand how they can play the roles just described—roles which, after all, are just the roles traditionally ascribed to laws.

If we admit the possibility that a generalization can count as a law and nonetheless fail to hold under some conditions, then the simple strategy described above for distinguishing between laws and accidents is no longer available. In *MTH*, I suggested an alternative partial solution to this problem along the following lines. Begin by restricting attention to those generalizations that may be interpreted as change-relating in the sense that they purport to describe how changes in the values of one or more variables are related to changes in some other variable. This category will include both many laws of nature (although perhaps not all[7]) and many accidental generalizations describing mere correlations such as the generalization (W). Consider a change-relating generalization G that associates different values of some dependent variable Y with different values of an independent variable X (where X may be a vector), according to some mapping F. That is, according to G, $Y = F(X)$. Now define a subclass of interventions called *testing interventions* as follows: A testing intervention for G on X with respect to Y is an intervention on X that changes some value of X, say x_1 to a different value of X, x_2, where x_1 and x_2 are claimed by G to be associated with different values of Y, y_1, and y_2. That is, $x_1 \neq x_2$ and (according to G) $F(x_1) = y_1 \neq F(x_2) = y_2$. G will be invariant under this testing intervention if and only if it correctly describes how the value of Y will change under this intervention—in this sense, the intervention 'tests' G. As an illustration, supposing (W) is understood in the change-relating way described above, the introduction of a copper wire onto L's table is not a testing intervention. However, an intervention introducing a non-copper wire *is* a testing intervention. A necessary condition N (not sufficient, as we will see shortly) for a generalization G to be a law is that G be stable/invariant under *some* testing interventions:

(N) If G is a change-relating generalization that is a law, then it is invariant under some testing interventions.

(W) fails to meet condition N—it is not invariant under any testing interventions. By contrast, a generalization like Coulomb's law will be invariant under some (in fact many) testing interventions and many other changes as well, so it meets condition N.

I said above that N is only a necessary condition for a generalization to count as a law. The picture I advocate is one in which there is both a threshold and above this a continuum with respect to lawfulness. Some generalizations, like (W), are 'pure accidents' in the sense that they are not invariant under any testing interventions. In this sense, they

---

[7] See *MTH*, pp. 246ff.

will be below the threshold represented by **N**. Other generalizations will be invariant under at least some testing interventions. Among these, some will be invariant under a larger or more significant range of changes, involving both testing interventions and other sorts of changes in background conditions than others, so that there will be a continuum of extent of invariance above the threshold represented by **N**. The generalizations that we regard as fundamental laws will be at the upper end of this hierarchy; causal generalizations of the sort found in the special sciences will be lower down in the hierarchy, but (I would claim) if they are genuinely causal, they must be above the threshold.

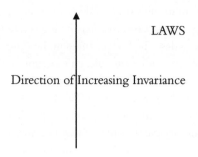

LAWS

Direction of Increasing Invariance

Generalizations are invariant under some interventions that we do not regard as laws (causal generalizations in the special sciences).

Threshold N

Accidents (e.g. W)

This system of classification contrasts with (or at least introduces additional structure that goes beyond) the way in which some philosophers use the notion of an 'accidental' generalization. Consider (cf. Haavelmo 1944) the relationship R between the angle of depression of the gas pedal of a particular model of car and its acceleration along a flat road meeting certain other conditions. Obviously R will be rather fragile in the sense that it may be readily disrupted by, e.g., changes in the grade of the road, the headwind, the condition of the engine, etc. Nonetheless, R is invariant under some testing interventions, as is reflected in the fact that under the right background conditions, it correctly describes how one can change the acceleration of the car by depressing the pedal to different degrees.

In discussing the generalization (R), Marc Lange (2009, p.13) describes it as an 'accident'. I agree there is a sense in which this is correct—(R) holds only because certain other conditions hold, and many of these hold only 'by accident', in the sense that it would not be inconsistent with the fundamental laws for these conditions to be different.

On the other hand, describing both (W) and (R) as accidental may be taken to suggest that there is no relevant difference between them, and this seems wrong-headed. Intuitively, (R) does describe a causal (or explanatory) connection (albeit one that is far less stable than a fundamental law) between the position of the pedal and the acceleration of the car—one that we appeal to when we say that the car was accelerating because the pedal had been pushed all the way to the floor. By contrast, (W) does not describe even a fragile causal connection, on an interventionist account like that embodied in (M). This is reflected in a real empirical difference between (W) and (R): One cannot make a non-copper wire turn into copper by placing it on L's desk, but one can make the car go faster by pushing on the pedal.

I am aware that many philosophers will take a dismissive attitude towards generalizations like (R), and will wonder why it is worth distinguishing them from pure accidents. In response, I would observe that many of the generalizations of the special sciences seem to have broadly the same features as (R)—they are invariant, but only under a limited range of background conditions. We need some way of distinguishing such generalizations from pure accidents like (W).

I turn now to some other features of my characterization of invariance. First, note that unlike the stability conditions on laws formulated by some other philosophers (e.g. Lange 2009, p. 22) (N) does not require that if a generalization is a law, it must continue to hold as (or be) a *law* under some suitable range of conditions (or counterfactual suppositions). Instead, (N) requires only that the generalization continues to hold, in the sense of being approximately *true*, under those suppositions. My suggestion is thus that there is nothing more to lawfulness than, so to speak, *de facto* invariance under some appropriately large range of changes in initial/boundary conditions, including changes involving interventions.

One reason for favouring this conception of lawfulness as (mere) *de facto* invariance is that there are empirical considerations (to be discussed below) that can be brought to bear on whether a generalization has this feature. By contrast, it is less clear there are similar procedures for answering questions about whether a generalization would remain a law under various conditions. Asking about whether the nomological status of a generalization (rather than just its truth) is contingent on other conditions seems to require a framework in which it makes sense to embed the 'it is a law' operator in more complex modal claims and put law-claims into the consequents of counterfactuals (so that we can ask whether L would be a law under counterfactual conditions C, etc.). If we can capture the role that laws play in science without journeying into such modal thickets, it would be desirable to do so.[8]

---

[8] Although the matter deserves more attention than I can give it here, it is worth noting that many familiar philosophical thought experiments bearing on Humean supervenience presuppose that claims about whether it is 'possible' that under certain conditions various claims L are laws are coherent and well posed. They thus presuppose the legitimacy of embedding of 'it is a law that' in modal contexts.

If we adopt the view that lawfulness has to do simply with whether a generalization would continue to be true under some appropriate range of conditions, this makes it easier to understand how there can be evidence supporting law claims. Consider the following example from Earman and Roberts (2005: 257):

Of the four Maxwell equations, the two curl equations entail that if the two divergence equations are true at one time, then they are true at all times. So we can consider two distinct physical theories: M, which says that all four Maxwell equations are laws of nature, and M*, which says that only the two curl equations are laws of nature, and the two divergence equations are contingently true at some particular time, from which it follows that they are true at all times, though only contingently so.

Like Earman and Roberts, I would not regard M and M* as distinct alternatives. Suppose we interpret their argument in the following way: if the curl equations are true at all times over the range of circumstances and conditions that constitute the domain of classical electromagnetism (hence invariant under these conditions) and the divergence equations hold at a particular time, then the divergence equations must also be true at all times over the range of circumstances that constitute the domain of classical electromagnetism (hence also invariant). I would say this argument shows, assuming these premises, that the divergence equations are laws—there is, so to speak, no gap between their being laws and their holding only contingently over all conditions (including those produced by interventions) in the domain of classical magnetism.

I turn now to another feature of my characterization which will seem unsatisfactory to some. This is, that in characterizing invariance in terms of stability under a range of ICs and background conditions, I have presupposed some notion of physical possibility. This feature has seemed 'circular' to some commentators. Psillos (2004: 300) writes:

Naturally, when checking whether a generalisation or a relationship among magnitudes or variables is invariant we need to subject it to some variations/changes/interventions. What changes will it be subjected to? The obvious answer is: those that are permitted, or are permissible, by the laws of nature. Suppose that we test Ohm's law. Suppose also that one of the interventions envisaged was to see whether it would remain invariant, if the measurement of the intensity of the current was made on a spaceship, which moved faster than light. This, of course, cannot be done, because it is a *law* that nothing travels faster than light. So, some *laws* must be in place before, based on considerations of invariance, it is established that some generalisation is invariant under some interventions. Hence, Woodward's notion of 'invariance under interventions' cannot offer an adequate analysis of lawhood, since laws are required to determine what interventions are possible.

As emphasized above, my proposal is not intended as an 'analysis' of lawhood if analysis means (as I believe Psillos intends) 'reductive analysis'. I will add, however, that the non-reductive character of my proposal does not mean that it is epistemically viciously circular or unilluminating. One reason is that we have (partial) independent access to whether the conditions we wish to consider in assessing invariance are physically possible on the basis of the consideration that whatever is actual must be physically possible. When an experimenter introduces a non-copper wire onto L's table and discovers that it does not become copper, hence that (W) is not invariant under an intervention leading to this IC, it is not as though she has to worry that she may by mistake have realized a condition that is not physically possible and hence one that is inappropriate for assessing invariance. In other words, from the point of view of methodology and epistemic access, we don't have to already know whether it is physically possible for a non-copper wire to be on L's desk in order to carry out the envisioned intervention—the intervention and its upshot tell us that this is physically possible. A parallel point holds if one simply observes that some generalization fails to hold when some condition is realized—this is enough to establish that the generalization is not stable/invariant under that condition.

5 The epistemology of law

Psillos's comments do, however, raise some important questions about the epistemology of laws, to which I now turn. Aside from some brief references to the role of experimental interventions, I have so far said little that is systematic about how one can tell whether or not a generalization exhibits the sort of invariance that qualifies it as a law. In fact, the whole question of the kinds of evidence and other considerations that (as a matter of empirical fact) lead scientists to conclude that some generalization is or is not a law has received surprisingly little attention from philosophers interested in laws. One place to begin would be with already existing historical studies of the considerations that led scientific communities to the judgment that universal gravitation, Maxwell's equations, the field equations of GR, and so on, were laws of nature. What one would like to see is the extraction from these studies of general patterns of reasoning that led to the identification of laws. In the absence of such work, I offer instead some very sketchy suggestions, which abstract from the much more complex considerations at work in real cases and which I hope may merit further exploration.

EXTRACTN OF RSNNG

1) Obviously one way of supporting the claim that a generalization continues to hold under some range of conditions is to observe that this is the case. Particularly when the range of conditions is substantial and some of these result from experimental manipulations, this can provide evidence for some non-trivial range of invariance. When Faraday found that under a variety of different conditions, experimentally manipulating a conductor by moving it through a magnetic field induced a current in it, with the magnitude of the current depending on the strength of the field, and the velocity of the conductor, there were obvious questions about the range of applicability of this generalization and about how to accurately represent it mathematically, but the hypothesis that this relationship was 'accidental' in the sense of being a misleading sample from an underlying population or in the sense that the relationship reflected an association between two factors that were causally unrelated but correlated because of the operation of some additional common cause, was effectively ruled out. This is because for the association to be produced by a third factor in this way, the factor would itself have to be

trauma

correlated both with Faraday's manipulations and the various other features of the experiment in a way that it is enormously implausible.

2) In many other cases one relies on 'theoretical' assumptions (including nomological assumptions) to evaluate claims about invariance. Appeal to such assumptions need not be circular in the sense that their application requires that we must already know whether the generalization of interest is invariant. Instead, we may be able to use known laws in conjunction with other information to determine whether *other*, distinct generalizations are invariant or not. (The example from Earman and Roberts involving Maxwell's equations provides one illustration.) Similarly, making use of known laws in delimiting the range of physically possible conditions relevant to assessing the invariance of some generalization, does not require that we must have already settled all questions about the invariance of that generalization.

As an illustration,[9] consider the status of various cosmological generalizations such as the large-scale flatness of the universe and the uniformity of the microwave background (apart from small inhomogeneities) in all directions in space. Most cosmologists do not regard these as laws of nature, despite their apparent simplicity and very wide scope. One reason is that, according to current understanding, these uniformities are contingent on initial conditions holding in the very early universe, these initial conditions might have been different, and had they been different, the cosmological uniformities would not have held. This in itself is taken to be enough to show that these cosmological generalizations are not invariant in the way that fundamental laws are expected to be. Of course one relies on previously accepted theoretical considerations to tell us that early initial conditions might have been different, but to reach this conclusion one does not have to already know or presuppose that the cosmological uniformities themselves are physically contingent.

It is interesting to note that this conclusion is very different from the conclusion apparently suggested by the BSA, which seems to imply these cosmological generalizations are laws, basically on the grounds that they are both very simple and very informative.[10] Assuming the BSA account is not being misapplied in such cases, this suggests that a generalization's having the property of being an axiom or theorem in a systemization that best balances simplicity and strength is a very different property than the property of being stable/invariant. Roughly, the difference is this: an invariant generalization

---

[9] Many other examples of the same overall pattern of reasoning are provided by cases of so-called deduction from the phenomena such as Newton's deduction of the gravitational inverse square law from the conjunction of his laws of motion and Kepler's result that the times for the planets to orbit the sun are in the ratio of the 3/2 power of the semi-major axis of their orbits.

[10] The conclusion that the BSA implies that cosmological facts (such as the existence of a low entropy past) are laws is endorsed by Callender 2004 and Loewer 2007. John Norton has suggested to me that this conclusion might be avoided by advocates of the BSA by denying that such cosmological claims are 'regularities', on the grounds that they are only instantiated once. But many cosmological claims can be written as though they are multiply instantiated regularities ('For each region of spacetime...') and there are independent reasons for not wanting whether or not a claim is a law to turn on the number of 'instances' it has.

continues to hold over a large range of possible ICs and background conditions, including those that are rarely or never realized—this is what allows us to combine the generalization with these different ICs to explain and predict. By contrast, it looks as though a generalization might be both simple and strong without having this sort of stability property. This might happen if the generalization is simple and strong with respect to those initial conditions that actually or usually obtain (where these might be very special cases among all possible initial conditions), but is not invariant under possible but unrealized or rarely realized conditions. The cosmological generalizations illustrate this.

I turn now to the bearing of these observations on a common philosophical argument (cf. Roberts 2009). Take a theory, T, having as part of its content the claim that L is a law. Rewrite T as:

T_1: It is a law that L and X (where X is whatever T says in addition to the claim that L is a law)

and also as:

T_2: L is true but not a law and X

It is then argued that no evidence could (even in principle) discriminate between T_1 and T_2.

Much might be said about this argument, but I will focus just on the following point: As an empirical matter, there seem to be few if any real-life cases of fundamental scientific theories that differ *only* in the way that T_1 and T_2 do. Instead, when two theories disagree about the nomological status of some true claim L, they will, in realistic cases, typically[11] disagree in other ways as well and this allows for the possibility that empirical evidence may be used to discriminate between them.

One reason is that while there may be cases in which T_1 and T_2 both regard L as true but differ over whether it is a law, it is not regarded as methodologically acceptable for T_2 to simply postulate as a brute fact that L holds but not as a law. Or at least this is so if L describes some relatively structured global uniformity, which presumably will be the case if L is even a *prima facie* candidate for a law. Instead, if L is true but not a law, it is taken to be extremely important for T_2 to explain *why* L holds, where this is taken to involve showing how L arises from the working of other generalizations that are laws on some prior set of initial conditions. In providing such an explanation T_2 will typically differ from T_1 in a variety of other ways, in addition to disagreeing about whether L is a law. In particular, if L is true but non-lawful, then since it is not (extensively) invariant, there must be possible ICs under which it fails to hold, in which case it makes sense to identify these conditions and to exhibit how whether L holds depends on which ICs

---

[11] I acknowledge that I have no proof that there are no real-life cases which differ only in the way that T_1 and T_2 do. However, in view of the considerations rehearsed below, it seems to me the burden of proof is very much on believers to actually produce such cases.

obtain. This will typically involve additional differences between T_1 and T_2 besides their disagreement about the nomological status of L.

As an illustration, although the cosmological generalizations discussed above are generally taken to be true but non-lawful, few scientists are willing to take them to be 'brute' accidents, holding without further explanation. Instead, various explanations are proposed for why these generalizations hold (involving different claims about earlier initial conditions) and these have distinctive evidential implications. For example, one popular class of explanations invokes a period of extremely rapid inflation in the very early universe. If some version of cosmic inflation is correct, we should expect to see evidence of this in the fine-grained detail of the microwave background, evidence that would not be present if the cosmological uniformities have some other explanation.

If this is correct, we can avoid two opposed but equally unattractive consequences that are suggested by a comparison of T_1 and T_2. The first is that because T_1 and T_2 are equally compatible with all evidence, there is no difference in literal content between them (and our account of law should reflect this fact, which presumably leads to some sophisticated version of a regularity theory). The other, diametrically opposed conclusion is that because T_1 and T_2 seem to have different content, we must opt for some trans-empirical conception of law to reflect this. On my view, both of these conclusions are unmotivated, in the absence of reasons to suppose there are actual examples of legitimate theories that differ only in the way that T_1 and T_2 are alleged to.

6 Simplicity, strength, and initial conditions

These points are closely related to another feature of 'initial conditions' and their relationship to laws that has received little philosophical attention. Many philosophers write as though all there is to the notion of an initial condition is that such conditions are 'contingent' or 'not (nomically) necessary'. But in fact the notion has more structure than this. To illustrate, consider some additional observations from Wigner (1979). He observes that while scientists try to formulate laws that describe structured regularities, it is also thought desirable, as a constraint on initial conditions, that these exhibit as *little* structure and regularity as possible. In other words, one looks for a split between laws and ICs such that as much structure as possible is put into the laws and as little as possible into the ICs. As Wigner puts it:

[the] existence of regularities in the initial conditions is considered so unsatisfactory that it is considered necessary to show that the regularities are but a consequence of a situation in which there were no regularities. (1979: 41)

Elsewhere, he suggests that, ideally, initial conditions should be as 'random as possible' and that when one is presented with apparent regularities in initial conditions, the ideal should be to show that 'this was preceded by a state in which the uncontrolled initial conditions were random', the more organized initial conditions arising from the operation of the laws on this random preceding state (1979: 41).

If, as I assume, this is an accurate description of how initial conditions are treated in science, it suggests that insofar as considerations of simplicity (and recall that the relevant notions of simplicity will be domain-dependent notions) and informativeness matter in science, they may have very different implications for hypotheses about laws and hypotheses about initial conditions.[12] If we think of a relatively random or structureless arrangement of ICs as non-simple in the sense that a great deal of information is required for its specification, then complexity in initial conditions may be desirable, or at least not something to be avoided. To the extent that simplicity is desirable in science, it is typically simplicity in laws rather than in initial conditions that is to be sought. To put the matter in the context of the BSA, rather than considering systemizations that lump together (what will later be identified as) hypotheses about both laws and ICs, asking which of these best balances simplicity and strength, and then using the results to identify the laws, perhaps we should think of ourselves as looking for a systemization according to which the laws come out relatively simple and informative, but hypotheses about ICs are allowed to be complex, or at least random and unstructured, if that is required for successful explanation of what is observed.

This is related to another feature of initial conditions worth emphasizing. As Hall (forthcoming) notes, strength is generally interpreted by Lewisians as a matter of excluding possibilities not actually realized in the HSB—the more such possibilities an assumption rules out, the 'stronger' it is taken to be. When applied indiscriminately to assumptions about initial conditions, this has consequences that seem at odds with assessments reached in scientific practice. To illustrate, consider some true global constraint on initial conditions (e.g. some cosmological uniformity) that is both simple and excludes many possibilities. As argued above, it seems misguided to conclude just on this basis that the constraint is nomologically necessary.

As Hall suggests, there is another, more plausible way of thinking of informativeness besides the exclusion of possibilities. As noted earlier, it is usually taken to be a desirable feature of fundamental theories, that they can be combined with a range of different assumptions about initial conditions to yield accurate predictions about what would happen under those conditions. This is closely connected to the idea that the fundamental laws should be invariant over different initial conditions and also to the idea (which I have emphasized elsewhere[13]) that ability of a theory to provide accurate answers to counterfactual or 'what-things-had-been-different' questions concerning what would happen under initial conditions is a mark of its ability to provide successful explanations. For example, understanding the impact of the moon's gravitational force on the tides is in part a matter of understanding how that impact would have been different if the mass of the moon or its distance from the earth had been different. As this example illustrates, the 'what if things had been different' questions a theory is expected to answer are not confined just to questions involving initial conditions that are actually realized.

---

[12] See Hall (forthcoming) for similar observations.
[13] See *MTH*, Chapter 4.

This feature of theorizing is in considerable tension with the conception of strength as the exclusion of alternatives. On this conception, it is a virtue rather than a defect in a theory that it fails to answer questions about what would happen under unrealized possibilities. Indeed, on the BSA conception, the ideal theory seems to be one that simply postulates that actually obtaining initial conditions (insofar as these are both simple and strong and correspond to regularities) are physically necessary and lawful. An alternative conception which seems more in accord with scientific practice is that it adds to the informativeness of a theory if its laws tell us what would happen under ranges of initial conditions that are not actually realized (assuming there is good reason to believe what the theory says about this, as there sometimes is[14]).

I take the upshot of this discussion to be that if we consider the features possessed by laws and causal claims (as these figure in scientific practice) and the considerations on which inferences to these are based, both look rather different than what we would expect on the basis of the BSA account. Inferences to both causal claims and laws typically rely on domain specific empirical assumptions having modal or causal or nomological content, rather than on very general considerations having to do with simplicity, strength, and achieving a best balance between them. This undercuts the argument that the BSA simply codifies the criteria that are used to identify laws in scientific practice. Status as a law (as well as status as a true causal generalization) is a matter of invariance and this notion leads us to an account of laws and the way in which they contrast with initial conditions, which is different conceptually from the way these notions are understood in the BSA. It also leads to different judgments about lawfulness in realistic cases, such as those involving cosmological generalizations.

[14] Some may find it tempting to argue there are no legitimate reasons to ever accept what a theory says about what would happen under initial conditions that are never realized. However, this involves unduly restrictive assumptions about empirical support. We may come to believe what a theory says about unrealized conditions on the basis of correct predictions it makes about actually realized phenomena.

4

How to explain the Lorentz transformations

Marc Lange

There are rival views regarding why the Lorentz transformations hold. To understand what would make one or another of these views correct, we must understand what it would be for the principle of relativity or a fact about spacetime geometry to 'transcend' the various force laws. Having cashed out this notion by appealing to subjunctive conditionals and their relation to natural laws, we will see what it would take for the principle of relativity or a fact about spacetime geometry to be explanatorily prior to the Lorentz transformations. I will ultimately argue that even if the Lorentz transformations are explained by the force laws, the transformations could additionally be explained by the principle of relativity and facts about spacetime geometry. Crucially, this latter explanation would then explain something about the transformations' status as laws that cannot be explained dynamically.

1 Introduction

The Lorentz transformations are central to Einstein's special theory of relativity, entailing such famous relativistic results as time dilation, length contraction, the relativity of simultaneity, and the velocity addition rule. The transformations specify how a point-like event's spacetime coordinates (x', y', z', t') in one reference frame S' relate to its coordinates (x, y, z, t) in another frame S, where the two frames are 'inertial': bodies feeling no external forces exhibit no acceleration there. For S and S' in 'standard configuration' (see figure: the corresponding primed and unprimed axes are parallel, the origin of the spatial coordinates in S' is moving uniformly in S with speed v in the +x direction, the spatial origins in S and S' coincide when the times at each are t = 0 and t' = 0,

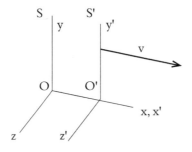

the frames are equivalent when v = 0), the Lorentz transformations are:

$$x' = (x - vt) / (1 - v^2 / c^2)^{1/2}$$
$$y' = y$$
$$z' = z$$
$$t' = (t - vx / c^2) / (1 - v^2 / c^2)^{1/2}$$

They replace the Galilean transformations from classical physics:

$$x' = x - vt$$
$$y' = y$$
$$z' = z$$
$$t' = t$$

Why do the Lorentz transformations hold? This question requests a scientific explanation of a law of nature. My main concern in this chapter will be to understand what it would take for the Lorentz transformations to have one or another possible explanation.

What kind(s) of explanation could coordinate transformation laws possess? The order of explanatory priority here cannot be the order of cause and effect, since laws are neither causes nor effects. My main aim shall be to understand the points of disagreement between rival views regarding the transformations' explanation. Ultimately, I shall use subjunctive conditionals (which are closely connected to laws) to elaborate these disagreements—which concern whether the transformation laws 'constrain' the force laws and, correspondingly, how the transformation laws' natural necessity compares to the force laws' modal status.

I believe that several rival views regarding the transformations' explanation represent genuine possibilities—ways that a world could be. Although my main aim is not to defend one of these rivals, I shall argue that a view according to which the transformations 'transcend' the force laws is the most plausible and fits best with scientific practice. In characterizing the Lorentz transformations as 'transcending' and 'constraining' the various force laws, I aim to cash out Einstein's own view, as expressed in remarks like these:

The new feature of [my work of 1905] was the realization of the fact that the bearing of the Lorentz transformation transcended its connection with Maxwell's equations and was concerned with the nature of space and time in general. A further new result was that the 'Lorentz invariance' is a general condition for any physical theory. This was for me of particular importance ... (Einstein 1955)

Many physicists and philosophers have interpreted the requirement that the dynamical laws be invariant under the Lorentz transformations (be 'Lorentz covariant'[1]) as

---

[1] That the laws are 'Lorentz covariant' means that they remain unchanged under the Lorentz transformations (i.e. when 'x' in the laws is replaced by '$(x - vt)/(1 - v^2/c^2)^{1/2}$', and so forth); phenomena in S' conform to the laws (expressed in primed coordinates) if and only if phenomena in S conform to the laws (in unprimed coordinates). That is, the result of taking any possible world that accords with the laws and putting it through Lorentz transformations is always another such world.

constraining what dynamical laws there could have been and thereby explaining the fact that all of the actual laws are Lorentz covariant. However, this notion of a 'constraint' on the laws is somewhat mysterious. Traditionally, of course, laws are distinguished from accidents by virtue of their possessing a kind of necessity that accidents lack—typically dubbed 'natural' (a.k.a. 'physical', 'nomic') necessity. (Natural necessity, in turn, is distinguished from other, stronger varieties of necessity: the 'broadly logical' necessities such as logical, conceptual, metaphysical, and mathematical necessity—all of which the laws of nature lack.) For there to be some 'constraints' limiting what the laws could have been, the constraints would have to possess some sort of necessity *stronger* than the actual laws possess (though presumably weaker than the broadly logical necessities).

My goal will be to reveal how such constraints are presupposed by certain explanations of the Lorentz transformations and what these constraints (and their necessity) would amount to. Only then can we understand how the Lorentz transformations are explained on the view that they 'transcend' the force laws. For example, we must understand what it would be for the 'principle of relativity' (which, on this view, helps to explain the Lorentz transformations) to be a 'meta-law' constraining 'first-order laws'. Likewise, we must understand what it would be for spatial and temporal homogeneity and spatial isotropy (which, on this view, join the principle of relativity in explaining the Lorentz transformations) to be first-order laws that have a stronger necessity than the force laws.

Although the modal status of such constraints requires unpacking, physicists do commonly characterize the principle of relativity as 'a sort of "super law"', as Lévy-Leblond (1976: 271) calls it (following Wigner 1985: 700), so that 'all the laws of physics are constrained' by it. Similarly, Earman (1989: 55) says that the special theory of relativity 'is not a theory in the usual sense but is better regarded as a second-level theory, or a theory of theories that constrains first-level theories'. Despite the frequency of such remarks in both the physics and philosophy literature, one has to dig only slightly beneath their surface to find oneself confronting some mysterious modal metaphysics. Consider, for instance, Penrose's (1987: 24) characterization of Einstein's insight as 'that one should take relativity as a *principle*, rather than as a seemingly accidental consequence of other laws'. Likewise, Janssen (2009: 39) says, 'Special relativity provid[ed] a new interpretation of Lorentz invariance . . . In this new interpretation, the property of Lorentz invariance is no longer accidentally shared by all dynamical laws . . .' What does this mean? After all, as Penrose's 'seemingly' acknowledges, a consequence of laws alone cannot really be accidental.

This chapter, then, is largely concerned with understanding the modal metaphysics needed to fund one scientific explanation of the Lorentz transformations. Some philosophers who have written recently about these issues deliberately avoid discussion of scientific explanation; Norton (2008: 824), for instance, says that such discussions 'seem only to lead to futile disputes over just what it means to explain, over which is the better explanation and, most opaquely, which is the "real" explanation'. In contrast, I see this case as affording us a good opportunity to understand one way in which Salmon's (1989:

180–2) distinction between 'top–down' and 'bottom–up' explanations figures in scientific practice, as well as to understand how a certain important kind of top–down explanation works. Salmon's distinction strikes me as very similar to Einstein's (1919/1954) distinction between 'principle' and 'constructive' theories, which many philosophers have invoked as supporting the view that the Lorentz transformations cannot be explained from the top down. I will take issue with that view as well as with the common interpretation of Einstein as denying the explanatory power of principle theories.

Some philosophers who (unlike Norton) do investigate the scientific explanation of the Lorentz transformations take the principle of relativity as a constraint on the dynamical laws, but do not elaborate this constraint in modal terms. Stachel (2002: 165), for instance, in taking a principle theory as supplying 'criteria that any constructive theory must satisfy', interprets this *must* epistemically rather than metaphysically: a principle theory will 'serve to limit and guide the search for a constructive theory'. Likewise, Janssen emphasizes how relativity transcends the details of the particular force laws that obtain, constraining those laws and explaining why they are all invariant under the Lorentz transformations:

> Special relativity does not decide which systems get to inhabit/carry Minkowski space-time. All it has to say about such systems is that their spatio-temporal behavior must obey the rules encoded in Minkowski space-time. This requirement is automatically met if the system is governed by Lorentz-invariant laws. Special relativity thus imposes a kinematical constraint on all dynamical systems. (Janssen 2009: 40)

But then he cashes out this constraint ('their spatio-temporal behavior *must* obey the rules') in terms of heuristics rather than metaphysics:

> So…special relativity plays the heuristic role of providing constraints on further theorizing. This heuristic role was the important feature of principle theories for Einstein. (Janssen 2009: 40, cf. 27)

Of course, Einstein saw the principle of relativity as enabling him to avoid having to rely on the unsatisfactory theories then available of the microstructure of matter. But there has got to be a more modally robust sense in which relativity transcends and constrains the motley collection of force laws if (as Janssen believes) relativity really explains why those laws are all Lorentz covariant. Relativity's explanatory power cannot arise from its utility as a heuristic. Rather, it is a useful heuristic because we know that whatever unknown dynamical laws there may actually be, they are Lorentz covariant—and (according to the top–down explanation) all of the actual laws are Lorentz covariant because the principle of relativity (together with other laws) requires them to be. My aim is to better understand what it would take for this to be the case.

In Section 2, I will contrast the two principal candidates for explanations of the Lorentz transformations: the view according to which they constrain the dynamical laws and the view, recently championed by Brown (2005), according to which they arise from the dynamical laws. In Section 3, I will elaborate the modal metaphysics needed to fund the former kind of explanation, thereby responding to Brown's arguments that no such explanation is possible. My strategy will draw upon ideas that I have developed elsewhere (2007, 2009). (As Janssen (2009: 28) noted, the machinery I developed there could be drawn upon to elaborate the sense in which the Lorentz transformations, in arising from the principle of relativity as a 'meta-law', impose constraints on the dynamical laws—though Janssen declined to use that machinery.) Finally, in Section 4, I will further demonstrate the power of this machinery by using it to account for the reason why (according to classical physics) Newton's first law of motion holds. Brown sees this law as positing a mysterious, inexplicable coordination among bodies. Like the Lorentz transformations according to relativity, Newton's first law according to classical physics is not *caused by* spacetime geometry, but can have a non-dynamical explanation. I will show what it would take for Newton's first law to be explained according to classical mechanics in much the same way as the Lorentz transformations may be explained according to relativity—namely, by various meta-laws and first-order laws that transcend the dynamical laws.

2 Two possible explanations of the Lorentz transformations

Einstein (1905/1989) originally derived the Lorentz transformations from two premises:

1. The 'principle of relativity', which entails that the laws of nature take the same form in all inertial frames.
2. The 'light postulate': that in one inertial frame (which Einstein initially dubs the 'stationary' system), light's speed is independent of the motion of its source.

Of course, not all deductions are explanations, and for various reasons, this sort of deduction is not generally regarded as explaining why the Lorentz transformations hold. For instance, many commentators regard the light postulate as unable to help explain the Lorentz transformations. Rather, they say, the arrow of explanatory priority points in the opposite direction: the Lorentz transformations are responsible for some of light's features. For example, Stachel (1995: 270–2) sees the light postulate as 'an unnecessary non-kinematical element' in Einstein's derivation:

His presentation of the special theory bears distinct traces of its origins. Mesmerized by the problem of the nature of light, he ignored the discrepancy between the relativity principle, kinematical in nature and universal in scope, and the light principle ... concerned with a particular type of electrodynamical phenomenon. [Stachel's footnote: The oddity of this reference to light would be even more apparent if one replaced it by a reference to some other massless field, basing the theory, for example, on the principle of the constancy of the speed of neutrinos.[2]] ... Einstein later recognized such defects in his original arguments.

[2] Today it is believed that neutrinos have small rest masses. But physicists have posited the photino (the photon's supersymmetric partner) and the graviton as massless.

'The special theory of relativity grew out of the Maxwell electromagnetic equations. So it came about that even in the derivation of the mechanical concepts and their relations the consideration of those of the electromagnetic field has played an essential role. The question as to the independence of those relations is a natural one because the Lorentz transformation, the real basis of the special relativity theory, in itself has nothing to do with the Maxwell theory...' [Einstein 1935: 223, with minor corrections to Stachel's quote]

On Stachel's view, the Lorentz transformations are explanatorily prior to the laws describing the particular sorts of things (e.g. light, electromagnetic fields) that happen to populate spacetime. (Note that 'happen'! We will shortly examine what it could mean, considering that these are *laws* that 'happen' to be true.)

This view regarding the reason why the Lorentz transformations hold has motivated a long tradition (at least from 1909) of trying to derive the Lorentz transformations without appealing to the light postulate.[3] For the sake of completeness (and because these derivations are omitted from most standard physics textbooks), I give such a derivation in the Appendix, drawn from the physics literature. One premise of the derivation is the principle of relativity. But since the derivation aims to be free of dynamical considerations, it cannot presuppose that Newton's first law of motion holds in various reference frames and so cannot use the concept of an 'inertial frame' in expressing the principle of relativity. Rather, the principle of relativity is given as follows:

there is a frame S such that for any frame S' in any allowed uniform motion relative to S, the laws in S and S' take the same form.

The derivation then seeks the transformation laws:

$$x' = X(t, v, x, y, z)$$
$$t' = T(t, v, x, y, z)$$

that relate the coordinates in any such frames S and S' when the coordinate axes are in the 'standard configuration' (see earlier figure). Along with the principle of relativity and the presuppositions implicit in the very possibility of such coordinate systems (such as that all events can be coordinatized in terms of a globally Euclidean geometry), the derivation also presupposes that the transformations X and T are differentiable and that the velocity of S in S' as a function of the velocity of S' in S is continuous and has a connected domain. Further premises are standardly entitled 'spatial (and temporal) homogeneity' and 'spatial isotropy':

in any S' in the family of frames satisfying the principle of relativity, the laws treat all locations and directions (and moments) alike and so are unchanged under arbitrary spatial (and temporal) displacement – that is, under the replacement of every location r in the laws with r + a, for

[3] For references to much of the early literature, see Berzi and Gorini 1969: 1518; for more recent references, see Pal 2003.

arbitrary a, and under arbitrary rotations (and under arbitrary temporal displacement – that is, under the replacement of t with t + a for arbitrary a).[4]

From these premises, it follows (see Appendix) that the transformations take the form:

$$x' = (1 - kv^2)^{-1/2}(x - vt)$$
$$t' = (1 - kv^2)^{-1/2}(-kvx + t)$$

for some constant k. The final premise needed to derive the Lorentz transformations is the law that the 'spacetime interval' $I = ([\Delta x]^2 + [\Delta y]^2 + [\Delta z]^2 - c^2[\Delta t]^2)^{1/2}$ between any two events is invariant (i.e. equal in S and in S'), where c is 'as yet arbitrary, and need not be identified with the speed of light', as Lee and Kalotas (1975: 436) say in emphasizing that the transformation laws are not owing to the laws about any particular force or other spacetime inhabitant (such as light). Rather, c is merely a constant having the dimensions of speed without being identified as the speed of any thing in particular. The interval's invariance entails[5] that:

$$k = c^{-2}$$

---

[4] Though nothing I say will turn on this point, we did not need to add homogeneity and isotropy as separate premises (contrary to Balashov and Janssen 2003: 333). From the principle of relativity, homogeneity and isotropy follow: if S' results merely from an arbitrary spatiotemporal displacement or rotation of S, then S' is forever at rest relative to S and so trivially in an allowed uniform motion relative to S, so by the principle of relativity, the laws in S cannot (e.g.) violate spatial homogeneity by privileging the spatial origin, since the laws in S' would then have to privilege a location other than the origin in S' and so would not take the same form as the laws in S. Minkowski (1908/1952: 75) emphasizes that the principle of relativity subsumes homogeneity and isotropy. Indeed, Minkowski argues that whereas homogeneity and isotropy have standardly been considered 'fundamental', invariance under velocity boosts has been treated at best 'with disdain', and that in unifying all of these symmetries under the principle of relativity, the latter are elevated to the same status as the former. (See also Barton 1999: 18.) What, then, is the difference between the lowly status to which invariance under velocity boosts had been assigned, before the advent of relativity theory, and its newly exalted status? We need the notion of a meta-law constraining first-order laws in order to understand the difference between the exalted and the lowly status; I shall ultimately elaborate it in terms of the way in which a regularity among first-order laws that holds as a matter of meta-law (the exalted status) differs from a regularity among first-order laws that does not hold as a matter of meta-law (the lowly status). As I noted in Section 1, the remarks that physicists make about this distinction quickly lead to some mysterious modal metaphysics. For instance, Cacciatori et al. (2008: 731) say that according to Minkowski, invariance under velocity boosts had formerly been regarded as 'somewhat accidental'. How can a consequence solely of the laws be accidental? My answer (in Section 3) will be: by not being a matter of meta-law—that is, by being just a fortuitous coincidence of the first-order laws.
[5] In S', if I is the spacetime interval between one event at the spacetime origin and another at (x',0,0,t'), then $I^2 = x'^2 - c^2 t'^2$. By using the previous result in the main text to transform x' and t' in this expression into x and t, and then (by virtue of the interval's invariance) equating this result to I^2 between these events in S, we find:

$$(1 - kv^2)^{-1}(x - vt)^2 - c^2(1 - kv^2)^{-1}(-kvx + t)^2 = x^2 - c^2 t^2$$

By boring algebra, this is

$$x^2 + v^2 t^2 - 2xvt - c^2 t^2 - k^2 v^2 x^2 c^2 + 2tkvxc^2 = (x^2 - c^2 t^2)(1 - kv^2)$$

which is

$$(x^2 v^2 k + t^2 v^2 - 2xvt)(1 - kc^2) = 0,$$

which is true for all x,v,t if and only if $k = c^{-2}$.

Thus we have the Lorentz transformations.

As we have seen, those commentators who show how the Lorentz transformations can be derived without using the light postulate aim to identify the reason why the transformations hold—and, in particular, to show that they do not depend on features of light or of any other inhabitants of space time. However, other commentators have a different view of the transformations' explanation. Brown (2005), for example, denies that the principle of relativity helps to explain the Lorentz transformations. On Brown's view, the principle of relativity and the Lorentz transformations have a common source: the Lorentz covariance of the fundamental equations of dynamics. On Brown's view, which consciously echoes Poincaré's (1905/2001) and others', an explanation of the Lorentz transformations must be dynamical, whereas the principle of relativity does not specify the forces holding the constituents of clocks and measuring rods together. On Brown's view, the Lorentz transformations arise from the way in which (in a given frame) the forces within a rod or clock depend upon its uniform speed: '[A] moving rod contracts, and a moving clock dilates, *because of how it is made up and not because of the nature of its spatio-temporal environment...*' (Brown 2005: 8).

This view is inspired by the fact that the electric field of a charge moving uniformly with speed v is diminished in the direction of its motion by a factor of $(1-v^2/c^2)$. Although nowadays this result is standardly derived by taking the electric field of a stationary charge and using the Lorentz transformations to determine what it looks like in a frame where the charge is moving, Oliver Heaviside originally derived it in 1888 directly from Maxwell's electromagnetic-field theory—that is, entirely within a single reference frame. As Brown says (2005: 144), 'Molecular forces inside chunks of matter might mimic electromagnetic forces in a specific sense'—in being Lorentz covariant—so that a bar's equilibrium length changes when it is moving. Brown might have added that if every bar at rest in S' and extending from the origin to x' has a length equal to L $(1 - v^2/c^2)^{1/2}$, where L is its length in S, then since in S the x-coordinate of the origin in S' is vt, the x-coordinate of x' is vt + x' $(1 - v^2/c^2)^{1/2}$. Solving for x' yields:

$$x' = (x - vt) / (1 - v^2 / c^2)^{1/2}$$

Thus we have a dynamical explanation of the x-component of the Lorentz transformation.[6]

This view's defenders are generally inspired by Einstein's (1919/1954) distinction between 'constructive theories' such as the kinetic-molecular theory of gases, which entail phenomena from the bottom up (by showing how they arise from the relatively simple behaviours of their constituents), and 'theories of principle' such as

---

[6] To explain the t-component, Brown might have added, suppose every clock in uniform motion is such that the laws governing its operation make it tick slower by a factor of $(1 - v^2/c^2)^{1/2}$ than it does at rest:

$$\Delta t' = \Delta t (1 - v^2/c^2)^{1/2}$$

thermodynamics, which entail phenomena from the top down (by invoking general conditions, such as energy conservation, that all natural processes must satisfy). Einstein took the principle of relativity to be a principle theory—

The principle of relativity is a principle that narrows the possibilities; it is not a model, just as the second law of thermodynamics is not a model (Einstein 1911/1993: 357)

—and Einstein is generally thought, on the strength of passages like the following, to have regarded only constructive theories as explanatorily potent:

When we say that we have succeeded in understanding a group of natural processes, we invariably mean that a constructive theory has been found which covers the processes in question. (1919/1954: 228)

Apparently, then, Einstein regarded the principle of relativity as unable to help explain the Lorentz transformations.[7]

Of course, this view runs contrary to the idea I mentioned earlier: that the Lorentz transformations somehow transcend the grubby, pedestrian details of the various forces

Suppose the dynamics also makes a clock measure light's speed to be the same regardless of the light's direction or the clock's uniform motion. Then the previous equation requires that clocks resting at different locations in S' be set so that (again taking the transformations to be linear):

$$t' + Fx' = t(1 - v^2/c^2)^{1/2}$$

where F is whatever quantity is needed for a momentary flash of light emitted at the frames' origins at $t = t' = 0$ to be accorded the same speed in the $+x'$ direction as in the $-x'$ direction. Hence:

$$t = (t' + Fx')(1 - v^2/c^2)^{-1/2}$$

The flash's x-coordinate is $x = \pm ct$, and since we found $x' = (x - vt)/(1 - v^2/c^2)^{1/2}$

$$x' = (\pm ct - vt)/(1 - v^2/c^2)^{1/2}$$

Substituting for t

$$x' = (t' + Fx')(\pm c - v)/(1 - v^2/c^2)$$

Rearranging

$$x'/t' = [-F + (1 - v^2/c^2)/(\pm c - v)]^{-1}$$

Since light's speed x'/t' in the $\pm x'$ directions must be equal in magnitude and opposite in sign,

$$-F + (1 - v^2/c^2)/(c - v) = F + (1 - v^2/c^2)/(c + v)$$

Solving

$$F = v/c^2$$

so

$$t' = t(1 - v^2/c^2)^{1/2} - Fx' = t(1 - v^2/c^2)^{1/2} - (v/c^2)(x - vt)/(1 - v^2/c^2)^{1/2}$$
$$= (t - vx/c^2)(1 - v^2/c^2)^{1/2}$$

[7] Even Janssen, who rejects Brown's dynamical explanation of the Lorentz transformations in favour of the view that the transformations are independent of all dynamical laws, now agrees with Brown that 'principle theories are not explanatory' (Janssen 2009: 38). Accordingly, he believes Einstein was incorrect to regard special relativity as a principle theory. I shall argue that Janssen is incorrect.

holding rods and clocks together and so cannot be explained by them. A closely related idea is that the transformations reflect the fundamental spacetime geometry whereas the force laws reflect the sorts of entities that happen to populate spacetime. As Michael Friedman (2002: 211–12) says, in contrasting Poincaré's interpretation of length contraction to Einstein's:

[T]he crucial difference between the two theories, of course, is that the Lorentz contraction, in the former theory, is viewed as a result of the (electromagnetic) forces responsible for the micro-structure of matter in the context of Lorentz's theory of the electron, whereas this same contraction, in Einstein's theory, is viewed as a direct reflection—independent of all hypotheses concerning microstructure and its dynamics—of a new kinematical structure for space and time involving essential relativized notions of duration, length, and simultaneity.

Similarly, Wolfgang Pauli (1958: 3) says of Lorentz that 'in contrast to Einstein, he tried to understand the contraction in a causal way'. Robert DiSalle (2006: 115), in contrast, doubts that facts about spacetime geometry can explain, since such geometry is not given by a constructive theory:

Minkowski spacetime is not presented as a deeper sort of reality underlying the phenomena described by Einstein, explaining them as, say, the kinetic theory of gases explains the phenomena described by the ideal gas law.

DiSalle seems prepared to recognize that facts about spacetime structure can supply a *kind* of explanation:

A more careful assertion would be one that acknowledged, at least, that a very different kind of explanation is at work.

But this concession turns out to be hollow:

We can certainly think of this representation as an explanation of a sort, provided that we don't confuse understanding a theory from a different viewpoint with deriving it from some deeper ontological ground.

That is, we can count it as an explanation provided we don't confuse it with a genuine explanation! Brown is more direct: facts about 'spacetime structure' and the Lorentz transformations have a common explainer: 'The appropriate structure is Minkowski geometry *precisely because* the laws of physics of the non-gravitational interactions are Lorentz covariant' (Brown 2005: 133).

But *why* are the force laws for the diverse kinds of fundamental non-gravitational forces (such as the strong and weak nuclear interactions) all Lorentz covariant? Brown answers:

In the dynamical approach to length contraction and time dilation... the Lorentz covariance of all the fundamental laws of physics is an unexplained brute fact. This, in and of itself, does not count against the approach: all explanation must stop somewhere. (2005: 143)[8]

---

[8] This remark together with many of the others I cite from Brown also appear in Brown and Pooley 2006: 84.

However, not all facts are equally plausibly brute, and the fact that all forces are Lorentz covariant, despite their diversity in other respects, is a humdinger. It seems highly unlikely to be coincidental. Presumably, a common reason lies behind each force's possessing this feature. That every clock, whatever its internal mechanism, ticks slower by the same rate when moving at the same uniform speed, and that every bar, whatever its constitution, shrinks by the same factor when moving at the same uniform speed, seems too suspicious to be plausibly coincidental.

To this argument (from e.g. Balashov and Janssen 2003: 340–2 and Nerlich 2006: 635), Brown (2005: 143) replies that to regard this similarity among all forces as *unlikely* to be brute is to acknowledge that it *could* be brute. Moreover, if the alternative to each force law's being independently Lorentz covariant is supposed to be for spacetime structure to be a common explainer, then this is no alternative:

[I]f one postulates space-time structure as a self-standing, autonomous element in one's theory, it need have no constraining role on the form of the laws governing the rest of content of the theory's models. (Brown 2005: 143; cf. Crisp 2008: 273)

For example, even if all spatial points are qualitatively identical, the laws could privilege some spatial regions (or directions) as a matter of brute fact, treating *here* differently from *there*, where these regions are not distinguished by any qualitative differences. Thus spacetime structure cannot explain the laws' Lorentz covariance because the fact that the laws possess such a feature is not necessitated by facts about spacetime structure:

[H]ow is [spacetime structure']s influence on these laws supposed to work? How in turn are rods and clocks supposed to know which space-time they are immersed in? (Brown 2005: 143)

They 'have no space-time feelers' (Brown 2005: 24).

I agree with Brown (2005: 143) that '[t]alk of Lorentz covariance "reflecting the structure of space-time posited by the theory" and of "tracing the invariance to a common origin" needs to be fleshed out if we are to be given a genuine explanation here'. I propose to do exactly that in the following section. Brown is correct that an explanation of the Lorentz transformations as transcending the dynamical laws cannot be an explanation that cites forces or any other causes of the Lorentz transformations. But Brown is incorrect to conclude that there are no such explanations in science. On the contrary, there are many scientific explanations where explanatory priority is not a matter of causal priority; as Salmon emphasized, that many scientific explanations are bottom–up does not preclude some scientific explanations from being top–down. (As Salmon often said, not every 'because' is a 'cause'.[9] For the same reason, it would be implausible to attribute to Einstein the view that only constructive theories can explain *anything*. After all, to explain why grandmother fails whenever she tries to divide thirty

[9] Possible varieties of non-causal scientific explanations include structural explanations (Hughes 1989: 256–7), dimensional explanations (Lange 2009), mathematical explanations (Colyvan 1998: 321–2), and geometric explanations (Lipton 2004: 9–10).

strawberries among her four grandchildren without cutting any (strawberries), we should not appeal to some constructive theory concerning her method of distributing them. The same outcome would have resulted no matter what method grandmother used—just as the same length contraction or time dilation would have occurred whatever the specific forces operating in the moving rod or clock.

Accordingly, I suggest that Einstein has been widely misunderstood as holding that only constructive theories can explain. What Einstein actually says is that to understand 'natural *processes*' (my emphasis), we need a constructive theory. Admittedly, a gas's expansion under increased temperature is a natural process (explained by the kinetic-molecular theory of gases). However, the relation among an event's coordinates in different reference frames is not obviously a *process*. It need not have a *cause* in order to have an explanation.

Of course, Brown is correct that those who say that 'Minkowski space-time explains by identifying the *kinematic nature* (rather than the cause) of the relevant phenomena' (Janssen 2009: 28) must lay out what this means, where the order of explanatory priority comes from, and how it allows the Lorentz transformations to 'transcend' (Janssen 2009: 27) the dynamical laws. I also agree with Brown that there is a possible world where every force law is independently Lorentz covariant, just as there is a possible world where the only reason that energy is conserved is because one kind of fundamental interaction conserves energy, another kind independently does too, and so forth for each kind of fundamental interaction. However, if scientists believed energy conservation to be just such a coincidence, then they could not consistently believe (as they do[10]) that were there additional kinds of fundamental interaction (perhaps taking place only under exotic, unfamiliar conditions), then they too would conserve energy. This subjunctive conditional is not merely *unlikely* to be true if energy conservation is coincidental. It is *false*. (In somewhat the same way, if a fair coin has been tossed ten times and landed heads each time, then this regularity is coincidental, and so had the coin been tossed again, it might have landed heads, but it might not—so it is false that if the coin had been tossed again, it would have landed heads. The coin tosses are independent, like the fundamental interaction laws on this view—though the coin tosses are stochastic, unlike the fundamental interaction laws.)

Likewise, if scientists believed that the Lorentz transformations arise from a coincidence of the fundamental force laws, they could not consistently believe that were there additional fundamental force laws or had the fundamental force laws been different, then the Lorentz transformations would still have held. (Nor could scientists justly use Lorentz covariance as a heuristic for discovering further laws, as Janssen emphasizes they do.) As Roger Penrose (1987: 21) says, if it is just 'a "fluke" ' that certain dynamical laws exhibit a kind of invariance, then '[t]here is no need to believe that this fluke should continue to hold when additional ingredients of physics are' discovered (cf. Barton 1999: 17). Physicists *do* generally regard special relativity as independent of the force laws. John-Marc

[10] See Bergmann 1962: 144; Feynman 1967: 59, 76, 83, 94; Planck quoted in Pais 1986: 107–8.

Lévy-Leblond (1976: 271) asserts that had the force laws been different so that photons, gravitons, and other kinds of particles that actually possess zero mass instead possessed non-zero mass, the Lorentz transformations would still have held (though these particles would not have moved with the speed c figuring in these transformations).[11]

In short, if the Lorentz transformations result from the fact that a given feature (Lorentz covariance) *happens* to be common to every force law, then certain subjunctive conditionals commonly accepted in science cannot be true. Of course, this response to Brown does not yet address his objection that spacetime's structure is unfit to explain the behaviour of rods and clocks. Moreover, it remains obscure what it would *be* for every force law to *happen* to possess a certain feature (since any consequence of the laws cannot be accidental)—and, by the same token, what would *make* the Lorentz transformations *more* than a 'fluke' (a consequence of the dynamical laws).

I will now lay out the modally robust sense in which relativity transcends and constrains the motley collection of force laws, thereby explaining why those laws must all be Lorentz covariant. In doing so, I will make use of exactly the kind of subjunctive conditional that I have repeatedly noted above. My account, then, will also explain why scientists associate these sorts of conditionals with top–down explanations. I will ultimately argue that even if the Lorentz transformations are explained by the force laws, the transformations could *additionally* be explained by the principle of relativity and facts about spacetime geometry. Crucially, this latter explanation would then explain something about the transformations' status as laws that cannot be explained dynamically—namely, their status as constraints on the dynamical laws.

3 How some laws can transcend others

'Broadly logical' truths, such as mathematical facts, are widely taken as transcending natural laws in that the laws' variety of necessity is weaker than the variety characteristic of broadly logical truths. Accordingly, science takes all broadly logical truths but not all natural laws as preserved under certain counterfactual antecedents. For instance, had the electric force been a bit stronger, the nuclear force would have been too weak to hold protons together in carbon nuclei considering their mutual electric repulsion (Barrow and Tipler 1986: 326). In ascertaining that this is so, we appeal to the fact that various mathematical truths would still have held, even if the force laws had been different. Likewise, as Augustine (1982: 112) said, six would still have been a perfect number even if the works of God's creation had not existed—and, I would add, even if there had been different natural laws.[12]

Even among the natural laws, there are several grades of necessity. To ascertain how bodies would have behaved had gravity been an inverse-cube force, we use the

---

[11] Although Brown (2005: 146) seems to acknowledge Lévy-Leblond's point, he does not seem to recognize that his view cannot embrace this conditional's truth.

[12] Six is a 'perfect' number because it is the sum of its divisors excepting itself (namely, 1, 2, and 3).

fundamental law of dynamics (in Newtonian physics: Newton's second law of motion). So Paul Ehrenfest (1917) famously showed that had gravity been an inverse-cube force, the planets would eventually have collided with the sun or escaped from the sun's gravity. Scientists regard the fundamental dynamical law as possessing a stronger variety of necessity than the gravitational force law does.[13] As I mentioned earlier, it is also commonly believed that energy and momentum conservation are not mere byproducts of the particular kinds of forces there happen to be, but rather would still have held even if there had been different force laws. The fundamental forces, whatever they are, have *got* to conserve energy and momentum.

To understand these strata of necessity, let us start with such facts as that my pocket now holds an emerald, all emeralds are green, etc.—but not that *it is a law* that all emeralds are green. That is, let us start with the 'sub-nomic' facts: the facts that hold, in any possible world where they do hold, independent of which facts are laws and which are not. Many philosophers (e.g. Goodman 1983) have suggested that the sub-nomic facts that are laws would still have held under any sub-nomic counterfactual antecedent that is logically consistent with all of the sub-nomic facts that are laws. Trivially, no sub-nomic fact that is an accident is preserved under all of these antecedents.

Of course, this suggestion takes all of the broadly logical truths as included by courtesy among the natural laws, since they have at least the same perseverance under counterfactual antecedents as mere laws do. The suggestion, more fully, is as follows:

It is a law that m (where m is sub-nomic) if and only if in all conversational contexts, it is true that had p been the case, m would still have been true [that is, $p \square \rightarrow m$], for any sub-nomic p that is logically consistent with all of the sub-nomic claims n (taken together) where it is a law that n.

This reference to the conditional's being true in *all conversational contexts* is required because the truth-values of counterfactual conditionals are notoriously context-sensitive.

This suggestion for distinguishing laws from accidents has an obvious problem: the laws appear on both sides of the 'if and only if'. The laws are picked out by their invariance under a range of antecedents that is, in turn, picked out by the laws. We have not only a vicious circularity in the analysis of lawhood, but also a privilege arbitrarily accorded to the laws: of designating the relevant range of antecedents. Invariance over this range makes the laws special only if there is already something special about this range—and hence about the laws.

But this problem can be avoided. The suggestion was roughly that the laws form a set of truths that would still have held under every antecedent with which the set is logically consistent. In contrast, take the set containing exactly the logical consequences of

---

[13] One might object that Ehrenfest was actually concerned with what would have happened, had gravity been an inverse-cube force *and the other laws remained the same*. However, there is no more reason to suppose that Ehrenfest's counterfactual antecedent contained this further proviso than to suppose that in an ordinary conversation. 'Had I struck the match, it would have lit' is really 'Had I struck the match and the match remained dry and oxygenated...' Just as the match would have remained dry and oxygenated, had it been struck, so (according to Ehrenfest) the dynamical laws would still have held, had gravity been inverse-cube.

the accident that all gold cubes are smaller than a cubic metre. This set's members are *not* all preserved under every antecedent that is logically consistent with them all. For instance, had Bill Gates wanted constructed a gold cube exceeding a cubic metre, I dare say such a cube would have existed—yet that Bill Gates wants such a cube constructed is logically consistent with all gold cubes being smaller than a cubic metre.

That is the idea behind the definition of 'sub-nomic stability':

Consider a non-empty set Γ of sub-nomic truths containing every sub-nomic logical conse-quence of its members. Γ possesses *sub-nomic stability* if and only if for each member *m* of Γ and for any sub-nomic claim p where $\Gamma \cup \{p\}$ is logically consistent (and in every conversational context), it is not the case that had p held, then m's negation might have held [that is, $\sim (p \,\Diamond\!\!\rightarrow\, \sim m)$, which entails $p \,\Box\!\!\rightarrow\, m$].

Sub-nomic stability avoids privileging the range of counterfactual antecedents that is logically consistent with the laws.

The set Λ containing exactly the sub-nomic truths that are laws is stable, whereas the set spanned by the gold-cubes accident is unstable. Let us look at another example. Take the accident g that whenever a certain car is on a dry flat road, its acceleration is given by a certain function of how far its gas pedal is being depressed. Had the gas pedal on a cer-tain occasion been depressed a bit farther, then g would still have held. Can a stable set include g? The set must also include the fact that the car has a four-cylinder engine, since had the engine used six cylinders, g might not still have held. (Once the set includes the fact that the car has a four-cylinder engine, the antecedent that the engine has six cylin-ders is logically *inconsistent* with the set, so to be stable, the set does not have to be pre-served under that antecedent.) But since the set includes a description of the car's engine, its stability also requires that it include a description of the engine factory, since had that factory been different, the engine might have been different. Had the price of steel been different, the engine might have been different. And so on—this ripple effect propagates endlessly. Take the antecedent: had either g been false or there been a gold cube larger than a cubic metre. Is g preserved? In every context? Certainly not. Therefore, to possess sub-nomic stability, a set that includes g must also include the fact that all gold cubes are smaller than a cubic metre (making the set logically inconsistent with the antecedent, so to be stable, the set does not have to be preserved under that antecedent). Since a stable set that includes g must include even the fact about gold cubes, I conclude that the only set containing g that might be stable is the set of *all* sub-nomic truths.[14]

I conclude that *no* nonmaximal set of sub-nomic truths that contains an accident pos-sesses sub-nomic stability. Stability *is* possessed by Λ. Are any other nonmaximal sets stable? The sub-nomic broadly logical truths form a stable set since they would still have

---

[14] According to many proposed logics of counterfactuals, $p \,\Box\!\!\rightarrow\, q$ is true trivially whenever $p\&q$ is true (a principle known as 'Centring'). If Centring is correct, then each member of the set of all sub-nomic truths is trivially preserved under every sub-nomic supposition p that is true. Of course, there are no sub-nomic suppositions p that are false and logically consistent with the set. (If p is a false sub-nomic supposition, then $\sim p$ is a member of the set.) In that case, the set of all sub-nomic truths trivially possesses sub-nomic stability. Accordingly, I will argue that Λ is the largest *nonmaximal* set that is sub-nomically stable.

held under any broadly logical possibility. Let us prove that for any two sub-nomically stable sets, one must be a proper subset of the other. The strategy is to consider an antecedent pitting the invariance of the two sets against each other:

1. Suppose (for *reductio*) that Γ and Σ are sub-nomically stable, t is a member of Γ but not of Σ, and s is a member of Σ but not of Γ.
2. Then ($\sim s$ or $\sim t$) is logically consistent with Γ.
3. Since Γ is sub-nomically stable, every member of Γ would still have been true, had ($\sim s$ or $\sim t$) been the case.
4. In particular, t would still have been true, had ($\sim s$ or $\sim t$) been the case. That is, ($\sim s$ or $\sim t$) $\square\rightarrow t$.
5. So t & ($\sim s$ or $\sim t$) would have held, had ($\sim s$ or $\sim t$). Hence, ($\sim s$ or $\sim t$) $\square\rightarrow \sim s$.
6. Since ($\sim s$ or $\sim t$) is logically consistent with Σ, and Σ is sub-nomically stable, no member of Σ would have been false had ($\sim s$ or $\sim t$) been the case.
7. In particular, s would not have been false, had ($\sim s$ or $\sim t$) been the case. That is, $\sim((\sim s$ or $\sim t$) $\square\rightarrow \sim s$).
8. Contradiction from 5 and 7.

We were asking about nonmaximal sub-nomically stable sets besides Λ. Since no nonmaximal *superset* of Λ is sub-nomically stable (since it would have to contain accidents), we must look for sub-nomically stable sets among Λ's proper subsets. Many of them are clearly unstable. For instance, take the law governing electric forces. Suppose we restrict it to times *after* today and take the set containing exactly this restricted law and its broadly logical, sub-nomic consequences. This set is unstable since it is false that the restricted law would still have held, had the electric-force law been violated sometime *before* today.

However, some of Λ's proper subsets *are* plausibly sub-nomically stable. For instance, take a set containing exactly the sub-nomic broadly logical consequences of the fundamental law of dynamics, the conservation laws, the parallelogram of forces, etc.—without the force laws. As I mentioned, it is widely thought that this set's members would still have held, had the force laws been different. The various strata of natural law form a hierarchy of sub-nomically stable sets:

Broadly logical truths among
the sub-nomic truths ·······························>

The above along with the fundamental
dynamical law, the law of the composition ·······················>
of forces, and conservation laws, among
others—but not the force laws

All of the laws among the sub-nomic truths ···············>
(Λ)

All sub-nomic truths? ···········>

Some (though perhaps not all) plausibly sub-nomically stable sets

For every grade of necessity, the truths possessing it form a nonmaximal stable set, and for each nonmaximal stable set, there is a variety of necessity that is possessed by all and only its members. There are good pretheoretic reasons to identify stability with necessity. A stable set has *maximal* staying power under antecedents: its members would all still have held under every sub-nomic supposition under which they *could* without contradiction all still have held. They are *collectively* as resilient under sub-nomic suppositions as they could *collectively* be. That sounds like necessity to me.

On this picture, there are many species of natural necessity—many strata of laws. A stable proper subset of Δ is associated with a stronger variety of necessity than Λ. That is, the range of antecedents under which the proper subset's members are all preserved, in connection with its stability, is wider than the range of antecedents under which Λ's members are all preserved, in connection with Λ's stability. The conservation laws thereby *transcend* the force laws. This picture of necessity as constituted by stability identifies what is common to broadly logical necessity and to the various grades of natural necessity in virtue of which they are all species of the same genus. My account not only teases the various grades of natural necessity apart, but also explains *why* there is a natural ordering among the genuine varieties of necessity: because for any two stable sets, one must be a proper subset of the other.

If the Lorentz transformation laws belong to some higher stratum on this pyramidal hierarchy than the force laws do, then even if the dynamical laws entail the transformation laws, their necessity is too weak to account for the stronger necessity possessed by the transformation laws. The dynamical laws are not preserved under some antecedents under which the transformation laws are preserved in connection with their membership in a stable set, so the dynamical laws cannot explain why the transformation laws are preserved under those antecedents. In elaborating what it would be for the transformation laws to be explanatorily prior to the force laws, I have appealed to precisely the sort of subjunctive conditionals to which we saw Lévy-Leblond appeal.

Let us now use this apparatus to understand what it would be for a fact such as the principle of relativity to be no coincidence of the force laws but rather a constraint upon them—that is, to be a 'meta-law'. Such a fact is not sub-nomic (since it concerns the sub-nomic facts *that are laws*), and so it appears in no sub-nomically stable set. It is a 'nomic' fact: it describes which sub-nomic facts are (or are not) laws. (For instance, that all emeralds are green is a sub-nomic fact, whereas that it is a law that all emeralds are green is a nomic fact.) Now consider the analogue of sub-nomic stability:

Consider a non-empty set Γ of truths that are nomic or sub-nomic containing every nomic or sub-nomic logical consequence of its members. Γ possesses *nomic stability* if and only if for each member m of Γ and for any nomic or sub-nomic claim where $\Gamma \cup \{p\}$ is logically consistent (and in every conversational context), $\sim (p \diamondsuit \rightarrow \sim m)$.

For instance, Λ lacks nomic stability because energy might not have been conserved had there been no *law* requiring its conservation. (That is a nomic antecedent logically consistent with Λ.) However, perhaps the principle of relativity transcends the force laws in that it would still have held even if there had been different fundamental forces (and hence different 'first-order' laws, i.e. laws among the sub-nomic truths)—and in that furthermore, it belongs to a nomically stable set that omits the force laws and various other first-order laws. Its members are then collectively as invariant under nomic or sub-nomic antecedents as they could collectively be. They possess a variety of necessity, and so it is not merely the case that the force laws *happen* to conform to the principle. They *must* do so—as a matter of meta-law.

As with the sub-nomically stable sets, the nomically stable sets must fall into a pyramidal hierarchy. Crucially, the two hierarchies are connected: for any nomically stable set, its sub-nomic members form a sub-nomically stable set. To show this, notice first that if p (a sub-nomic claim) is logically inconsistent with a nomically stable set Γ, then Γ must entail $\sim p$ (also sub-nomic), and so p is logically inconsistent with the set Σ containing exactly Γ's sub-nomic logical consequences. Conversely, if p is logically inconsistent with Σ, then obviously p is logically inconsistent with Γ. By Γ's nomic stability, Σ is preserved under all sub-nomic antecedents p that are logically consistent with Γ—which (we have just seen) are exactly those that are logically consistent with Σ. Hence, Σ is sub-nomically stable.

Therefore, any sub-nomic truth that follows from a 'meta-law' belongs to a sub-nomically stable set—one higher on the pyramid than Λ (since presumably not all first-order laws follow from meta-laws). This is the way that the meta-laws constrain the first-order laws: any sub-nomic truth that follows from the meta-laws is a constraint imposed by the meta-laws on the first-order laws in that it is a first-order law belonging to a sub-nomically stable set located higher on the pyramid than Λ. Insofar as the Lorentz transformations follow from meta-laws, then, they will have a stronger variety of necessity than, say, the force laws. Thus, my account is in a position to capture the thought of those like the Cambridge physicist L. A. Pars (1921: 249–50) who maintain, in arguing that the principle of relativity explains the Lorentz transformations, that the principle of relativity 'is altogether more deep-seated in the scheme of things than the consequent phenomena of' length contraction and light's having the same speed in all inertial frames. 'Its inevitableness lies deeper', Pars says—a view that we need grades of natural necessity to cash out. Likewise, Minkowski (Corry 1997: 280, 286) compares the principle of relativity to energy conservation in that both hold of whatever unknown forces there might be or have been; he places the principle of relativity at the top or peak ('Spitze') of mechanics, as in my pyramidal hierarchy. I have used stability to understand the modal metaphysics behind this common idea.

What I hope to have shown so far in this section is how a meta-law or a first-order law belonging to a sub-nomically stable set located above Λ in the pyramidal hierarchy can *constrain* other first-order laws by limiting what those laws *could have been*. They can thereby explain features of those first-order laws by making it the case that the first-order laws *had* to exhibit those features. I thus hope to have gone some way towards meeting Brown's challenge to 'flesh out' the notion of 'tracing' features of the various force laws 'to a common origin'.

Now let us apply this machinery to the derivation of the Lorentz transformations that I described earlier (and detail in the Appendix). If the principle of relativity is a meta-law, then it (along with spatial and temporal homogeneity, spatial isotropy, and the other premises of the derivation given in the Appendix) belongs to a nomically stable set. Therefore, as we just saw, the set's sub-nomic members form a sub-nomically stable set higher in the pyramidal hierarchy than Λ. One sub-nomic member of the set is the conclusion of the derivation in the Appendix: the fact that the transformations take the form:

$$x' = (1 - kv^2)^{-1/2}(x - vt)$$

$$t' = (1 - kv^2)^{-1/2}(-kvx + t)$$

Therefore, this fact *must* hold, where this *must* involves a stronger variety of necessity than the force laws exhibit. As a meta-law, the principle of relativity would help to explain why the transformations would have still taken the above form even if the force laws had been different (as per the conditional endorsed by Lévy-Leblond). The force laws have insufficient necessity to explain that fact.[15]

The final step in the derivation uses the spacetime interval's invariance to arrive at the Lorentz transformations. If the principle of relativity is a meta-law and the spacetime interval's invariance is a first-order law higher than Λ on the pyramid, then both transcend the first-order laws. Hence, the Lorentz transformations do, too. Since the spacetime interval's invariance belongs to a sub-nomically stable set higher than the force laws on the hierarchy, it constrains what the force laws could have been. That the spacetime interval is a frame-independent measure of the separation between two events is commonly characterized as a matter of the spacetime geometry on the grounds that the frame-independent quantities are exactly the physically significant ones (e.g. Angel 1980: 82; Norton 1992: 198, 216). Here, then, we have spacetime's geometry helping to explain the transformations without bodies having to possess spacetime 'feelers'. I hope thus to have responded to Brown's challenge by fleshing out how a feature of spacetime structure could help to explain a feature of the laws.

The point of this section was to lay out what would make it the case that the Lorentz transformations are explained by the principle of relativity, spatial and temporal homogeneity, a feature of spacetime geometry, and so forth—that is, what would make those facts explanatorily prior to the Lorentz transformations and how the transformations would transcend the force laws if they were so explained. I have used

[15] I have followed convention in entitling certain symmetry principles used in this explanation 'spatial homogeneity' and 'spatial isotropy'. (I gave the principles in Section 2; the role they play in the derivation is specified in the Appendix.) Physics textbooks commonly say that each 'reflects a property of spacetime itself' (Bais 2007: 67). But this is hyperbole: as I mentioned earlier (following Brown), spatial points could be qualitatively identical without the laws exhibiting the symmetries expressed by 'spatial homogeneity' and 'spatial isotropy'. So for 'spatial homogeneity' and 'spatial isotropy' to help explain why the Lorentz transformations hold is not for spacetime structure to necessitate something about the laws. Brown's challenge to flesh out that idea will be met in the remainder of this section.

various subjunctive conditionals to express what it takes for this explanation to go through. Importantly, I have argued that advocates of this approach to explaining the Lorentz transformations regard these subjunctive conditionals as capturing what makes this explanation go through. I will now present another reason to regard this machinery as unpacking the modal metaphysics behind this explanation: the same machinery applies nicely to another scientific explanation that poses some of the same philosophical questions as the explanation that we have just considered.

4 Another application of this approach: to explanations of Newton's first law by classical physics

Brown (2005: 142) asks, '[H]ow do all the free particles in the world know how to behave in a mutually coordinated way' so that they are unaccelerated relative to the same family of reference frames? 'Anyone who is not amazed by this conspiracy', Brown (2005: 15) says, 'has not understood it.' It cannot be explained by spacetime's structure, according to Brown, because 'there is no *dynamic coupling*' between spacetime and matter (2005: 142, cf. 25)—no 'mechanism' by which a body is 'informed as to what this structure is' (2005: 8). But as we have just seen in connection with an explanation of the Lorentz transformations, an explanation does not require a mechanism or coupling: a force. A feature of spacetime structure can help to explain without spacetime being a cause. According to classical physics, I shall now argue, bodies obey Newton's first law—that is to say, inertial frames exist—because various laws *constrain* the dynamics so that there must be a family of frames in which Newton's first law holds. No force is needed to explain how bodies 'know' what the natural laws are.

In classical physics, Newton's first law is explained in the manner I elaborated in the previous section—namely, by:

(i) various meta-laws: that there is a reference frame where 'spatial homogeneity' and 'isotropy' hold and where a free body's subsequent trajectory is determined by its initial position and velocity, and

(ii) various first-order laws that transcend dynamical laws: that the Galilean transformations hold between any reference frame in (i) and any other frame in arbitrary uniform motion relative to it. (Hence, the meta-laws in (i) hold in any such reference frame.)

In classical physics, the Galilean transformations transcend the dynamics in the same way as the Lorentz transformations transcend the dynamics according to special relativity. In fact, the explanation detailed in the Appendix also serves in classical physics to explain why the Galilean transformations hold. That argument explains why the transformations take the form

$$x' = (1 - kv^2)^{-1/2}(x - vt)$$

$$t' = (1 - kv^2)^{-1/2}(-kvx + t)$$

From this result, t = t' yields k = 0 and hence the Galilean transformations. Therefore, within classical physics, an explanation of the Galilean transformations can proceed from the principle of relativity, spatial and temporal homogeneity, and spatial isotropy (and the other premises of the derivation given in the Appendix), and that t = t'.[16] Like the spacetime interval's invariance in relativistic physics, the fact that t = t' can be understood in Galilean spacetime (Geroch 1978) as a matter of the spacetime geometry on the grounds that time intervals are physically significant and the frame-independent quantities are exactly the physically significant ones.

From (i) and (ii), Newton's first law can be explained by an argument given by Wigner (1992: 340–1). Take a free body in a reference frame in this family where it starts from rest at the origin. Since space is isotropic and the body's motion is determined by its initial position and velocity, it must stay put. Now suppose the body starts from rest at any other location r. By spatial homogeneity, the body must stay put at r, too. Now view this case from a frame moving uniformly at −v relative to the first frame. The body begins there with velocity v. By the Galilean transformations, the body's position at t must be x + vt. Thus it is a law that in any of these frames, free bodies undergo no acceleration.

Therefore, no conspiracy or mysterious coordination among the free bodies is needed to explain why they are all unaccelerated in the very same frames. Rather, the explanation is that these are the frames where various symmetries and other laws transcending the dynamics hold. Here we have another scientific explanation (this time within classical rather than relativistic physics) that uses meta-laws and first-order laws transcending the dynamics.

This explanation, like the earlier explanation of the Lorentz transformations, appears to contravene the thought commonly attributed to Einstein that principle theories are explanatorily impotent. But I have suggested that Einstein's remark may be widely misunderstood. It requires constructive explanations of natural *processes*. Like the relation among coordinates in two reference frames, the behaviour of a body that is free is not obviously a causal process. After all, the body is experiencing no forces. The existence of a family of inertial reference frames is not a *process*.

5 Conclusion

I have argued that the key difference between a dynamical explanation of the Lorentz transformations and an explanation according to which the transformations transcend the force laws is that on the latter, but not the former, the transformations would still have held even if the force laws had been different. If this conditional is true, then even if the transformations are *entailed* by a dynamical argument, the dynamical laws are not

---

[16] Accordingly, the meta-laws explaining the Lorentz transformations also entail that *had* t = t' held, then the Galilean transformations would have held. That is because the meta-laws entailing the conclusion reached in the Appendix would still have held under this counterfactual antecedent.

responsible for the transformations' characteristic necessity. In that case, the dynamical laws can explain the *truth* of the transformations and even why they possess the variety of necessity characteristic of the dynamical laws. But the dynamical laws cannot explain why the transformations possess a stronger variety of necessity. I have used the notion of stability to elaborate these different varieties of necessity and the sense in which the principle of relativity could be a 'constraint' on force laws—a sense that does not involve merely our finding the principle useful for arriving at promising dynamical theories.

If the dynamical laws can explain why the transformations hold, but not why they possess their characteristic necessity, then a dynamical explanation of the transformations co-exists with an explanation from spacetime geometry and symmetry principles transcending the dynamics.[17] Dorato (2007: 100) had anticipated the possibility that the two explanations do not exclude each other—though not that the explanation from meta-laws would then explain something about the transformations' status that cannot be explained dynamically. Dorato aptly compares this example to the two compatible explanations offered by Salmon's (1989: 183) 'friendly physicist': that a helium-filled balloon in an airplane accelerating for take-off moves toward the front of the cabin can be explained either from the bottom up (by the pressure gradient of the air in the cabin) or from the top down (by general relativity's principle of equivalence). Dorato maintains that Brown does not consider this possibility. It seems to me that Salmon's example could be treated in the same way as I have treated the two approaches to explaining the Lorentz transformations.

If Einstein regards the principle of relativity as a meta-law, thereby constraining the first-order laws in the sense I have elaborated, then the contrast between Einstein and Newton is quite stark—contrary to Brown (2005: 145), who says that 'in Einstein's hands [the principle of relativity] was not essentially different from the principle defended by Newton—a constraint on the nature of the fundamental interactions'. The contrast concerns the nature of this 'constraint'. In the *Principia*, Newton presents the fact that the laws take the same form in all inertial frames as just a byproduct of the laws of motion; it is Corollary 5 to them, not explanatorily prior to them.[18] If, by contrast, the principle of relativity is a meta-law on Einstein's view, then David Gross (1996: 14256) correctly interprets Einstein's 'great advance of 1905' as having been to take symmetries not as mere 'consequences of the dynamical laws of nature', but rather 'as the primary feature of nature that constrains the allowable dynamical laws'. Here the relativity principle 'constrains' not merely by joining our evidence in limiting which hypotheses for the dynamical laws could actually be true (a matter of epistemic possibility), but as limiting what the dynamical laws could have been (a matter of alethic possibility). I have tried to explain what it would be for the principle of relativity to possess this status.

---

[17] In his exchange with Prašil, Einstein (1911: 354–5) seems to regard both arguments as explanatory without one rendering the other redundant.

[18] Newton's proof of the Corollary presupposes that mass is velocity-independent and that all forces on bodies are independent of their absolute positions and velocities over and above their positions and velocities relative to other bodies (Barbour 1989: 31–2, 577–8). If any of these features are *coincidentally* common to all forces, then it also makes the principle of relativity just a byproduct of the laws of motion and force laws.

Appendix

We seek the transformation laws:

$$x' = X(t, v, x, y, z)$$
$$t' = T(t, v, x, y, z)$$

The only privileged axis is x, along which the origin of S' is moving in S. By spatial isotropy, then, x' and t' are independent of y and z. By spatial homogeneity, the x'-separation of (x, y, z, t) and $(x + \Delta, y, z, t)$ depends only on Δ, not on x. Therefore:

$$\left(\frac{\partial}{\partial x}\right)[X(t, v, x + \Delta) - X(t, v, x)]_{\Delta, t, v} = 0$$

Dropping the remainder of what's being held fixed as we take the partial derivative with respect to x:

$$\left(\frac{\partial}{\partial x}\right)X(t, v, x + \Delta) = \left(\frac{\partial}{\partial x}\right)X(t, v, x)$$

Thus $\left(\dfrac{\partial X}{\partial x}\right)$ is equal for all x, so X is linear in x—and, by analogous reasoning, T is linear in x and (using temporal homogeneity) X and T are linear in t:

(1) $x' = X(t, v, x) = A_v x + B_v t$

(2) $t' = T(t, v, x, y, z) = C_v x + D_v t$

where the subscripts indicate that A–D are functions exclusively of v. (For simplicity, I omit the subscripts when the function is understood to be evaluated at v.[19])

Let us derive 'reciprocity': that the origin of S is moving in S' with velocity $w = -v$.[20] Since the frames are in 'standard configuration' (recall figure), the $+ x$ and $+ x'$ directions are the same: $A = (\partial x' / \partial x) > 0$. Without loss of generality, suppose that the $+ t$ and $+ t'$ directions are the same: $D = (\partial t' / \partial t) > 0$. From (1), the x and t coordinates of $x' = 0$ obey $x = (-B/A)t$, so $v = -B/A$. Take S (S') and invert the direction of the x (x') axis, yielding $\mathbf{S}$ ($\mathbf{S'}$). By the principle of relativity, the laws transforming coordinates in S to coordinates in S' take the same form as the laws transforming $\mathbf{S}$ to $\mathbf{S'}$:

$$x' = A_v x + B_v t$$
$$t' = C_v x + D_v t$$

[19] Einstein (1905/1989: 146) says, without elaboration, that spatiotemporal homogeneity implies linearity. The argument I have given is roughly from Terletskii (1968: 18–19). Gannett (2007) replaces the assumption of X's differentiability with its boundedness on a compact set (i.e. that X takes all of the spatiotemporal points within a given finite R from the origin to points that, for some finite R*, are within R* from the origin).

[20] This argument is adapted from Berzi and Gorini 1969.

where v is the velocity in S of the origin of S'. Since $x = -x$, $t = t$, $x' = -x'$, and $t' = t'$, (1) and (2) yield:

$$x' = A_v x - B_v t$$

$$t' = -C_v x + D_v t$$

Hence:

$$A_v = A_v$$
$$B_v = -B_v$$
$$C_v = -C_v$$
$$D_v = D_v$$

and the x and t coordinates of $x' = 0$ obey $x = (B_v/A_v) t$, so $v = B/A = -v$. Therefore:

$$\left. \begin{array}{l} A_{-v} = A_v \\ B_{-v} = -B_v \\ C_{-v} = -C_v \\ D_{-v} = D_v \end{array} \right\} \quad (3)$$

For $x = 0$ and $t' = 1$, (1) and (2) yield:

$$x' = B_v t$$
$$1 = D_v t$$

so at $t' = 1$, $x' = B_v/D_v$. That is, in S', the origin of S moves a distance of B_v/D_v in one unit of time, so its velocity $w = B_v/D_v$, which is some unknown function $\varphi(v)$. Since $B_{-v} = -B_v$ and $D_{-v} = D_v$, $\varphi(-v) = -\varphi(v)$. By the principle of relativity, the function φ that takes us from the velocity of S' in S to the velocity of S in S' also takes us from the velocity of S in S' to the velocity of S' in S: $v = \varphi(w)$. Therefore, $v = \varphi(\varphi(v))$. Because φ takes us from S to S' and vice versa, φ is 1–1 and (since, by the principle of relativity, the same range of relative velocities must be allowed in each frame) φ maps its domain onto itself—and (assuming any real number between two velocities that one frame may have relative to another is also an allowed velocity) it follows that $\varphi(v)$ is either strictly increasing (i.e. if $v_2 > v_1$, then $\varphi(v_2) > \varphi(v_1)$) or strictly decreasing. Take these two options in turn.

If φ is strictly increasing and $v < w$, then $\varphi(v) < \varphi(w)$. But $\varphi(w) = \varphi(\varphi(v)) = v$, so $w = \varphi(v) < v$, contradicting $v < w$. A contradiction likewise arises from $v > w$. So the only possibility is $v = w$, i.e. $v = \varphi(v)$. Then since we found $\varphi(v) = B/D$, $D = B/v$, and since we found $B = -vA$, $D = -A$. By substitution into (1) and (2):

$$x' = Ax - vAt$$
$$t' = Cx - At$$

so $(\partial x'/\partial x) = A$ and $(\partial t'/\partial t) = -A$. These cannot both be greater than zero, contrary to our initial supposition.

If φ is strictly decreasing then if $\zeta = -\varphi$, then ζ is strictly increasing. We found $\varphi(\varphi(v)) = v$, so $\zeta(-\zeta(v)) = -v$. We found $\varphi(-v) = -\varphi(v)$, so $\zeta(-v) = -\zeta(v)$. Putting these together, we find $\zeta(\zeta(-v)) = -v$. So ζ is a strictly increasing function whose double application is the identity function. By the previous paragraph's argument, $\zeta(v) = v$, so $\varphi(v) = -v$, i.e. reciprocity (!).

By the principle of relativity, the laws transforming coordinates from S to S' take the same form as the laws transforming S' to S (but, by reciprocity, with '−v' replacing 'v'):[21]

$$x = A_{-v}x' + B_{-v}t'$$
$$t = C_{-v}x' + D_{-v}t'$$

Substituting these into (1) and (2):

$$x' = A_v(A_{-v}x' + B_{-v}t') + B_v(C_{-v}x' + D_{-v}t')$$
$$t' = C_v(A_{-v}x' + B_{-v}t') + D_v(C_{-v}x' + D_{-v}t')$$

By (3):

$$x' = A_v(A_vx' - B_vt') + B_v(-C_vx' + D_vt') = (A^2 - BC)\,x' + (-AB + BD)t'$$
$$t' = C_v(A_vx' - B_vt') + D_v(-C_vx' + D_vt') = (AC - CD)\,x' + (-BC + D^2)\,t'$$

So:

$$A^2 - BC = 1$$
$$B(D - A) = 0$$
$$C(A - D) = 0$$
$$D^2 - BC = 1$$

The two middle equations have two solutions: (i) $B = C = 0$, yielding the identity coordinate transformations—the trivial result; not what we were seeking—and (ii):

$$D = A$$
$$C = (A^2 - 1)/B$$

Since $v = -B/A$, the latter equation yields $C = (1 - A^2)/vA$. Thus:

$$x' = A_vx - vA_vt$$

(4)

$$t' = \left[(1 - A_v^2)/vA_v\right]x + A_vt$$

Consider a frame S" in standard configuration whose origin is moving uniformly with speed u relative to S'. By the principle of relativity, the laws transforming coordinates from S to S' take the same form as the laws transforming S' to S". So:

---

[21] The following argument is taken directly from Pal 2003.

$$x'' = A_u x' - u A_u t'$$

$$= A_u [A_v x - v A_v t] - u A_u ([(1 - A_v^2) / v A_v] x + A_v t)$$

$$t'' = [(1 - A_u^2) / u A_u] x' + A_u t'$$

$$= [(1 - A_u^2) / u A_u][A_v x - v A_v t] + A_u([(1 - A_v^2) / v A_v] x + A_v t)$$

By the principle of relativity, the laws transforming coordinates from S to S", given above, take the same form as the laws transforming S to S', where we found $D = A$. Hence the coefficient of t in the equation for t" must equal the coefficient of x in the equation for x":

$$[(1 - A_u^2) / u A_u](-v A_v) + A_u A_v = A_u A_v - u A_u[(1 - A_v^2) / v A_v]$$

Simplifying and rearranging:

$$(A_u^2 - 1) / u^2 A_u^2 = (A_v^2 - 1) / v^2 A_v^2$$

Since these quantities are equal for all u and v, they must be independent of u and v: For some constant k,

$$(A_v^2 - 1) / v^2 A_v^2 = k$$

So $A = (1 - kv^2)^{-1/2}$. By (4):

$$x' = (1 - kv^2)^{-1/2} x - v(1 - kv^2)^{-1/2} t = (1 - kv^2)^{-1/2}(x - vt)$$

$$t' = -kv(1 - kv^2)^{-1/2} x + (1 - kv^2)^{-1/2} t = (1 - kv^2)^{-1/2}(-kvx + t)$$

The constant k is fixed by the invariance of the spacetime interval, as I explain in the main text.[22]

---

[22] We could instead follow Pal (2003) in using the fact that light's speed c is the same in S and S' to derive $k = c^{-2}$ and hence the Lorentz transformations. But this would be for a peculiarity of a particular force to be responsible for the transformations, and so the explanation would fail to accord the transformations a variety of necessity stronger than the force laws possess.

PART II

Dispositions and Causes

5

A disposition-based process-theory of causation

Andreas Hüttemann

Given certain well-known observations by Mach and Russell, the question arises what place there is for causation in the physical world. My aim in this chapter is to understand under what conditions we can use causal terminology and how it fits in with what physics has to say. I will argue for a disposition-based process-theory of causation. After addressing Mach's and Russell's concerns I will start by outlining the kind of problem the disposition-based process-theory of causation is meant to solve. In a second step I will discuss the nature of those dispositions that will be relevant for our question. In Section 3 I will discuss existing dispositional accounts of causation before I proceed to present my own account (Sections 4 to 6) and contrast it with traditional process-theories (Section 7).

1 Problems of causation

There are many problems of causation. Michael Tooley and Ernest Sosa for instance present a list of five fundamental issues: (1) the relation of causal laws and causal relations; (2) do causal states of affairs logically supervene on non-causal ones? (3) if not, is an a posteriori reduction feasible? (4) are causal relations immediately given in experience? (5) do causal concepts need to be analysed, or can they be taken to be basic? (Sosa and Tooley 1993: 5). While all of these are important issues, I will not attempt to answer any of these—at least not directly. Rather, I will approach the issue of causation from a different angle. In what follows I will focus on 'probably the central problem in the metaphysics of causation' (Field 2003: 443).

At the turn of the 20th century Mach and Russell suggested that the terms 'cause' and 'effect' ought to be eliminated because they are imprecise and their conditions of application inconsistent with what physics says about reality. However, causal notions play an important role in everyday life and in the special sciences, and, as Nancy Cartwright (1983: 21ff.) has pointed out, they seem indispensable in order to distinguish efficient from non-efficient strategies. How are these observations to be reconciled? What place have causes and effects in a world as described by physics—for short: in a physical world?

1.1 Historical background

In 1874 Gustav Kirchhoff criticized the notion of causation in the well-known preface to his *Lectures on Mechanics*:

It is common to define mechanics as the science of forces and forces as causes that bring about motions or tend to bring them about. [...]. [This definition] is tainted by an obscurity that is due to the notion of cause and tendency [...]. For this reason I propose that the aim of mechanics is to describe the movements that take place in nature—more specifically to describe them completely and as simple as possible. What I want to say is that we should aim at stating what phenomena there are rather than to determine their causes. (Kirchhoff 1874: preface)

Kirchhoff's criticism concerns causation in a productive sense or understood as a force, which was indeed the main concept of cause that was used by physicists in the first half of the 19th century.[1] Eliminating productive causes from physics still leaves room for other conceptions. Gustav Theodor Fechner and the early Ernst Mach for example turned to John Stuart Mill. Mill had repudiated productive causes and defended a regularity view according to which the cause is an instance of the antecedent in a law, which is a sufficient condition for the occurrence of the effect:

To certain facts certain facts always do, and, as we believe, will continue to, succeed. The invariable antecedent is termed the cause; the invariable consequent the effect. (Mill 1843/1891: 213)

When at the turn of the century Mach and Bertrand Russell criticized the notion of cause it was a Millian regularity view of causation they had in mind.

Mach argued that for at least three reasons the concept of cause cannot be applied to reality as described by physics and should therefore be given up.

(i) Taking seriously the concept of cause as a set of conditions implies that you need to consider every single factor on which an event depends. That is practically impossible.

If one attempts to eliminate the traces of fetishism, which are still associated with the concept of cause, and takes into consideration that in general you cannot specify a cause since a phenomenon most of the times is determined by a whole system of conditions, you are led to the conclusion to give up the concept of cause altogether. (Mach 1896: 435–6)

(ii) The concept of cause requires strict regularities. However, there are no such regularities:

In nature there are no causes and no effects. Nature is there only once. Repetitions of identical cases, such that A is always correlated with B, the same outcome under the same conditions, i.e. what's essential for the relation between cause and effect, exists only in abstraction [...] (Mach 1883: 459)

---

[1] See Hüttemann, 'The Elimination of Causal Vocabulary from Physics', manuscript.

(iii) Finally, the advanced sciences replace causal terminology by the concept of a mathematical function, which is a more precise notion.

In the higher developed natural sciences the use of the concepts cause and effect becomes more and more limited. There is a perfectly good reason for this, namely that these concepts describe a state of affairs provisionally and incompletely – they are imprecise [...]. As soon as it is possible to characterise the elements of events through measurable quantities, [...] the dependence of the elements on each other can be characterized more completely and more precisely through the concept of a function, rather than through the insufficiently determined concepts cause and effect. (Mach 1883: 278)

Russell in his well-known paper 'On the notion of Cause' adds two important considerations:

(iv) Causes are usually conceived as localized events (locality). However, no localized event is sufficient for the occurrence of any other event, because there may always be an interfering factor.

In order to be sure of the expected effect, we must know that there is nothing in the environment to interfere with it. But this means that the supposed cause is not, by itself, adequate to insure the effect. And as soon as we include the environment, the probability of repetition is diminished, until at last, when the whole environment is included, the probability becomes *nil*. (Russell 1912–13: 7–8)

Thus, if the fact that causes determine their effects is spelled out in terms of conditional regularities such that the cause is the antecedent, we cannot have both locality and determination.

(v) In a physical system as described by fundamental physics, the future determines the past in exactly the same way as vice versa.

[...] the future 'determines' the past in exactly the same sense in which the past 'determines' the future. The word 'determine', here, has a purely logical significance: a certain number of variables 'determine' another variable if that variable is a function of them. (Russell 1912–13: 15)

Therefore, the asymmetry which we associate with the causal relation is inconsistent with fundamental physics.

Mach and Russell both conclude that there is no place for causation in the advanced sciences. Even though this latter claim has been proven false for today's advanced sciences,[2] the issue has been raised of how to reconcile Mach's and Russell's observations with the persistence and usefulness of causal terminology.

---

[2] See, for instance Suppes (1970: 5–6), Hitchcock (2007: 55), and Williamson (2009: 195–7).

1.2 The folk-conception of causation

As others have observed (Norton 2007), there is probably no univocal conception of causation as we usually (pre-theoretically) understand it, let alone a conception that furthermore applies to the special sciences. What people mean by causation has probably changed over time and even within historical periods of time there might be different conceptions. Be that as it may, I will present some features that are often associated with causation in everyday life as well as in the special sciences, and will ask to what extent a relation that has these features has its place in a physical world.

- *Modal Force*: A cause brings about the effect. It somehow *forces* the effect to occur. The cause determines the effect to occur.
- *Asymmetry*: Causes bring about effects, but not vice versa.
- *Time-precedence*: Causes precede their effects.
- *Locality*: Causes and effects are events that can be localized in spacetime, in some definite kind of region.
- *Dominant Cause*: There is a distinction between a main cause and secondary factors (between causes and conditions).
- *Objectivity*: Whether or not something is a cause is independent of human interests or convictions.
- *Multi-level*: Causal relations obtain on all kinds of 'levels': in physics, the special sciences in everyday life.[3]

As we have seen, some of these characteristics are somewhat problematic in the light of the early 20th-century criticism. In what follows, I will focus on the problem of modal force, and occasionally mention how I think the other features might be dealt with. I will not have anything to say about the problem of the asymmetry of the causal relation, but assume that an account can be given that explains this feature in terms of statistical mechanics somewhere along the lines of Albert (2000) or Field (2003, section 4).

In what follows I will argue that, even though causation in the above-mentioned sense probably has no place in a physical world, a near relative can be shown to be compatible with physics—at least given the right conditions. That will allow us to understand why and under what conditions we are successfully applying causal terminology. I take it that the relation between causes and effects does not describe *sui generis* facts over and above those described by the various sciences. Causal facts—I will argue—are partly determined by the facts of physics, biology, economics, etc., but they are also partly determined by pragmatic considerations.

---

[3] Some of these characteristics are mentioned in Norton (2007). *Modal Force* and *Asymmetry* have been called the hard problems of a theory of causation (Hitchcock 2007: 58).

2 Laws and dispositions

One of the central claims I will argue for is that we need to understand the roles of dispositions for physical laws. This then allows us to understand how causal relations emerge from compound systems given the right kind of conditions (as well as certain pragmatic considerations that I will talk about towards the end).

Law, disposition, and causation are closely related concepts. All three are concerned with some kind of natural necessity. The cause *forces* the effect to occur. Given a disposition and the right circumstances the disposition *cannot but* manifest, and the law *forces* or *necessitates* bodies to behave in some way rather than another. Furthermore, all three notions are closely tied to counterfactual conditionals. Laws support counterfactuals, causal relations can often be spelled out in terms of counterfactual claims, and the conditional analysis of disposition is at least a helpful device for the explication of dispositional properties. It thus seems to be reasonable to see how laws, dispositions, and causation are in fact related so as to give a unified account of these concepts and maybe of the kind of natural necessity involved.[4]

I will argue that at least most laws of nature are grounded in dispositions. Given a detailed understanding of these dispositions, we will also be able to understand how causal relations fit into a physical world.

2.1 Part–whole explanation

In this section I will explain why it is reasonable to assume that physical systems have dispositions and how to understand these dispositions.

I will argue that we need to assume that physical systems have dispositional properties because this assumption provides the best explanation for the way physics treats compound systems and their parts.

Let me start with an example of a part–whole explanation from quantum mechanics: carbon monoxide molecules consist of two atoms of mass m_1 and m_2 at a distance x. Besides vibrations along the x-axis, the atoms can perform rotations in three-dimensional space around its centre of mass. This provides the motivation for describing the molecule as a rotating oscillator, rather than as a simple harmonic oscillator. The compound's (the molecule's) behaviour is explained in terms of the behaviour of two subsystems, the oscillator and the rotator. In this case the parts are not spatial parts, they are sets of degrees of freedom. The physicist Arno Bohm, who discusses this example in his textbook on quantum mechanics, describes this procedure as follows:

We shall therefore first study the rigid-rotator model by itself. This will provide us with a description of the CO states that are characterised by the quantum number n = 0, and will also approximately describe each set of states with a given vibrational quantum number n. Then we shall see how these two models [The harmonic oscillator has already been discussed in a previous

---

[4] For a discussion of these connections see Handfield (2009: 4) and McKitrick (2009: 31).

chapter. A.H.] are combined to form the vibrating rotator or the rotating vibrator. (Bohm 1986: 128)

Thus, the first step consists in considering how each subsystem behaves if considered as an isolated system. The second step consists in combining the two systems.

This is a perfect illustration of a quantum-mechanical part–whole explanation. In carrying out this programme Bohm considers the following subsystems: (i) a rotator, which can be described by the Schrödinger equation with the Hamiltonian: $H_{rot} = L^2/2I$, where L is the angular momentum operator and I the moment of inertia; (ii) an oscillator, which can be described by the Schrödinger equation with the following Hamiltonian: $H_{osc} = P^2/2\mu + \mu\omega^2 Q^2/2$, where P is the momentum operator, Q the position operator, ω the frequency of the oscillating entity and μ the reduced mass.

He adds up the contributions of the subsystem by invoking a law of composition (for short: COMP):

IVa. Let one physical system be described by an algebra of operators, A_1, in the space R_1, and the other physical system by an algebra A_2 in R_2. The direct-product space $R_1 \otimes R_2$ is then the space of physical states of the physical combinations of these two systems, and its observables are operators in the direct-product space. The particular observables of the first system alone are given by $A_1 \otimes I$, and the observables of the second system alone are given by $I \otimes A_2$ (I = identity operator). (Bohm 1986: 147)

Thus, four laws are involved in this part–whole explanation:

(1) The law for the compound: The compound behaves according to the Schrödinger-equation with the Hamiltonian $H_{comp} = H_{rot} + H_{osc}$. (This is the *explanandum*; it describes the behaviour of the compound.)

(2) The law for the rotator: The rotator behaves according to the Schrödinger equation with the Hamiltonian: $H_{rot} = L^2/2I$.

(3) The law for the oscillator: The oscillator behaves according to the Schrödinger equation with the Hamiltonian: $H_{osc} = P^2/2\mu + \mu\omega^2 Q^2/2$.

(4) The law of composition (COMP) that tells us how to combine (2) and (3).

We explain the behaviour of the compound (the *explanandum*) as described in (1) in terms of (2), (3), and (4) (the *explanans*).

The solar system provides another example of a part–whole explanation. Even in the case of a highly integrated system as the solar system, you make the same steps. In the dynamic equations for the solar system (Lagrange-equation) you write the terms for the kinetic energy of the planets, etc. (that's the term that describes how the part would behave if it were on its own). You then combine these subsystems, i.e. you describe them by a single Hamilton function or operator. The only significant difference to the case above is that you need to add gravitational interaction terms. As in the case above, we rely on laws of composition, namely laws that tell us how to add up the various contributions.

Let me add as a final example of a compound system a falling stone in a medium. The subsystems are the freely falling stone on the one hand and the medium on the other. Both contribute to the overall behaviour.

2.2 An argument for dispositions

In this section I will argue that we need to assume that systems have dispositional properties in order to understand how part–whole explanations work.

As working definitions I employ the notions of categorical and dispositional properties as follows: A dispositional property is a property that, if instantiated by an object, is manifest under specific conditions only. A categorical property by contrast is a property that, if instantiated by an object, is manifest under all conditions. So, according to this distinction, categorical properties are limiting cases of dispositional properties. Note: In the limiting case of a categorical property, the distinction between a property and its manifestation doesn't do any work.

This is certainly not the orthodox way to draw the distinction, but the usual suspects fall on the right sides. Solubility and fragility, if instantiated by an object, become manifest under specific conditions. On the other hand, triangularity or massiveness (the best candidates for categorical properties), if instantiated by an object, are manifest under all conditions.

Why do we need dispositions to understand part–whole explanations? A basic ingredient of the explanans in a part–whole explanation is the reference to the behaviour the parts would manifest if they were on their own. However, this behaviour of the parts is not manifest while they are parts of a compound.

The vibrating rotator illustrates this: the subsystems contribute to the overall energy of the compound. But the behaviour of the subsystems is not manifest.[5] If they were manifest, the associated spectral lines could be measured—at least in principle. But they can't. The only spectral lines there are, are those of the compound.

The explanation relies on how the parts would behave if they were isolated, i.e. on how the rotator would behave if the oscillator were absent. The manifestation of the behaviour of the rotator is interfered with by the presence of the oscillator. The oscillator serves as an antidote with respect to the rotator's manifestation (and vice versa). It is, however, a *partial* antidote, because it does not suppress the manifestation completely. It prevents (complete) manifestation—however, it allows for *contributing* to the behaviour of the compound and thus partial manifestation.

The behaviour of the falling stone is—in general—not (completely) manifest either, because the medium serves as a (partial) antidote. Still, the behaviour of the falling stone in the absence of interfering factors plays an essential role in the explanation of the behaviour of the compound (falling stone in a medium).

---

[5] That is, they are not completely manifest. The distinction between complete and partial manifestation will be drawn in the next section. When I talk about manifestation simpliciter this has to be read as *complete* manifestation rather than partial manifestation (see section. 2.4).

The description of the temporal evolution of the solar system relies among other things on how the parts (the planets and the sun) would behave if they were isolated (the kinetic energy terms). That behaviour is, however, not manifest. The other parts or planets as well as their interactions serve as partial antidotes.

To sum up: In part–whole explanations the behaviour of compound systems is explained in terms of the behaviour of the parts. The behaviour of these parts is not manifest because there are antidotes, namely the other parts or factors. The behaviour that we attribute to the parts is thus a behaviour that becomes manifest given certain circumstances obtain—the absence of antidotes or disturbing factors. A fortiori, we assume that the parts have dispositional properties. Their behaviour is not manifest under all circumstances (see Hüttemann 1998 and 2004. For a similar argument see Corry 2009).

2.3 Inertial and quasi-inertial laws

The above argument is not an argument for dispositional monism, i.e. the view that *all* properties are dispositional. I merely claim that at least some of the properties of physical systems, namely those appealed to in part–whole explanations, need to be construed as dispositional properties. Similarly, the argument does not claim that all laws need to be understood in terms of dispositions. According to the argument, those laws that describe the behaviour (properties) of systems that can play the role of parts need to be construed as attributing dispositions to physical systems.

The laws, which went into the explanations we looked at, are laws that describe the temporal evolution of systems: the temporal evolution of rotators, oscillators, stones, or planets. They describe *processes*. The temporal behaviour (or process) that such a law describes becomes manifest when there are no disturbing factors or antidotes, as for instance the medium or other systems. I will call these laws 'quasi-inertial laws' by analogy to Newton's first law:

Every body continues in its state of rest or of uniform motion in a straight line, unless it is compelled to change that state by forces impressed upon it. (Newton 1999: 416)

The behaviour Newton's first law attributes to bodies becomes manifest, given nothing interferes. My claim is that many law-statements ought to be understood as making similar claims. Some temporal behaviour (process) is classified as in some sense 'inertial'. The law-statement says that unless something intervenes, some kind of behaviour will become manifest. So in a sense many laws, e.g. Galileo's law of free fall or the law that describes the behaviour of a rotator, can be classified as 'quasi-inertial' laws in the following sense: They describe what happens *if nothing intervenes*. They describe the *default-*behaviour of a system (or a default process).

2.4 Dispositions as contributors

The properties we rely on in part–whole explanations are dispositional in the sense outlined at the outset: The property/behaviour becomes manifest under special circumstances only. This is a feature they share (by definition) with dispositions we come across in everyday situations such as solubility or fragility. However, the dispositions appealed to in physical part–whole explanations have certain special features, which are not in general associated with everyday dispositions. These special features are responsible for the fact that my disposition-based theory of causation differs significantly from other dispositionalist accounts of causation (e.g. Molnar 2003 or Mumford 2009a).

First, as already said, the behaviour appealed to in the part–whole explanations under consideration is typically temporal behaviour. The point is not that the manifestation itself takes time, but rather that the behaviour—when it is manifest—has a temporal dimension. It is a process.

Second, the triggering conditions for the dispositions appealed to are purely negative. The quasi-inertial behaviour becomes manifest in the *absence* of disturbing factors (antidotes).

Third, the dispositions in question can be *partially* manifest; they *contribute* to the behaviour of the compound. Traditionally it is assumed the following possibilities obtain: either (i) a system S has a disposition D and D is manifest; or (ii) S has D, but D fails to be manifest; or, finally, (iii) S does not have D. In the case of various factors or parts contributing to a compound, a further situation has to be considered: S has D and D is partially manifest, i.e. it is not completely manifest but it contributes.[6] Partial manifestation and contribution may appear at first sight to be rather vague terms. This appearance is, however, deceptive in the case of physical part–whole explanation. It is in virtue of the laws of composition that contribution/partial manifestation can be made quantitatively precise. In our examples it can be made quantitatively precise how the rotator and the oscillator contribute to the compound system; similarly it can be made quantitatively precise how the medium affects a falling stone. So what I mean by calling dispositions 'contributors' is that the presence of a subsystem's disposition makes a difference to the behaviour of the compound and that the difference it makes depends on the law of composition.[7]

Let me add that my aim is not to provide a general theory of dispositions but rather to characterize those dispositions that we have to postulate in order to understand part–whole explanations in physics. The characteristics I have just highlighted are thus not to be taken to be those of dispositions in general.

---

[6] Why is partial manifestation not just a separate set of dispositions that are manifest in cases of non-isolation? Answer: That would not explain why it is the *same* disposition that is measured in different contexts (isolated and non-isolated cases alike).

[7] The notion of contribution developed here has to be distinguished from that of Molnar. According to Molnar, 'A manifestation is typically a contribution to an effect, an effect is typically a combination of contributory manifestations' (Molnar 2003: 195). Molnar's 'effect' is what I call 'the behaviour of the compound'; in my terms, the 'effect' is the manifestation of the dispositions of the compound. As I understand it, the contributions/manifestations for Molnar are real entities that mediate between the disposition and the overt behaviour (effect). I try to get along without such mediating entities.

3 Dispositions as contributors are not causes

In the special sciences and in everyday contexts we apply causal terminology. *Prima facie* it is difficult to see how we could do without. This raises the problem of how to reconcile the apparent indispensability of causal talk with Mach's and Russell's claims to the effect that causal statements are incompatible with what physics has to say about the world.

In Section 2 I have argued that physical part–whole *explanations* presuppose that the properties/behaviours of physical systems that can play the role of parts ought to be understood as dispositional properties. One way to go from here is to argue for the thesis that causes are dispositions (Handfield 2009; Molnar 2003; Mumford 2009a). The idea is that dispositions cause their manifestations (I take this to be the standard dispositionalist account). I will, however, argue that this is a blind alley. While I am not denying that everyday dispositions such as fragility can be conceived of as causes of their manifestations, this move is not possible with regard to the dispositions introduced in Section 2.

So the claim I am arguing for in this section is: Contribution and causation are different relations and thus not to be identified. Why is this so?

There may be cases of simultaneous causation, but the standard causal relation is a *temporal* determination relation: An *earlier* event causes a *later* event. Here a *temporal* determination relation is one in which a property, a state, or an event at t determines another property, state, or event at $t^\star$, with $t^\star > t$ (or $t^\star < t$, though I will not consider this case). Given this definition, the part–whole relation and a fortiori the relation of contribution is an atemporal relation. The reason is that the laws of composition do not involve time.

As a consequence, causation (in general) cannot be identified with (reduced to) contribution (i.e. to the relation of a disposition to its manifestation). At best, *simultaneous* causation (if there is such a thing) can be identified with contribution. So we would have a theory for simultaneous (or instantaneous) causation and would need a different theory for cases in which the cause precedes the effect.

But maybe we should conversely consider contribution as a particular kind of (instantaneous) causation? The problem here seems to be that the alleged causes and effects are not in an appropriate way independent. The part–whole relation is constitutive. The relevant events, for instance, the rotator contributing to the compound and the compound being in a certain energy state, fail to be *distinct* events. It is, however, generally accepted that causes and effects have to be distinct events (cf. Lewis 1973: 165).[8]

---

[8] Some authors such as Martin (2008), Molnar (2003), and Mumford (2009a) argue that causation does not necessarily obtain between distinct events, but is rather a relation between identical events. 'It is not a matter of two events, but of one and the same event—a reciprocal dispositional partnering as a mutual manifesting. This surprising identity of what we had dimly thought of as the two-event cause and effect loses its surprise in the clear light of day' (Martin 2008: 46). There are several difficulties connected with this view. For our purposes the essential point is that we set out to explain our use of the causal terminology in the special sciences and in everyday contexts. This clearly involves that in general, the cause precedes the effect

So I conclude that this approach is a blind alley—dispositions (in our sense) do not cause their manifestations. It should be stressed that my argument relies essentially on the fact that the manifestation of the dispositions I consider is regulated by laws of composition, which do not contain a time parameter. It is for this reason that the standard dispositionalist account of causation is not tenable in a world as described by physics.

4 A disposition-based account of causation

We have just seen one attempt to ground the modal force of causes. The idea was to identify it with the disposition bringing about its manifestation. We have seen that this suggestion does not work. The dispositions in physics are contributors rather than causes.

More traditionally the modal force of causes (that in virtue of which the cause determines the effect to occur) has been grounded in laws of nature, conceived of as strict regularities. There are *laws* according to which the cause is a sufficient condition for the occurrence of the effect. As an illustration consider the following simple idealized case: Two billiard balls bounce against each other and are deflected.

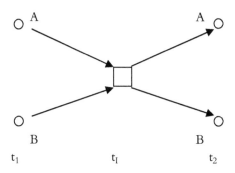

Billiard ball A bouncing into B is the cause for B's deflection. According to the regularity view, the effect (B's deflection) had to occur in virtue of a regularity according to which the cause is a sufficient condition for the effect to occur. The law or regularity might be the following:

If at time t_1 billiard ball A is at x_{A1} and has velocity v_{A1} and B is at x_{B1} and has v_{B1}, then B at t_2 is at x_{B2} and has v_{B2}.

The problem with this kind of regularity account, as Russell has pointed out, is that there are not enough strict regularities. It is always possible that some factor interferes

and it is not easy to see how what we called temporal priority in Section 1 emerges from Martin's and related accounts. Following Martin et al. would require us to reject a substantial part of the folk conception of causation—a rejection that will turn out not to be necessary.

(and as a matter of fact, such things do often happen). As a consequence, the alleged cause is not a sufficient condition of the occurrence of the alleged effect.

A second major account of causation is the counterfactual account. It explains how the cause partially determines the effect ('partial' because it allows for interfering factors): According to the counterfactual account, the cause partially determines the effect in the sense that if the cause had not occurred, the effect would not have occurred either. So with respect to the above example, the modal force of the cause is spelled out as follows: If at t_1 billiard ball A had not been at x_{A1} with velocity v_{A1}, B at t_2 would not have been at x_{B2} with v_{B2}. However, there are well-known problems with the counterfactual account of causation in general and with the account of modal force in particular. There are cases of causation and a fortiori of causes determining the effects to occur, in which the counterfactual conditionals do not hold (pre-emption).[9]

The challenge is thus to give an account of the modal force of causes that neither runs into the problem of interferences nor into the problem of pre-emption.

4.1 Central idea

The overall aim is to explain why in everyday life and in the special sciences we can successfully employ causal terminology despite Mach's and Russell's observations, which seemed to imply that the concept of causation is incompatible with fundamental physics. As I already mentioned, in this chapter I will focus on the problem of modal force. My account of the modal force of causation will proceed as follows. In a first step I will explain how causation and its modal force can be integrated into an idealized world as described by physics. In a second step I will explain how this accounts for our ordinary applications of causal terminology outside idealized physical models. The essential point with respect to the second step is that pragmatic considerations will play an important role. Finally, I will discuss some advantages of this view and relate it to other accounts of causation.

Let me start with a remark by Mach. 'In general we only feel the need to ask for a cause, if a (unexpected) change has occurred' (Mach 1896: 432). Similarly, Hart and Honoré have observed:

The notion, that a cause is essentially something which interferes with or intervenes in the course of events which would normally take place, is central to the common-sense concept of cause. (Hart and Honoré 1959: 27)

Apparently, very often what we mean by applying the word 'cause' is that a certain factor disturbs a *default* process of some kind.[10] This observation will be my starting point and I will argue that it suffices to give an account of the modal force of causes that is at the same time compatible with physics.

---

[9] See Collins et al. (2004) for a discussion of these problems.

[10] Maudlin (2004) and Menzies (2007) develop similar ideas. Menzies has also developed an account of the kinds of context-sensitivities I discuss in Section 5.

Let me return to the simple idealized case: Two billiard balls bounce against each other and are deflected.

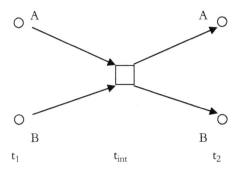

We take the presence of the ball A at a particular place at t_{int} as the cause for B's deflection.

If we disregard the problem of asymmetry, we can explain in terms of physics why A's collision with B at t_{Int} is the cause for B's deflection.

B behaves according to Newton's first law, i.e. it has the disposition to simply continue in a straight line with uniform motion unless there is a disturbing factor. Newton's first law describes the inertial or default behaviour of B.

If the default behaviour does not occur, the law tells us that there must be some factor that interacted with B. The event of this factor interacting with the default process is the cause of the later non-occurrence of the default behaviour. Thus, in the idealized case we are considering here, the cause is something that prevents some system's default behaviour to occur.

In the idealized case under consideration, a cause is an actual disturbing factor (antidote) to the default behaviour that a system is disposed to display.

(I will discuss in Sections 5 and 6 how this definition has to be augmented in less idealized cases.)

As we have seen, laws are typically quasi-inertial or default laws. They tell us what happens if nothing interferes. Deflections, i.e. deviations from quasi-inertial or default behaviour, require an interfering factor—an interaction to have occurred. That is what the quasi-inertial laws of physics tell us. Causes are precisely these interfering factors that the quasi-inertial laws require in cases of deviations. Causes are thus the antidotes that explain why the dispositions that are ascribed by the quasi-inertial laws fail to be (completely) manifest.

4.2 The origin of the causal counterfactuals

We can now explain why typically—though not always—counterfactual conditionals obtain according to which if the cause had not occurred, the effect would have occurred neither.

$\sim O(c)\,\square\!\!\rightarrow\sim O(e)$ (Lewis (1986b): 167).

Why is this counterfactual true in many cases of causation? Consider again our simple example:

My claim is that we hold this counterfactual true in virtue of Newton's first law: If A had not collided with B, B would have taken path b* rather than path b—as it actually has (see the figure below).

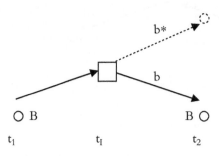

b: B's actual path
b*: the path B would have taken if A had not interfered at time t_I

Laws of nature describe how systems would behave in the absence of disturbing factors, i.e. they attribute dispositions to physical systems. Laws of nature usually describe counterfactual situations and should therefore be read as saying, for instance, 'If the hydrogen atom were isolated it would behave according to the Schrödinger equation with a Coulomb potential.' According to my proposal, it is exactly the underlying dispositions that make true the relevant counterfactuals. So we can understand why in many cases of causation, causal counterfactuals are true if we assume that the systems in questions have the relevant dispositions (see Hüttemann 2004: 110–15).

4.3 Pre-emption and interference

I promised an account of causation that does not run into the problems of interference and pre-emption. So how are these problems evaded?

As is well known, sometimes backup causes may be around. We do think that backup causes do not undermine causation. However, they undermine counterfactual dependence. Since according to our account causation is not identified with counterfactual dependence, there is no problem of (either early or late) pre-emption. Counterfactual dependence is not necessary for causation. For this solution of the pre-emption problem it is essential that the cause, i.e. the occurrence of the disturbing factor or antidote, can be spelled out in terms of *actual* facts about interactions rather than in terms of counterfactual claims about what would have happened if the factor in question had been absent. All that is needed for singular causation is the disposition of a system to behave according to a (quasi-)inertial law and the *actual* disturbing factor. The presence of *poten-*

tial disturbing factors is irrelevant on the account presented here (see Maudlin (2004) for a similar approach).

How does our account evade the interference problem? After all, laws play quite a significant role in our account. The main move is to understand laws as ascriptions of dispositions rather than as strict regularities concerning manifest behaviour. Newton's first law is not a strict regularity concerning manifest behaviour. It is no strict regularity because in fact there are often (maybe always) interfering factors around (impressed forces). However, strict regularities are not needed for our account. All that we need for our account of causation are laws based on dispositions that tell us what would happen if nothing disturbs the default behaviour. The problem of interferences does not apply.

5 Causal fields

The example we have considered so far was highly idealized. Relative to this idealized setting a cause was defined as a disturbing factor to the default behaviour that a system is disposed to display. The situation was idealized because we have abstracted away from diverse factors. In non-idealized situations there are always further interference factors besides what we identify as 'the cause', e.g. the molecules in the air collide with the billiard ball in question. Furthermore, certain constitutive conditions obtain, such as the presence of the billiard-ball table.

John Mackie has described this as the *causal field*:

> Both cause and effect are seen as differences within a field; anything that is part of the assumed (but commonly unstated) description of the field itself will, then, be automatically ruled out as a candidate for the role of cause. (Mackie 1980: 35)

It is for instance taken for granted that the gravitational field is stable, the history of the universe is kept fixed, etc. It is only relative to these and other background assumptions that a default process can be defined. If, for example, the billiard-ball table had not been smooth but bumpy, and if this were part of the background assumptions (causal field), the default process would have been different.

It is important to notice that in one and the same situation different people may make different assumptions about the background. In a case of a car accident one observer might take the dirt on the street as part of the background. The default process in this case might be that the car starts to skid slightly and that the driver is able to stabilize the car afterwards. The cause for the accident is the driver's drunkenness and his/her inability to control the car in difficult circumstances. Someone else might take the drunkenness of the driver as part of the background conditions. The default process is the driver driving the car home safely (provided no difficult situations occur). In this case the dirt on the street is the cause of the accident.

What counts as a quasi-inertial or default process and what counts as a cause will be determined relative to a causal field and thus relative to pragmatic or subjective concerns. However, this relativity does not imply that quasi-inertial processes are arbitrary.

If one has chosen a particular field, whether or not a certain process is an inertial process is an objective matter. If the smoothness of the billiard-ball table is part of the causal field, it is no longer a subjective matter whether the default process of the billiard ball consists in a uniform and rectilinear motion rather than in some kind of non-uniform motion.

To sum up: An augmented definition of 'cause' has to take the causal field into account:

> **Relative to a causal field, a cause is an actual disturbing factor (antidote) to the default behaviour that a system is disposed to display.**

The introduction of causal fields allows us to explain some of the features that are usually associated with the causal relation.

First, it allows to distinguish between causes and conditions. The smoothness of the billiard-ball table (as part of the causal field) is a mere condition of the deviation of ball B, whereas the interaction with A is its cause.

Second, it allows causes to be local. While it may be true that the conjunction of all relevant factors for a certain event is non-local in the sense that an indefinite environment has to be taken into account, the introduction of the causal field allows us to relegate the environment to the field. Thus, the intuition that causes are local can be respected.

It is, however, a consequence of this conception that whether or not a particular event is considered to be part of the causal field—and thus a condition rather than a cause—is a matter of pragmatic and subjective concerns. Whether or not an event is a cause is thus not an entirely objective fact. This consequence seems, however, to capture how we actually employ causal terminology (as illustrated in the case of the car accident). Objectivity seems to be an issue where the folk-conception and the actual use of the terminology point in different directions.

6 Limiting conditions

What we have shown is that—given our conception of causation—causal terminology is applicable in certain cases (such as the billiard ball example). However, we have no guarantee that the terminology is generally applicable.

I would like to suggest that causal terminology is applicable given that certain limiting conditions obtain, but that it might not be applicable in other cases.[11] What are these limiting conditions?

In some compound systems (such as the system consisting of the two interacting billiard balls) we can identify two subsystems and their default behaviour (because they are isolated prior to their interaction and afterwards), as well as their spatio-temporally localized interaction. If these conditions are met, the application of the causal termin-

---

[11] Dennis Dieks has developed similar ideas in his dissertation (Dieks 1981, chapter. 3). For a recent articulation of this strategy see Norton 2007.

ology is plausible. In other words: As long as the (compound) system we are investigating can reasonably be described as having the 'two colliding billiard balls'-structure (local-ized interaction, isolated systems prior to and after the interaction), causal terminology is applicable.

While the above-mentioned conditions are sufficient for the application of causal terminology, they do not seem to be necessary. For instance, in real cases, to which we apply causal terminology, the disturbed systems are never completely isolated. The bil-liard balls collide with molecules in the air, the moon exerts a gravitational pull, etc. Some of these factors can be relegated to the causal field while others are simply neglected. Thus, classifying certain interfering factors as negligible is a further pragmatic aspect that is presupposed by the application of causal terminology.

Furthermore, the interaction we considered in the billiard-ball case was local (colli-sion). That seems not to be a necessary condition for the applicability of causal termi-nology. Consider the following case:

A compound system consisting of a large massive system A and small massive system B that is deflected:

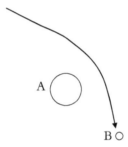

Let us assume that A simply sits there and by gravitational attraction deflects the path of B. Even though the interaction is not local, we would still say that the gravitational potential generated by A is the cause of B's path being deflected. The interaction is always on and thus B never actually instantiates the default or quasi-inertial behaviour. Still, since in this situation B approaches inertial behaviour if it is very distant from A, we can understand why in this case causal terminology is applicable. In this case the essen-tial point seems to be that we have theoretical and/or experimental means on the basis of which we can attribute a certain default behaviour to B that is then disturbed by A.

In the end there may not be a clear-cut line that distinguishes cases in which the terms 'cause' and 'effect' are applicable from those in which they are not. There are, how-ever, clear cases. We have come across systems to which the causal terminology is clearly applicable. On the other hand, there are, for example, closed deterministic systems with nothing remotely similar to the billiard-ball structure. They seem to be clear candidates where the application of causal terminology is inappropriate. It was these cases that Russell had in mind:

The law of gravitation will illustrate what occurs in any advanced science. In the motions of mutually gravitating bodies, there is nothing that can be called an effect; there is merely a formula. Certain differential equations can be found, which hold at every instant for every particle of the system, and which, given the configurations and the velocities at one instant, or the configurations at two instants, render the configuration at any other earlier or later instant calculable. That is to say, the configuration at any instant is a function of that instant and the configurations at two given instants. [...]. But there is nothing that could be properly called 'cause' and nothing that could properly be called 'effect' in such a system. (Russell 1912–13: 14)

Russell's claim was of course meant not only to apply to this special case. However, as we have seen, there are limiting conditions such that the application of causal terminology is plausible. The limiting condition we have identified is this: It must be plausible to attribute default behaviour to a subsystem of a compound and to identify a disturbing factor for the deviation of the default behaviour. And this does indeed often seem to be case, at least relative to certain pragmatic considerations.

7 Relation to other process-theories

I argued that the application of causal terminology can be best understood if a cause is taken to be an actual disturbing factor (antidote) to the default behaviour that a system is disposed to display (relative to a causal field). This is a claim about processes, because the default behaviour concerns the temporal evolution of a system (e.g. the process that is described in Newton's first law). So how exactly is the disposition-based view related to traditional process-theories?

Process-theories tend to take 'causation to be the transfer or persistence of properties of a specific sort' (Dowe 2009: 214). The default processes we have talked about can indeed be characterized in terms of the persistence of properties: The behaviour in question is persistently manifest as long as nothing intervenes. Process-theories consider interferences with these processes as cases of causation. Thus far I agree. There are two important disagreements: First, I do not take the processes themselves to constitute causation. A statue being at a certain place at 2 p.m. today is not a cause of its being there at 5 p.m.—even though it may be a condition. Therefore, I do not talk about *causal* processes but rather about *default* processes. Second, the characterization of the relevant processes and disturbances (interactions) is different. Whereas Dowe and Salmon characterize these processes either by the mark-criterion or in terms of invariant or conserved quantities (Dowe 2009 provides an overview), I characterize them in terms of the underlying systems' dispositions. A ball rolling on a flat surface is classified by traditional process-theorists as a causal process because it conserves kinetic energy and momentum. I characterize it as a default process, because it manifests a disposition, namely the one that is attributed in Newton's first law. Having certain invariant/conserved physical properties is thus not necessary to qualify as a default process. The essential question is whether or not the relevant system has a certain disposition. It is for the physicists to decide whether or not bodies have the disposition to continue in uniform rectilinear motion if no forces are impressed. Similarly it is for economists to decide whether or not (within a certain causal field) an economic system in which inflation rises will yield higher unemployment rates (if nothing interferes).

As a consequence whether or not something qualifies as a default process need not be spelled out in terms of physics. To the extent that biology or economics attributes dispositions to systems that concern their temporal evolution, these disciplines are dealing with biological or economical default processes.

Similarly, what qualifies as a disturbance of a default process needs to be spelled out in terms of physics. I want to leave room for various kinds of disturbances that have to be specified locally. It is the job of the sciences in question to provide a more detailed description of the disturbance. While physics considers a certain repertoire of disturbance factors that can be described in terms of physical interaction or, maybe, conserved quantities, economy considers state interventions, decisions of the Federal Reserve Bank, or natural catastrophes.

The disposition-based process-theory thus promises to take account of the fact that causal relations may obtain on various 'levels'.

A further advantage of the disposition-based process-theory vis-à-vis traditional process-theories is its ability to cope with double prevention cases. Ned Hall has described a paradigm case:

Suzy is piloting a bomber on a mission to blow up an enemy target, and Billy is piloting a fighter as her lone escort. Along comes an enemy fighter plane, piloted by Enemy. Sharp-eyed Billy spots Enemy, zooms in, pulls the trigger, and Enemy's plane goes down in flames. Suzy's mission is undisturbed, and the bombing takes place as planned. (Hall 2004: 241)

We want to say that Billy's pulling the trigger is a cause of the bombing of the target. Traditional process-theories have a problem with this example because there is no continuous physical process leading from Billy's pulling the trigger to the actual bombing.

Here is how the situation can be described given the disposition-based process-theory:

Let's start with the simple case. Suzy's bombing being the cause for the destruction of the target. Here the *target sitting around peacefully* is the default process that is disturbed. Second case: If Enemy would prevent Suzy from bombing the target, we consider *Suzy bombing the target* as the default process that is disturbed by Enemy's intervention. So, Enemy's intervention is the cause of the target's survival. Third, if Billy shoots down Enemy, the default process we are considering is *Enemy preventing Suzy from bombing the target*. This process is disturbed by Billy's pulling the trigger. Billy's pulling the trigger is therefore the cause that *Enemy preventing Suzy from bombing the target* does not take place and thus a cause of the bombing of the target.

So the disposition-based process-theory is able to cope with at least some objections to traditional process-theories.

8 Probabilistic causation

One might wonder how the account outlined so far is relevant for causal claims in the special sciences, since many of these are probabilistic causal claims. Probabilistic causal claims such as 'Smoking causes lung-cancer' are typically type-level causal claims in contrast to the token-level claims I have considered so far. Thus the question is whether and how probabilistic causal type-level claims fit into the picture outlined so far.

There are two different ways in which the truth of such claims may depend on underlying processes and disturbances, depending on whether the underlying processes are deterministic or genuinely indeterministic.

(1) Deterministic case: The probabilistic type-level claim obtains in virtue of coarse graining over different kinds of different causings. Suppose the claim is that some event type X probabilistically causes Y to occur. This may be true in virtue of the fact that two different kinds of situations are involved:

situation type A: X disturbs process P, Y occurs as a result of ensuing process P⋆.
situation type B: X disturbs process P, X⋆ disturbs ensuing process P⋆, Y does not occur.

Coarse graining over heterogeneous situations of type A and type B makes probabilistic type-level claims true. If $Pr(Y|X) > Pr(Y)$ one might say that X is likely to cause Y. In this deterministic case no new element has to be introduced in order to understand probabilistic causal claims at the type-level.

The situation is different if one wants to accept genuine chancy causation:

(2) Indeterministic case: The probabilistic type-level claim obtains in virtue of genuine chancy causation. Suppose the chance of receiving a certain illness I is 0.5 per cent. Excessive consumption of X raises the probability to 2 per cent. We furthermore assume that the relevant type-level claim 'Excessive consumption of X *causes* I' cannot be explained in terms of coarse-graining over heterogeneous situations. This case requires the introduction of genuinely indeterministic processes, i.e. processes that have various outcomes and a probability distribution over the outcomes. It might be the case that human beings (in the usual contexts) develop illness I in 0.5 per cent of the cases and non-I (i.e. fail to develop I) in 99.5 per cent of the cases. Take this to be the default process. I take it that x is the cause of i (lower case for instantiations of types) if the person in question excessively consumes x, if the person furthermore develops I, and if the original probability distribution changes in virtue of the consumption of x such that it is more likely to develop I.

Genuine chancy causation (at the token level) can then be understood as follows:

x causes i, if x occurs, i occurs, and the default process probability distribution has been disturbed by x so that $Pr(I/X)>Pr(I)$ is true.

The central idea is that genuinely indeterministic processes have a probability distribution over outcomes, which might be disturbed by interfering factors. If the disturbance raises the probability of the outcome, then the interfering factor may be said to have caused a certain outcome. This is an extension of the original account to the case of chancy causation. There are certain well-known difficulties with the probability raising requirement (see, e.g., Hitchcock 2011); however, I hope the sketch suffices to indicate how genuine chancy causation may be adumbrated.

Probabilistic causal type-level claims in the special sciences may thus be true in virtue of underlying disturbances of deterministic processes or in virtue of disturbances of indeterministic processes or both.

9 The origin of causal modality

In this chapter I have argued that causation can be explained in terms of laws that describe default processes and that these laws should be understood in terms of dispositions. What does that tell us about the origin of causal modality or causal determination?

In the case of the billiard balls the origin of this determination becomes apparent if we consider the situation as the behaviour of a compound system. What is relevant in this case is the law of the conservation of momentum. A's state and the law of the conservation of momentum determine how B behaves.

More generally: The law for the compound system (plus the states of the other parts) determine the effect, i.e. the behaviour of the part that is disturbed.

The modal force or determination is thus due to those laws that determine the behaviour of the compound system.

(N) The effect occurs necessarily because the compound system manifests its behaviour necessarily.

But what kind of necessity is involved here?

Let me present a somewhat speculative sketch that provides an answer to this question. In what follows I take metaphysical necessity to be necessity that obtains in virtue of the essence of a system. So if a system has a certain property with metaphysical necessity it has it in virtue of its essence. Now let us assume that the systems we are considering have their dispositions essentially. This will not yet give us the explanation of the modal force or determination we are looking for (N).

The essential point is that two issues have to be distinguished:

a) the claim that an object or property has a disposition necessarily (dispositional essentialism) and
b) the claim that a disposition displays its manifestation necessarily.

Dispositional essentialism (a) does not explain why the dispositions in question manifest their behaviour necessarily. In fact, they don't. As long as antidotes are possible, manifestation cannot occur with necessity, i.e. it is still not clear what kind of necessity is involved in (N) (for a discussion of these points see Schrenk 2010).

A possible solution to this problem is the following: What happens if the compound (consisting of the disturbed system and the interferer) is itself disturbed, is determined by the disposition(s) of this compound, the disposition(s) of the new interference factor as well as the law(s) of composition. Now assume that it is part of the *essence* of systems that they behave according to the laws of composition. Then the following holds: It is necessarily the case that, if nothing interferes, the compound system manifests its behaviour. It is furthermore necessarily the case that, if something interferes, the system displays a different behaviour of this or that kind. In other words, if we assume that the laws of composition hold with metaphysical necessity, then the manifestation of the dispositions of the systems happens with conditional metaphysical necessity. The conditions in question are the disturbing factors. So it holds with metaphysical necessity that—if nothing interferes—billiard ball A deflects billiard ball B. The modal force of causes obtains in virtue of the essence of the systems involved. The necessity involved in (N) is conditional metaphysical necessity.

The assumption of conditional metaphysical necessity allows us to give a unified account of dispositional, nomological, and causal modalities. It is conditional metaphysical necessity that is at work in all of these cases. If the systems have not only their dispositions essentially but furthermore conform to the laws of composition in virtue of their essence, then, first, with metaphysical necessity—if nothing interferes—the disposition becomes manifest. Second, with metaphysical necessity—if nothing interferes—the law that attributes the disposition in question is true. And, third, with metaphysical necessity—if nothing interferes—the disposition of compound systems such as the system consisting of the two billiard balls becomes manifest, i.e. with metaphysical necessity—given the right conditions—the cause determines the effect.

10 Conclusion

To sum up: I have asked in this chapter how and under what circumstances causal terminology can be applied to the physical world. The focus was the question how to understand that the cause determines the effect to occur (I disregarded the problem of the asymmetry of causation). I argued that we should conceive a cause as an actual disturbing factor (antidote) to the default process that a system is disposed to display (relative to a causal field). Given this disposition-based process-theory we can understand how causation is part of the physical world. We can furthermore understand how causation can have many of the features that the folk-conception of causation associates with it: modal force, locality, the distinction between causes and conditions, and the multi-level character of causation. The idea that whether or not something is a cause (as opposed to a condition) is an objective matter could not be vindicated. It should also be stressed, that causal terminology is only applicable given certain limiting conditions that need to be realized by all kind of (physical) systems.[12]

[12] I would like to thank two anonymous referees, the audience in Nottingham, the members of the DFG-funded Research Group FOR 1063 on *Causation and Explanation*, as well as John Roberts for their very helpful comments on an earlier version of this chapter.

6

How to activate a power

Jennifer McKitrick

According to most views of dispositions or powers, they have 'triggers' or activation conditions. Fragile things break *when they are struck*; explosive things explode *when ignited*. The notion of an activation event, or 'trigger', is central to the notion of a disposition. Dispositions are defined not only by their manifestations, but also by their triggers. Not everyone who grumbles and complains counts as irritable—just those who do so with little inducement. Not everything that can be broken counts as fragile—just things that can be broken with relatively little force. The idea that triggers are part of the identity conditions of powers is evident in conditional analyses of powers, and even in the claim that certain conditionals are typically true of things with certain powers. The antecedent of the conditional corresponds to a trigger of that power: 'If it's struck, it will break' is true of a fragile thing, and 'being struck' is the trigger.

In this chapter, I explore the nature of activation events and their relation to the powers they activate. In particular, I will consider what triggers would look like if all properties were powers, as the dispositional monist or pandispositionalist tells us they are. While many have expressed worries about *manifestations* involving instantiations of only dispositional properties, it is also worth noting that, on a pandispositionalist scenario, the activation event must be equally dispositional. If all properties are powers, it seems that a triggering event must be an acquisition of a power. But how does something acquiring a power activate another power to produce its manifestation? I suggest and evaluate possible answers. I will argue that, as with the case of manifestations, a vicious regress threatens the pandispositionalist picture of power activation. I go on to consider several possible pandispositionalist responses.

1 Triggers

The kind of thing I'm talking about goes by various names, such as 'trigger', 'stimulus', 'circumstances of manifestation', 'activation conditions', and 'activation event'. I suspect that any distinction one might draw between the stimulus and the background conditions is a matter of pragmatics. What counts as the stimulus as opposed to the background depends on what's salient to an audience in a context. In some contexts, a spark is a trigger for flammability. In other contexts, the availability of oxygen might be. Perhaps it's best to think of the total set of circumstances necessary for the activation of a power as the 'circumstances of manifestation' or 'activation conditions', and the 'trigger' or 'stimulus' as a salient part of those conditions singled out for discussion. However, for simplicity, I'm going to use the expression 'trigger' indiscriminately as a name for any part or whole of the circumstances of manifestation, and 'activate' as a verb describing what a trigger does. In short, a trigger activates a power.

You might say triggering a power *produces* its manifestation. So, if one wanted to analyse the relation between a power and its manifestation, one might do well to offer an analysis of production. But seeing as all parties to the debates that I am considering agree that powers produce their manifestations, I do not think that the nature of production is central to this discussion, and I will not attempt to analyse it here. My concern in this chapter is not so much the relation between a power and its manifestation, but rather the relation between a trigger and the power it activates. Since the existence of the power typically pre-dates its trigger, I do not think the relation between these two is one of production.

What kind of thing is a trigger? Examples such as 'dropping a glass' or 'striking a match' suggest that they are events. When a power is activated, a certain event occurs which activates that power. This event is what I'm calling the power's 'trigger'. When one says that a power has a trigger, one usually means that a certain type of event tends to activate that kind of power. I am not assuming any particular account of events. Thinking of events as property exemplifications[1] is helpful, but not essential, to what I have to say about triggers. I am merely assuming that the occurrence of an event somehow involves the instantiation of some property. I'll start with the assumption that when a trigger occurs, a new property is acquired, but also consider the possibility that merely having a property may be sufficient to activate a power.

Do powers necessarily have triggers? One might think that it's part of the concept of a power that it has a trigger. According to Andreas Hüttemann, 'A dispositional property is a property that, if instantiated by an object, is manifest under specific conditions only.'[2] This suggests that a dispositional property must have a trigger. However, he goes on to say, 'A categorical property by contrast is a property that, if instantiated by an object, is manifest under all conditions. So, according to this distinction categorical properties are limiting cases of dispositional properties.'[3] This suggests that

---

[1] Kim, Jaegwon (1976) 'Events as Property Exemplifications', in M. Brand and D. Walton (eds) *Action Theory*, Dordrecht: Reidel, pp. 159–77.

[2] Hüttemann, Andreas (2009) 'Dispositions in Physics', in Gregor Damschen, Robert Schnepf, and Karsten R. Stuber (eds), *Debating Dispositions: Issues in Metaphysics, Epistemology and Philosophy of Mind*, Berlin, Germany: Walter de Gruyter, p. 3.

[3] Hüttemann (2009), p. 3.

categorical properties are powers that are activated by anything and everything. But one could equally say that such powers do not need to be activated at all. If a power is constantly manifesting, there is no need for a trigger to activate that power. So, it seems reasonable to think of constantly manifesting powers as 'trigger-less' powers. Notice, however, that to say that a power is constantly manifesting is not to say that it is constantly possessed, nor that the power is essential to objects that have it. Rather, it is just to say that an object manifests that power whenever it has that power. So an object could gain or lose a constantly manifesting power.

Another possible trigger-less power is a spontaneously manifesting power. One might say that uranium has a disposition to decay, but no event activates that power; it just happens spontaneously. But even if there are powers that have no triggers, there may be some that do. These are the ones I'm going to focus on. But perhaps, in the end, the pandispositionalist will need powers without triggers.[4]

2 Triggers for the pandispositionalist (take one)

The idea that all properties are powers has received a lot of recent attention.[5] A noted implication of pandispositionalism is that the manifestations of powers consist of acquisitions of further powers. Some have regarded this implication as problematic, leading to some sort of vicious regress.[6] Similar worries apply to triggers as well. If powers *producing* nothing but powers is problematic, one would expect that powers *being activated by* nothing but powers to be problematic, too. Consider the following implications:

T1. A power's trigger is an event.
T2. Events essentially involve something acquiring a property.
T3. Therefore, a power's trigger essentially involves something acquiring a property.
T4. According to pandispositionalism, all properties are powers.
T5. Therefore, according to pandispositionalism, a power's trigger essentially involves something acquiring a power.

[4] Stephen Mumford and Rani L. Anjum (2011) *Getting Causes from Powers*, and Barbara Vetter 'Dispositions without Conditionals' (forthcoming) suggest that dispositions do not have triggers. Though they have independent motivations, perhaps this chapter will give them further reason to think that dispositions are not triggered by events.

[5] For example, see Bird, Alexander (2007a) *Nature's Metaphysics*. Oxford, UK: Oxford University Press.

[6] For regress arguments against pandispositionalism, see Armstrong, David (1997) *A World of States of Affairs*, Cambridge, UK: Cambridge University Press; Swinburne, Richard (1980) 'Properties, causation, and projectibility: Reply to Shoemaker', in L. J. Cohen and M. Hesse (eds) *Applications of Inductive Logic*, Oxford, UK: Oxford University Press, pp. 313–20. For replies, see Molnar, George (2003) *Powers: A Study in Metaphysics.* Stephen Mumford (ed.) Oxford, UK: Oxford University Press; Bird, Alexander (2007b) 'The Regress of Pure Powers?' *The Philosophical Quarterly* 57, pp. 513–34; Mumford, Stephen (2009a) 'Passing Powers Around', *The Monist* 92, pp. 94–111; and McKitrick, Jennifer (2010) 'Manifestations as Effects', in Anna Marmodoro (ed.) *The Metaphysics of Powers: Their Grounding and their Manifestations*, New York, NY: Routledge, pp. 73–83.

So, a power being activated, resulting in its manifestation, is, on this view, a matter of something acquiring a power, thereby activating the first power to make something acquire yet another power. Putting things this way might already strike those without pandispositionalist sympathies as unattractive. But I think there are deeper worries.

Let me introduce some terminology in order to try to avoid confusion. I'll call the power to be activated the 'target power' and the manifestation of the target power the 'target manifestation'. I'll call the power the acquisition of which activates the target power the 'triggering power'. So, the view in question is that the target power is activated by something acquiring a triggering power, resulting in the target manifestation. If 'power A' is the triggering power, and 'power B' is the target power, power B is triggered by something acquiring power A, resulting in the manifestation of B, or the target manifestation.

Let me try to further clarify the picture of power activation that I think is emerging. Suppose the target power is the flammability of some gasoline. One trigger for this power is striking a match close to the gasoline. If that event is a matter of something acquiring a power, perhaps the match acquires a power when it activates the flammability of the gasoline, resulting in a fire. But what power does the match acquire? If the gasoline's flammability is 'power B' in this case, what is 'power A'?

Perhaps the triggering power is the flammability of the match? Note that the match and the gasoline are both flammable. They have the same type of power but different tokens. The suggestion is that the gasoline's token flammability is the target power and the match's flammability is the triggering power. Casting some doubt on this suggestion is the fact that the match's flammability is not a newly acquired power, but one that the match had prior to the occurrence of the trigger.

Another possibility is that the triggering power is the match's power to ignite gasoline. But even if we want to allow for such powers, this also seems like a power that the match already had; not a new power, just a newly activated power. Perhaps it would help to make a distinction between having a power A and having a power to acquire power A. I suppose one could say that the match did not, strictly speaking, have the power to ignite the gasoline prior to being struck, but that it had the power to acquire the power to ignite the gasoline. Now 'the power to ignite the gasoline' is a newly acquired power, and can perhaps play the role of triggering power.

Note that whether a property is a considered (a) a triggering power, (b) a target power, or (c) a power of the target manifestation, is a relative matter. 'The power to ignite gasoline' is: (a) a triggering power, relative to the flammability of the gasoline; (b) a target power, relative to the power of the striking surface to light matches; and (c) a power of the target manifestation, relative to the match's power to acquire the power to ignite gasoline. To consider a different example, 'being magnetic' could be (a) a triggering power, relative to the dispositions of things that are attracted to magnets, (b) a target power of magnetic things that can be activated by the proximity of metal objects, and (c) a manifestation of magnetizability—the disposition to become magnetic.

So, according to the suggestion under consideration, the match starts off with flammability (or perhaps the power to acquire the power to ignite the gasoline) and then the match is struck, thereby acquiring the power to ignite the gasoline. The acquisition of this power is the trigger which activates the target power (the gasoline's flammability) resulting in the target manifestation (the gasoline burning). This strikes me as a *prima facie* plausible account of power activation for the pandispositionalist.

However, I think trouble arises for the pandispositionalist when one asks: Is it possible for something to acquire a triggering power without manifesting it? Is it possible for the match to possess the power to ignite the gasoline without activating the gasoline's flammability and starting a fire? If this power is acquired merely by the match being struck, it seems that it can be possessed without manifesting. A match can burn without igniting some gasoline, for all sorts of reasons. *Perhaps* if the power to ignite the gasoline is acquired only in ideal conditions—that is, conditions ideal for igniting gasoline—the power cannot fail to manifest. But I am not sure that we want to say that when a trigger occurs, something acquires a sure-fire power to activate another power, and that the match's power cannot fail to activate the gasoline's flammability, resulting in combustion. Sometimes a trigger occurs, but something such as a gust of wind interferes with the target power being activated. Perhaps we could say that the struck match is just part of a potential circumstance of manifestation, and we need all the other factors to come together to produce the target manifestation. However, given a seemingly infinite number of possible defeaters, it does not look like there is any set of circumstances that will guarantee the occurrence of a manifestation.

So, it looks like it is more plausible to say that the triggering power might be latent, or dormant. (The distinction between an active and dormant power is simply this: an *active* power is currently manifesting, whereas a *dormant* power is not currently exhibiting its manifestation, though it could possibly exhibit its manifestation at some other time. For example, while the switch is off, the power of the light bulb to illuminate is dormant, not manifesting; when the switch is turned on, the bulb lights up, its power to illuminate is active and manifest.) If a trigger is a matter of something acquiring a power to activate a target power, even when the triggering power is acquired, it might be dormant. So even after the match acquires the power to ignite gasoline, it could fail to light the gasoline on fire. This suggests that, if A is the triggering power and B is the target power, merely acquiring power A is not sufficient for activating power B: Power A must be manifest.

As for igniting the gasoline, we might cite additional conditions such as the air being sufficiently oxygenated, the gasoline being nearby and accessible, lack of strong winds or rainstorms, etc. But recall that, on the view under consideration, every feature of the activation conditions is a matter of something acquiring a power. Perhaps the air being sufficiently oxygenated can be construed as the possession of a power, but I am not sure how to think of the proximity of the gasoline, or the absence of wind and rain, as the possession of powers.

3 The regress

The intuition that some properties do not seem like powers is nothing new. What is more problematic is that the triggering power must not only be acquired, it must be manifest. It may be puzzling to think that acquiring one power can activate another power to manifest. It is utterly mysterious how the acquisition of a latent power could do the job. So, the triggering power must itself be manifest. Now, if the triggering power must be activated in order to manifest and activate the target power, there is a regress in the making. The trigger of the triggering power is itself an event. According to the view under consideration, this event is itself a matter of something acquiring a power. By the same reasoning, in order for this power to activate the triggering power, it must itself be activated. This regress can be employed in a *reductio* against pandispositionalism as follows:

R1. Suppose that, in order for a power to be activated, something must acquire a triggering power.

R2. Suppose that, in order for a triggering power to activate a target power, the triggering power must be activated.

R3. It follows that something must acquire another triggering power in order to activate the first triggering power.

R4. Furthermore, in order for this second triggering power to be activated, something must acquire a third triggering power, and so on.

R5. Consequently, in order for a power to be activated, infinitely many triggering powers must be acquired and activated.

R6. That is absurd.

R7. Therefore, our suppositions must be rejected.

It follows from the suppositions of the argument (R1 and R2) that, for any power B, in order for B to be activated, some power A must be activated. Plug that principle in to power A's activation, and the regress begins. Consider the sequence of events that must occur in order to activate the gasoline's flammability. Suppose striking a match is the trigger. The striking occurs at t_1, and the gasoline catches on fire at t_n. On the view under consideration, in order to activate the gasoline's flammability, the striking must involve something acquiring a power. Perhaps the match acquires the power to ignite the gasoline at t_1. In order for that power to activate the gasoline's flammability, it cannot be latent—it must itself be activated. The activation of the match's power to ignite the gasoline is itself an event, which must occur after the triggering power is acquired at t_1. So the triggering power is itself activated at t_2, say. On the view under consideration, this second trigger must also be a matter of something acquiring a power. I do not know what object acquires what power in this scenario, but in any case, the problem is that it seems like this power must also be activated. Therefore, there must be a trigger which occurs at some t_3, and this trigger is itself the acquisition of a power, which itself must be activated, necessitating another trigger, and so on.

4 Possible replies

An initial reaction one may have to this regress is that the pandispositionalist shares it with anyone who thinks that all causes have causes. If A causes B, and A is itself an effect, then A must have a cause as well, and that cause must have a cause, and so on. While one may wonder about the possibility of a chain of causes and effects stretching infinitely back into the past, this type of regress does not seem especially vicious. But even if it were, it would not put the pandispositionalist in any worse position than anyone else who believes in a universal causal principle.

This response would be fair if the regress I was worried about was that something having a power is itself the manifestation of an earlier power. So, if power B were the manifestation of power A, and power A were itself a manifestation of an earlier power, etc., there would be a chain of manifestations and the powers they were manifestations of stretching back into the past. Like the causal regress, such a regress may be harmless.

However, the pandispositionalist picture of power activation I described differs from an innocent causal regress in several ways. Suppose that, in order for power B to manifest, a trigger must occur, and this event essentially involves something acquiring a power, call it power A. The acquisition of power A is the trigger for power B to manifest. It is not the case that power A brings about power B, or that power B is the manifestation of power A. Power B was already there, dormant. Something acquiring A is the event that activates power B to produce its manifestation. The question is not 'where did power A come from?' but 'how did it activate power B?' In other words, how does something acquiring a triggering power result in something manifesting a target power? What is puzzling to me is not what comes before the trigger, but the process that is supposed to commence upon the acquisition of the triggering power.

The regress is not a matter of powers being activated by powers that were activated by powers. Rather, it is a matter of infinitely many triggers needing to occur in order to bring about the manifestation, with the result that we never seem to get there. The problem is not that there are potentially infinitely many triggering events before the striking at t_1. It is that we seem to need infinitely many triggering events between the striking at t_1 and the gasoline fire at t_n. To see this, note that the striking is the acquisition of the triggering power at t_1. Since a power cannot be activated until it is acquired, the activation of the triggering power must occur between t_1 and t_n. Let's call that time t_2. If the activation of the triggering power is the acquisition of power that must be activated, this activation must occur sometime t_3 which is after t_2, but before the target manifestation at t_n. (t_3 cannot occur before t_2. t_2 is the time that the first triggering power is activated, that is, when the second triggering power is acquired. t_3 is the time that the second triggering power is activated. A power cannot be activated before it is acquired. Therefore, t_3 cannot occur before t_2.) If the activation of the second triggering power happens at t_3, that is an acquisition of a power that must be activated sometime between t_3 and t_n, and so on.

One way to break out of this regress is to deny (R1)—that a trigger is the acquisition of a power. The pandispositionalist cannot say that a trigger is an acquisition of some nondispositional property, but perhaps he can say that an activation event is a matter of continuing to have a power. If an event merely involves an object *having* a property at a time, a trigger can occur without something *acquiring* a *new* property. Does this help?

Let us reconsider the activation of the gasoline's flammability. Let us suppose that this does not have to be a matter of the match acquiring a new property; it is acceptable if the triggering power is a power that the match had all along. However, if this power needs to be activated, there needs to be another trigger. In accordance with the current suggestion, this trigger could also be a matter of something maintaining one of its powers. However, if this power must also be activated, the regress still looms. Whether a trigger is a matter of acquiring a power or maintaining one does not seem to matter.

There is further reason to reject the idea that a trigger is a matter of maintaining a power, rather than acquiring one. If merely having the power were enough to activate a target power, there is no clear reason why the target manifestation did not occur as soon as the triggering power was acquired. In our example, if the match retaining some power that it had prior to t_1 was an event that could activate the gasoline's flammability, then it is not clear why the gasoline did not catch on fire prior to t_1. It seems that even if the triggering power is not newly acquired, it at least needs to be newly activated. And again, if this second trigger is a matter of something having a power that needs to be activated, we have a regress.

But, one may wonder, do we still have the same kind of regress? Perhaps if the triggering power only needs to be activated, then the regress looks more like the innocent causal regress discussed above.[7] Suppose again that the trigger occurs at t_1 and the target manifestation occurs at t_n. The present suggestion is that the triggering power was instantiated prior to t_1 but that it was recently activated. The principle that a power must be acquired before it can be activated no longer mandates that the activation of the triggering power occurred after t_1. So while there may be an endless chain of triggering events, it is no longer the case that they must occur between t_1 and t_n, and the picture looks like powers that were activated by previously triggered triggering powers, back into the past, which looks innocent enough.

In response, consider when is the activation of the triggering power supposed to occur? If it occurs after t_1, the situation is essentially the same as it would be for a newly acquired power. If it occurs prior to t_1, then there is an unexplained delay between the activation of the triggering power and the occurrence of the target manifestation. If it occurs at t_1, then something activates the triggering power at the same moment that the triggering power activates the target power. And 'that something' activating the triggering power is a matter of something activating another power, which of course must be activated as well. The result would be that a triggering event would require infinitely many powers being activated simultaneously.

What seems to be causing the problem, then, is not whether the triggering power is newly acquired; it is the triggering power's need for its own trigger. This suggests that

---

[7] Thanks to Landon Hedrick for this point.

the way for the pandispositionalist to escape the regress is to deny (R2)—that a trigger-ing power needs to be activated. So, according to this suggestion, what happens when the target power is activated is that something instantiates a triggering power, and with-out itself being activated, this triggering power activates the target power to exhibit its manifestation.

In other words, the suggestion is that the triggering power is what we called earlier a 'trigger-less power'. Recall that there seem to be two kinds of trigger-less powers: spon-taneously manifesting and constantly manifesting. Perhaps there are some cases where a trigger is a matter of something acquiring a spontaneously manifesting power. So, when a trigger occurs in certain circumstances, even if they are ideal, it is a stochastic matter whether the triggering power will manifest and activate the target power. But if deter-minism is true, or if there are some sure-fire dispositions that always manifest when activated in ideal circumstances, power activation would still be problematic for the pandispositionalist in those cases. However, the pandispostitionalist can appeal to the other possible kind of trigger-less powers—constantly manifesting powers. A triggering power could be a power that does not need its own trigger because it is constantly manifesting.

Now, the issue of whether a trigger involves acquiring a power or maintaining a power arises again. If a trigger can be a matter of maintaining a power, and that power is constantly manifesting, then, again, there is no explanation of the time lapse between the acquisition of the trigger power and the target manifestation. So, we are back to the view that a trigger must be a matter of *acquiring* a power, with the new stipulation that it must be a constantly manifesting power, so no additional triggers are needed in order to the bring about the target manifestation.

But recall what this means in terms of our original example. We already noted how a match can acquire a power to ignite gasoline without that power ever being manifest—without the gasoline catching on fire. So, if the match acquires some constantly mani-festing power, it cannot be the power to ignite the gasoline—that power might not manifest at all. So, if the match acquires some constantly manifesting power, it must be some other power. (Recall that an object can gain or lose a constantly manifesting power.) What power could it be?

In the case of the match, an important property the match acquires is *being on fire*. Being on fire is often considered an occurrent property—something that is happening to the match now, not a matter of what it would do in certain circumstances. But recall Hüttemann's view—that there is no real difference between a constantly manifesting power and a categorical property. So perhaps we can think of 'being on fire' as a con-stantly manifesting power that is acquired when the match is struck.

Note that the manifestation of the triggering power is not the same as the manifestation of the target power—the match being on fire is not the same event as the gasoline being on fire. This suggests that even after the triggering power is manifest, its work is not done, as far as bringing about the target manifestation is concerned. However, as we have seen, we do not want to say we need another trigger to bring about the target manifestation. So we need a different account of how the triggering power helps to bring about the target manifestation.

5 Triggers for the pandispositionalist (take two)

One alternative, which I think will be a welcome suggestion to some, is that the constantly manifesting triggering power *contributes* to the target manifestation. The other factors, such as the oxygenation of the air, the proximity of the gasoline, are not to be construed as triggers, but as co-contributors. We had been talking about the acquisition of the triggering power as the triggering event, but since it is the triggering power that contributes to the manifestation, perhaps it would be better to think of the power itself as the trigger. The picture that is now emerging is that when there is a confluence of a target power, a triggering power, and certain powers in their environment, they all jointly contribute to the manifestation. This picture now resembles Heil's view according to which dispositions have mutual manifestation partners.[8] When a disposition stands in the right relation to its partner(s), the manifestation ensues.

Notice that, in this picture, there is little to distinguish a trigger from other powers that are needed for the manifestation. We have already seen that distinguishing a trigger from the total circumstances of manifestation seems to be a matter of pragmatics: We usually count the match's power as the trigger, but the atmosphere's being oxygenated is an equally qualified candidate. And we've already noted that the same power can be a triggering power relative to one power, and a target power relative to another: Recall that the power of the match to ignite the gasoline was a triggering power relative to the flammability of the gasoline and a target power relative to the power of the striking surface to light matches. Moreover, if powers are mutual manifestation partners, there is no principled reason to call one power a target and the other power a trigger. Which power counts as being targeted and which power counts as doing the triggering is an interest-relative matter. We have been supposing that the match's power triggers the gasoline's flammability. But we could equally say that gasoline's flammability triggers the match's power to ignite flammable substances, or the atmosphere's power to fuel fires, for that matter.

So, if all properties are powers, what do triggers look like? Well, not surprisingly, they look like powers. Triggers cease to be a category of much metaphysical interest, above and beyond that of powers in general. A triggering power is just one of the powers which interact with other powers to produce a manifestation. I do not know if there is any significance to the concept of 'interaction' on this view, other than to say that certain combinations and arrangements of powers result in the occurrence of the manifestation. There are all sorts of pragmatic reasons why one power might be singled

---

[8] Heil, J. (2005) 'Dispositions', *Synthese* 144: 343–56. On the view I am describing, however, there will typically be more than two contributing powers. See also Mumford and Anjum (2011).

out as a trigger. If a power is part of normal background conditions, its contribution to a manifestation might be taken for granted rather than noted as salient. Such is usually the case with local gravitational fields or typical atmospheric conditions. However, if a power is newly introduced into a situation, it is more apt to be considered a trigger. Moreover, if a power is the last power acquired before the assembled powers culminate in a manifestation, that power is likely to be called a trigger.[9] But the fact that a power is new, or the final contribution to the manifestation, does not mean that it is a different kind of thing than any of the other powers that contribute to the manifestation. The answer to the question 'how does a pandispositionalist activate a power?' is: He brings it together with all its mutual manifestation partners.

To summarize, the possibility that survived the regress discussion was that triggers must be trigger-less. In particular, they must be constantly manifesting. This suggestion raised the question as to how these constantly manifesting triggering powers can be active, and yet not guarantee the occurrence of the target manifestation. The answer to that question is the view currently under consideration, that the triggering power needs its mutual manifestation partners in order for the target manifestation to occur. On this metaphysical picture, even a relative distinction between triggering powers and target powers is merely pragmatic.

6 Remaining doubts

The picture according to which a trigger is one of the powers which gets together with other powers to produce a manifestation suggests there is no real role for activation. Powers are inherently active, making their contributions, and all one needs to do is to combine them to get a manifestation. But is there ever a sense in which powers are *inactive*, in addition to being insufficient for a certain effect? Perhaps the flammability of the gasoline that is just lying on the ground in a puddle is not making any contribution towards a fire yet. The sulphur on the tip of the match that is tucked away in a match book—its power seems dormant too. The idea that both of these powers are making their small contribution to the fire before the match is even struck seems odd. The fragility of the intact glass, the dark light bulb's power to illuminate, the soporiferousness of the sleeping pill still in its bottle—these all seem like dormant powers.

Remember, dispositional monism is the view that all properties are powers, not necessarily that all properties are *active* powers. On some views, the possibility of not manifesting, or being manifest in certain circumstances only, is what distinguished dispositions from other properties. If there is no clear difference between a categorical property and a constantly manifesting power, there is no clear difference between the view that all properties are constantly manifesting powers and the view that all properties are

---

[9] Here, I am following Mumford and Anjum (2011), p. 37.

categorical properties. If dispositional monism is a real alternative to categorical monism, it should allow for dormant powers.

If powers jointly produce manifestations, these powers need to be active. The question of how to activate a power does not arise for powers that are already active. But it seems possible that some powers are sometimes dormant. And a dormant power cannot contribute anything to a manifestation unless it is activated. But how does that happen? The answer under consideration seems to be that we add its co-contributors to the mix. But if an inactive power cannot contribute, it is not a contributor, and therefore has no co-contributors. More to the point, positing contributing powers does not explain how a dormant power becomes active.

7 Triggers for the pandispositionalist (take three?)

There is another option for the pandispositionalist. The view that 'powers contribute to manifestations' should be distinguished from another view, associated with Molnar, Cartwright, and others.[10] Such views note that most events are not manifestations of a single power, but are instead the result of complex interactions between multiple powers. According to Molnar, a power is one thing, its contribution is another thing, and the actual effect is yet a third. Accordingly, we should distinguish between a power, its manifestation, and the effect that occurs. In a similar vein, Cartwright favours a tripartite distinction between a capacity, its exercise, and the manifest result. For example, perhaps the manifestation of 'gravitational mass' is 'gravitational force', and that force contributes to the movements of bodies, along with all of the other forces present in any particular set of circumstances. On these views, it is not the power that contributes to an effect; rather, the capacity's exercise, or the power's manifestation, is the contribution. In what follows, I'll adhere to Molnar's terminology, according to which 'powers' have 'manifestations' that contribute to 'effects'.

Where are triggers in this picture? A trigger is no longer one of the powers that contribute to an effect, since it is the power's manifestation, not the power itself, which contributes to the effect. Perhaps one of the powers whose manifestation contributes to the effect could still be called a trigger. Keeping with an earlier suggestion, perhaps the power whose manifestation is the final contribution to the effect is apt to be considered a trigger (the only difference from the earlier view being that the power is distinguished from the contribution it makes). This picture is slightly more complicated, but the role for the triggering power is essentially the same. While the triggering power does not contribute to the effect directly, its manifestation does.

---

[10] See Molnar (2003) and Mumford (2009a) for defence of the view that manifestations are contributions to effects rather than effects themselves. See McKitrick (2010) for criticism. See also Cartwright and Corry in Handfield, T. (2009) *Dispositions and Causes*, Oxford, UK: Oxford University Press. I am not saying that these views about exercising powers are offered in service of pandispositionalism, but that they can be put to that end.

However, there is still the issue of the relationship between a power and its manifestation (keeping in mind that a power's manifestation is something that contributes to an effect, rather than being an effect itself). Some powers might manifest constantly, as is perhaps the case with massive objects which constantly exert gravitational force. Some powers manifest spontaneously. But perhaps there are some powers that are such that, not only do they have certain effects in certain circumstances, but they only manifest in certain circumstances. If so, there are times at which such powers are not manifesting, and need to be activated to produce their manifestations.

So, this third take on power activation for the pandispositionalist is subject to essentially the same worries expressed about the second take. If powers are always manifesting, while combining those manifestations to get a resultant effect is surely an intriguing and at times complex process, there is no need for activation. However, if any powers are ever dormant, any story about combining manifestations will not explain how they get activated. This suggests that when such a power has a manifestation that contributes to an effect, there is another element of this scenario—a trigger. Are we any closer to understanding the nature of this trigger?

8 Conclusion

A power must be active in order to contribute to an effect, or to have a manifestation that contributes to an effect. While a power is dormant, it contributes nothing, and has no manifestation to contribute. If any powers are ever dormant, either (a) they stay that way, (b) they manifest spontaneously, or c) something happens that activates them, i.e. a trigger occurs. Before such a trigger occurs, the target power is a dormant power. We have discussed a sense in which any power that contributes to an effect can be considered a target power. But on second thought, there is no need to activate powers that are already active and making their contributions. I submit that there is a more central sense of power activation, according to which a target power must be a dormant power.

So let us return to the view that, when a trigger occurs, something acquires a property, and for the pandispositionalist, this property must be a power. And it must be manifest. If the triggering power were dormant like the target power, it is not clear how it could do any triggering.[11] Furthermore, if the triggering power were dormant, the triggering power would need its own trigger, and would itself be a target power, and of course, a vicious regress looms. So it looks like insofar as a power is playing the role of triggering power, it must be active.

---

[11] I suppose it is possible that a manifestation could result from two latent powers coming together. Perhaps a manifestation results from the collusion of two dormant powers in accordance with some law of nature. I see two difficulties for the possibility. This explanation of power activation may interfere with another desiderata of the powers theorist—reduction of laws to powers. And relatedly, it is not clear why these properties should be thought of as powers rather than categorical properties governed by laws. Thanks to Luke Elwonger for this suggestion.

So now we *do* have a metaphysical distinction between a target power and a triggering power: When a power is a target power, it is latent, dormant, not manifesting; when a power is a triggering power, it must be active, exercising, manifesting. And so there is no unexplained delay between the trigger and the manifestation, the triggering power must be recently acquired or recently activated. We do not want to say that all triggering powers are activated just prior to the occurrence of the target manifestation, if that means they needed triggers, due to by now familiar regress concerns. I think, also, we do not want to say that the triggering power manifests spontaneously because (a) we do not want to presuppose indeterminism, and (b) our own abilities to activate powers (light matches, remove stains, make phone calls, etc.) are too reliable to be purely chancy affairs. So, it looks like the best account of triggers for the pandispositionalist is that they are a matter of acquiring constantly manifesting powers not far in advance of the occurrence of the target manifestation.

One might wonder if another regress looms. If the power is newly acquired, what caused it to be acquired? Was yet another power needed to bring about the instantiation of the triggering power? But if there is a regress here, I think it is akin to the innocent causal regress discussed earlier. In a pandispositionalist scenario, the instantiation of a triggering power is a manifestation of another power that was activated previously, just as the cause of an effect is itself an effect that was caused by an earlier cause.

There was also concern over the fact that a triggering power does not guarantee the occurrence of the target manifestation, even when the triggering power is itself manifest. And if something else is needed, it had better not be another trigger. But perhaps there are aspects of the views considered that we can retain and make use of. The activation circumstances might be multi-faceted, involving several different triggering powers. The presence of one constantly manifesting power might not be sufficient, and other powers are needed to contribute and activate the target power.

Or, it might be that the triggering power has successfully activated the target power, and the target power is now contributing its manifestation, but the presence of co-contributing manifestations is insufficient to produce the expected effect. Note that when employing the Cartwright/Molnar tripartite distinction, we must watch for ambiguous references to 'manifestations'. The triggering power may be constantly manifesting, and it might get the target power to manifest, but they might fail to jointly result in what we have been calling the 'target manifestation' if that is, in fact, an effect that would result from the complex interaction of multiple contributions.

If there are dormant powers that do not manifest spontaneously, they need triggers. And to avoid a regress, they need triggers that do not need triggers themselves. So, I suggest, the pandispositionalist needs constantly manifesting powers to trigger dormant powers. But is there any difference between a constantly manifesting power and a categorical property? It would be ironic if the only way a pandispositionalist can activate a power is by positing what is effectively a categorical property. If the pandispositionalist accepts my solution, has he in effect compromised his pandispositionalism?

Again, I think it depends on what we mean by 'manifestation'. If there were such a thing as a constantly manifesting power to be cubicle, for example, I would be hard-pressed to explain how that is any different than the categorical property of being cubicle. But what if a manifestation is not a state of affairs like being cubicle, but something less tangible, like the force of gravity? What if constantly manifesting powers have manifestations that are forces, not effects? It is not clear that there is any place for such a constantly manifesting power in a categorical monist ontology. Its manifestation seems insufficiently categorical. So, if pandispositionalism is true, even if a trigger of a power is a constantly manifesting power, it will be distinguishable from a categorical property, since the manifestation is itself the instantiation of a power.

In sum, I have considered several accounts of triggers for the pandispositionalist: acquisitions of dormant powers, activations of dormant powers, acquisitions of spontaneously manifesting powers, acquisitions of constantly manifesting powers, powers that contribute to a manifestation, and powers whose manifestations contribute to effects. I have noted what I take to be drawbacks to each approach. While I tend to favour thinking of triggers as acquisitions of constantly manifesting powers, I leave it to the pandispositionalists to determine which approach works best in their ontology, and to live with or overcome the drawbacks I have highlighted, or to present an alternative account of activation I have yet to consider.

PART III

Natural Kinds

7

How to carve across the joints in nature without abandoning Kripke–Putnam semantics[1]

Helen Beebee

1 Introduction

The topic of this chapter is the connection—or rather, I shall argue, the lack of connection—between what I shall call 'natural kind essentialism' and the Kripke–Putnam semantics for natural kind terms ('KP' for short). Natural kind essentialism is not a well-defined philosophical position, and in particular the question of exactly what one is committed to when one is committed to 'essentialism' gets different answers from different authors in both 'essentialist' and 'anti-essentialist' camps.[2] For the purposes of this chapter I shall take natural kind essentialism to enshrine a commitment to three theses: first, that which natural kinds exist is a fully mind- and theory-independent matter; second, that natural kinds have intrinsic essences; and, third, that natural kinds have a hierarchical structure (what Tobin (2010) calls the 'hierarchy thesis').[3]

Those who endorse natural kind essentialism as just defined typically endorse Kripke and Putnam's claim that theoretical identifications, such as 'water is H_2O' and 'gold is the element with atomic number 79', are metaphysically necessary but knowable only a posteriori.[4] Indeed, some go further and take the truth of this claim to constitute grounds for believing natural kind essentialism. Nathan Salmon, by contrast, argues that

[1] I am hugely indebted to Nigel Sabbarton-Leary, without whom I would never have been able to write this chapter. Thanks also to Alexander Bird, Genoveva Martí, L. A. Paul, Emma Tobin, and many other people who heard and commented on a distant ancestor of this chapter.

[2] For example, there is a large amount of middle ground in between the essentialist position defended by Brian Ellis (2001) and the anti-essentialist positions defended by Stephen Mumford (2005) and Paul Griffiths (1999). The contested meaning of 'essentialism' is clear from the fact that Joseph LaPorte (2010: 118) takes himself to be an essentialist, while John Dupré (2004) argues that he isn't (see Beebee and Sabbarton-Leary 2010b: 19–20 for a brief discussion of this latter dispute).

[3] Actually some defenders of natural kind essentialism subscribe to a weaker hierarchy thesis than this; see section 4 below.

[4] An exception is Oderberg (2007).

the alleged necessary a posteriori status of theoretical identities is secured only by pre-supposing a 'nontrivial' essentialism at the outset; in other words, *contra* many of its defenders—and indeed some of its detractors—the semantics of natural kind terms just by itself does nothing to justify natural kind essentialism. I shall argue, however, that what Salmon regards as 'nontrivial' essentialism is in fact pretty innocuous by the lights of most contemporary metaphysicians. This being so, it remains an open question whether KP entails natural kind essentialism as just defined—a highly nontrivial brand of essentialism. I shall argue that it does not. In particular, KP is compatible with species pluralism (where some species concepts that one might be pluralist about are ones that assign extrinsic essences to species), and hence does not entail either the hierarchy thesis or the thesis that natural kinds have intrinsic essences. In addition—and contrary to Putnam's original intentions—KP is compatible with Kuhnian relativism, and hence does not entail the mind- or theory-independence of natural kinds. In other words, one can sign up to KP and the 'nontrivial' essentialism it entails, and still reject all of the three theses just described.

The basic idea is this. We have, on the one hand, the sorts of vernacular kind term that Kripke and Putnam were originally concerned with: 'gold', 'water', 'tiger', 'magpie', 'lemon', and so on. We correspondingly presuppose certain pre-theoretical sameness-of-kind relations: *same substance, same animal, same fruit*, and so on. In such cases, we defer (if KP is correct) to scientific investigation to tell us what it is for something to be the same *NK* as something else for a given kind *NK*, where '*NK*' refers to some higher-order kind—what I'll call a 'category'—that is pre-theoretically specifiable (*substance, fruit*, and so on) and the vernacular kind term designates the relevant lower-level natural kind (*gold* and *water* are both kinds of substance, *tiger* and *magpie* are both kinds of animal, and so on). Thus, for example, we defer to chemical investigation to tell us whether *this* (the contents of my glass) is the *same substance* as *that* (the contents of my ice-cube tray), where *substance* is a category; if the answer is 'yes', then there is some lower-level natural kind (namely, *water*) of which both samples are a member.

On the other hand, we have natural kind terms that are manifestly *not* vernacular—'electron', 'ununbium', 'enzyme', '*Coracias tibicen telonocua*', and so on. In many such cases, no such pre-theoretical sameness-of-kind relation is available to us. The blank in 'same ...' can only be replaced by appealing to the classificatory framework of the relevant science: *elementary particle, element, species*, and so on are no part of our pre-theoretical framework. In such cases, we defer to the classificatory framework of the relevant science not only to tell us what it is to be the same *NK* as something else for a given *NK*, but also to specify the category *NK* itself. For example, there is no determinate answer, from the point of view of biology, to the question whether *this* (pointing at an African elephant) is the same *animal* as *that* (pointing at an Asian elephant): the answer is 'yes (if you mean "same family") and no (if you mean "same species" or "same genus")'. But 'same animal' does not determinately mean any one of these alternatives. In the case of, say, ununbium (the element with atomic number 112), again one cannot ask the relevant question ('is this the same *NK* as that?') without deploying a distinctively theoretical framework—in this case the periodic table—since the only vernacular kind available is *substance*, and it is unclear that ununbium is a *substance* at all in the pre-theoretical sense, given that it has a half-life of 0.24 milliseconds.

If we are to hold that for *every* natural kind there is some necessary a posteriori theoretical identity that specifies the essence of the kind, then, we must leave vernacular kind terms and their associated categories (*substance, animal*, and so on) behind. But once we are in the business of deferring to the classificatory framework(s) of the relevant science, I shall argue, the 'essentialism' we are left with is—in the absence of further, independent metaphysical requirements on natural-kind essences that have nothing to do with KP—an extremely weak thesis that falls a very long way short of natural kind essentialism.

I shall proceed as follows. In Section 2, I very briefly outline KP and make the case that the position I am arguing against is no straw man by providing three examples of philosophers (Brian Ellis, John Dupré, and Joseph LaPorte) who (I shall later argue) overstate the metaphysical implications of KP. In Section 3, I outline Nathan Salmon's '*OK*-mechanism'—a template for deriving necessary a posteriori theoretical identifications—and argue that the sense of 'nontrivial' essentialism enshrined in its third premise is, in fact, a very weak form of essentialism. Hence the question remains whether KP (plus nontrivial essentialism) provides any justification for endorsing natural kind essentialism. In Section 4, I define four different ways in which a kind might be thought to 'cut across' nature's joints, and which one might hope (and, in some cases, some authors explicitly claim) are ruled out by KP. In Section 5–7, I take three of these varieties of crosscutting in turn (leaving artificial kinds to one side), and argue that none of them are, in fact, ruled out by KP. I conclude, in Section 8, by explaining how KP is consistent with a 'shallow' form of essentialism, in a sense roughly analogous to the 'shallow essentialism' defined for individuals in Paul 2006. Thus just as Kripke's account of the semantics of names does not—in the absence of independent substantive metaphysical assumptions—adjudicate between deep and shallow essentialism when it comes to individuals, so KP does not adjudicate between deep and shallow essentialism (in a slightly different sense) when it comes to kinds.

2 The Kripke–Putnam programme and the wonders it (allegedly) performs

As is well known, according to Kripke, 'theoretical identity statements' such as 'gold is the element with atomic number 79' and 'water is H_2O' are metaphysically necessary but knowable only a posteriori. So, for example, 'gold' rigidly designates the kind *gold*— 'gold' is a nondescriptive *name* for that kind[5]—and the 'essence' of that kind (*being the*

---

[5] The ontological status of natural kinds is a matter for dispute. In the philosophy of language, kinds are normally taken to be abstract objects, so that kind terms are genuine names of kinds; Devitt and Sterelny (1999), by contrast, take natural kind terms to 'rigidly apply' to members of their extensions, thus avoiding commitment to abstract objects. I shall proceed as though kind terms are names of kinds, but nothing directly relevant to the argument hangs on this.

element with atomic number 79) is discovered by scientific investigation. Hence 'gold is the element with atomic number 79' is necessary if true, since if *E* is the essence of *K*, all *K*s will be *E*s, and vice versa, across all possible worlds. But it is knowable only a posteriori because only empirical investigation can reveal what gold's essence is. Thus:

[A] material object is (pure) gold if and only if the only element contained therein is that with atomic number 79. Here the 'if and only if' can be taken to be strict (necessary). In general, science attempts, by investigating basic structural traits, to find the nature, and thus the essence (in the philosophical sense) of the kind. (Kripke 1980: 138)

Putnam (1975) turns more or less the same trick, but without explicit appeal to essences. On his view:

When I say '*this* (liquid) is water', the 'this' is, so to speak, a *de re* 'this' – i.e. the force of my explanation is that 'water' is whatever bears a certain equivalence relation [namely the *same-liquid* or *same$_L$* relation] to the liquid referred to as 'this' *in the actual world*. (1975: 231)

The *same$_L$* relation is a '*theoretical* relation—whether something is or is not the same liquid as *this* may take an indeterminate amount of scientific investigation to determine' (1975: 225)—and its cross-world import, giving us the rigidity of 'water', is demonstrated by the standard twin earth thought experiment. So we get the necessary status of 'water is H_2O' from the fact that the *same$_L$* relation has cross-world import—something at any possible world is the same liquid as *this* liquid if it bears the *same$_L$* relation to it—and a posteriority from the fact that the *same$_L$* relation is a relation whose obtaining is discovered by scientific investigation. Similarly for other ostensive definitions: ' "this (animal) is a tiger"; "this (fruit) is a lemon"; where the parentheses are meant to indicate that the "markers" *liquid, animal, fruit*, may be explicit or implicit' (1975: 229).

So much for the machinery of necessary a posteriori theoretical identification; what of its metaphysical significance? The argument of this chapter will be that its significance has been overstated, both by those who endorse KP and by those who reject it. Here is a selection of claims that have been made, starting with philosophers who endorse KP.

I'll start with Brian Ellis. Ellis (2001) has perhaps the most extreme conception of the significance of KP. On Ellis's view, which he dubs 'scientific essentialism', the laws of nature describe the essences of natural kinds (which include natural kinds of substance, process, and property), and hence are metaphysically necessary. But what *is* it for a proposition to be metaphysically necessary? He says:

Analytic propositions are true in virtue in virtue of the meanings of words–that is, they depend for their truth on some conventionally established criterion for including something in some linguistically defined class. Metaphysically necessary propositions, on the other hand, are true in virtue of the essential natures of things–for example, they state correctly, or otherwise depend for their truth on, what makes something a thing of the natural kind it is. (2001: 235)

He goes on to explain how to distinguish between analytic truths on the one hand and metaphysically necessary propositions on the other:

…one technique is to abstract from the descriptive language used to refer to [some class of objects], and replace the general name used with an ostensive 'kind-referring' expression, such as 'stuff of this kind' or 'things of this kind'. If the necessity survives this process, then we know that it cannot be grounded in the descriptive language we had been using. 'Water is H_2O', for example, clearly survives this test, because 'stuff of this kind is H_2O', said pointing to a glass of water, is no less necessary than 'water is H_2O'. If there is any doubt about it, then it can only be a doubt about what the intended object of reference is [e.g. about whether one is referring to the glass or its contents], or ignorance about what its nature is. (2001: 235–6)

On Ellis's view, then, natural kind terms (and ostensive expressions) rigidly designate kinds whose essences are knowable only a posteriori ('stuff of this kind is H_2O' is manifestly not knowable a priori, and yet is metaphysically necessary, just as 'water is H_2O' is). And it is the a posteriority that tells us that the proposition in question is metaphysically necessary, or a matter of what he sometimes calls 'real necessity'—that is, 'true in virtue of the essential natures of things'. In other words, the existence of necessary a posteriori theoretical identifications is the cornerstone of scientific essentialism: it is KP that shows that there is such a thing as 'real necessity'.

Turning now to some philosophers hostile to KP but who nonetheless hold that it has significant implications, second up is Joseph LaPorte (2004). LaPorte argues that a broadly causal story about reference-fixing is consistent with a degree of 'vagueness' of reference at the pre-scientific stage at which reference (of, say, 'water' or 'gold') is fixed by the folk: 'causal baptisms, which according to the causal theory endow terms with their reference conditions, are performed by speakers whose conceptual development is not yet sophisticated enough to allow the speakers to coin a term in such a way as to preclude the possibility of open texture, or vague application not yet recognized' (2004: 118). The meaning of the term is then precisified by scientists at the point at which a decision needs to be made; hence scientists do not *discover* the essence of (say) water, but rather stipulate a new meaning. Hence—contrary to KP (though not, LaPorte argues, contrary to a broadly causal theory of reference that rejects a posteriori necessity)— 'water is H_2O' is necessary but not a posteriori: empirical investigation engenders a *decision* about, for example, whether to classify D_2O as water, and so—that decision having been made—'water is H_2O' is true by definition.

LaPorte's conclusion is that, because it does not deliver the full machinery of KP, and in particular does not deliver necessary a posteriori theoretical identities, a broadly causal theory of reference does not block referential instability across theory change: it does not 'dispel the threat of incommensurability' (2004: 172). So LaPorte—along with Putnam (1975) himself—clearly thinks KP itself *does* (or would, if true) dispel the threat of incommensurability. I shall argue in Section 7 that KP (suitably extended to cover all the natural kinds recognized by the sciences) does not in fact have the resources to do this.

My third and final example is John Dupré, who says:

To assert that there are real essences is, in part, to claim that there are fundamental properties that determine the existence and extensions of kinds that instantiate them. The existence of such properties would have profound metaphysical consequences. In particular it would imply that the existence of kinds of things was as much a matter of fact about the world as was the existence of particular things. Such kinds would be quite independent of our attempts to distinguish them, and their discovery would be an integral part of the agenda of science. The majority of contemporary usage takes such independent existence of kinds defined by real essences and awaiting scientific discovery as constituting the necessary and sufficient condition for the existence of a *natural* kind. Certainly, the existence of a natural kind . . . will follow from the existence of a real essence. (1993: 62–3)

While Dupré does not mention Kripke or Putnam by name here, KP is clearly the view he is describing. On that view, natural kinds are just those kinds that have 'independent existence', are 'defined by real essences', and await scientific discovery. So theoretical identities such as 'gold is the element with atomic number 79' are necessary (since having atomic number 79 is the 'real essence' of gold) and knowable only a posteriori (since it is a matter of scientific discovery what the real essence of gold is). He thus credits KP with 'profound metaphysical consequences'. One such alleged consequence, alluded to here, is that the essences of natural kinds—in effect, whatever appears on the right-hand side of a theoretical identification—are, always and everywhere, Lockean *real* essences; that is to say, underlying intrinsic features which causally explain manifest properties. Thus Dupré takes it that an evolutionary approach to taxonomy in biology is incompatible with the 'essentialism' of Kripke and Putnam (1993: 38). A second alleged consequence is the claim that kinds are 'independent of our attempts to distinguish them'. Whatever exactly this means, it is a claim that Dupré clearly takes to be incompatible with his own 'promiscuous realism' and, in particular, with species pluralism.

The central contention of this chapter is that the claims made by Ellis, LaPorte, and Dupré, amongst others, concerning the metaphysical consequences of KP are significantly overstated. KP does not, just by itself, deliver a metaphysically significant brand of necessity ('real' necessity). Nor, *pace* LaPorte, would it (if true) ward off the threat of incommensurability; nor, *pace* Dupré, would it establish the falsity of species pluralism.

My argument will turn on a fact that it is worth making explicit, namely that any *prima facie* plausible version of natural kind essentialism (of the sort that Ellis, Dupré, and LaPorte are interested in) relies on a very significant extension of KP to the non-vernacular 'substantial' natural kind terms of physics, chemistry, and (perhaps) biology. In other words, what goes for 'water' and 'gold' goes also for 'phosphorus trichloride', 'ununbium', 'Higgs boson', '*Coracias tibicen telonocua*', and so on.[6]

Nigel Sabbarton-Leary and I argue elsewhere (2010c) that such an extension is not warranted. Moreover, as LaPorte's (2004) and Dupré's (1993) arguments against KP show, it is not even clear that KP really works even for the vernacular terms for which it was designed. (My beef with LaPorte and Dupré is not that there is something wrong

---

[6] Ellis himself holds on independent metaphysical grounds that there are no natural biological species kinds (see Ellis 2001: 167–70). But he does assume that KP holds for the natural substance kinds terms of physics and chemistry; indeed he also assumes that it holds for 'natural kinds' of process and property.

with their anti-KP arguments; only that they overstate the metaphysical implications of their opponents' view.) Nonetheless, I shall assume for the sake of the argument that KP does work for vernacular kind terms, and that the required extension to non-vernacular kind terms can, in principle, be made to work. But, I shall argue, the very moves that would be needed in order to *make* it work for non-vernacular kind terms render KP unable to perform the metaphysical wonders that have been claimed for it. So the view I have in my sights is not, strictly speaking, KP just by itself, but KP combined with the assumption just described: roughly, the view that KP holds for all the natural kind terms of the sciences.

3 The *OK*-mechanism and 'nontrivial' essentialism

Let's start with Nathan Salmon's account—which itself draws on unpublished work of Keith Donellan—of how Kripke and Putnam secure the necessary a posteriori status of 'water is H_2O', which he calls the '*OK*-mechanism' (Salmon 2005: 166–7; sentences renumbered):

(1) It is necessarily the case that: something is a sample of water if and only if it is a sample of *dthat* (the same substance as *this* is a sample of).
(2) *This* (liquid sample) has the chemical structure H_2O.
(3) Being a sample of the same substance as something consists in having the same chemical structure.

Therefore,

(4) It is necessarily the case that: every sample of water has the chemical structure H_2O.

This argument, Salmon says, is 'intuitively valid' (though (3) needs further tinkering in order to make the argument genuinely modally valid; more on this below), and, since (at least) one of the premises, namely (2), is knowable only a posteriori, (4) can also only be known a posteriori. Thus we derive our necessary a posteriori theoretical identification: every sample of water has the chemical structure H_2O.

Before proceeding, we need to pause briefly to consider the inadequacy of (3) as it stands. The most important problem for present purposes is that it only provides an intra-world condition on consubstantiality, whereas what is needed to make the argument modally valid is an inter-world condition. Salmon therefore replaces it with:

(3★) [I]f x exists in w_1 and y exists in w_2, and if furthermore x is a sample in w_1 of the same substance that y is a sample of in w_2, then whatever chemical structure x has in w_1, y has that same chemical structure in w_2, and *vice versa*. (2005: 179–80)[7]

---

[7] Salmon deliberately replaces the necessary and sufficient conditions on consubstantiality implicit in 'consists in', in (3), with a merely necessary condition in (3★) (i.e. (3★) has 'if...then', and not 'iff'), because sufficiency is irrelevant to the validity of the argument; see Salmon 2005: 179.

Because it's easier on the eye, however, I shall continue to refer to (3), and take it as read that the *same substance* relation is to be conceived as an inter-world relation.

My interest in this section is in Salmon's charge that (3) has 'nontrivial essentialist import' (2005: 185). This has been noted by enemies of natural kind essentialism (e.g. Mumford 2005); but what, exactly, does this import amount to? I want to argue that while KP's essentialist import is indeed nontrivial in Salmon's very specific sense, it isn't *highly* nontrivial; in fact, it's something most contemporary metaphysicians wouldn't think twice about signing up to, and it falls a long way short of the kind of highly non-trivial essentialism embraced by natural kind essentialism.

Salmon regards (3) as enshrining 'nontrivial' essentialism because he contrasts it with 'trivial' essentialism. Thus:

> Given that 'Hesperus' rigidly denotes the planet Venus, the identity sentence 'Hesperus is identical with Phosphorus' is necessary . . . if and only if Venus is such that it could not fail to have the property of *being identical with Phosphorus*. Hence, using only some elementary modal semantics and the established fact that Hesperus is Phosphorus, we are able to derive from the theory of direct reference the result that the planet Venus has a certain essential property, namely the property of *being Phosphorus*. (2005: 82)

> This derived result, however, if it is a brand of essentialism at all, is a brand of essentialism of the most trivial and innocuous kind. It is not the deeply metaphysical sort of essentialism that has come under so much criticism. (2005, 83–4)

Roughly speaking, the idea here is, first, that *being identical with Phosphorus* is a pretty innocuous essential property for Venus to possess because its instantiation follows trivially from the fact that all identities are necessary, and, second, that this 'trivial' form of essentialism is all that Kripke's semantics for proper names delivers. KP, by contrast—the claim that theoretical identities are necessary a posteriori—entails, and on Salmon's view entails because it presupposes, essentialism of a 'deeply metaphysical sort'.

What *is* this 'deeply metaphysical sort' of essentialism? The answer is implicit in a footnote to the passage just quoted, where Salmon says, 'Quine is the best known and most outspoken critic of essentialism' (2005: 84, n.4). Indeed so, on a certain understanding of 'essentialism', namely what Quine calls 'Aristotelian essentialism': the view that 'some of the attributes of a thing (quite independently of the language in which the thing is referred to, if at all) may be essential to the thing but others accidental' (Quine 1966: 175–6). Kripke similarly characterizes essentialism as 'the belief in modality *de re*' (1980: 39). In other words, all that 'nontrivial essentialism' amounts to is a belief in *de re* modality, and/or the belief that there is a language-independent distinction to be drawn between the essential and accidental properties of a thing (or, in the case of natural kinds, *kinds* of thing).

Essentialism thus conceived is not, by the lights of contemporary metaphysics, a very strong thesis.[8] This may be obvious to those readers who appeal to *de re* modality on a

---

[8] Indeed, Kit Fine (1994) argues that the resources of *de re* modality are insufficient for accounting for essences; on Fine's view, then, 'nontrivial essentialism' in Salmon's sense isn't really 'essentialism' at all.

daily basis without considering themselves to be essentialists in any robust sense; but it is worth spelling out. We can shed a little more light on the matter by drawing an analogy with essentialism about individuals. L. A. Paul (2006) draws a useful distinction between 'deep' and 'shallow' essentialism. She says:

> Deep essentialists take the (nontrivial) essential properties of an object to determine its nature–such properties give sense to the idea that an object has a unique and distinctive character, and make it the case that an object has to be a certain way in order for it to be at all . . . Intuitively, on the deep essentialist picture, an ordinary object has essential properties, and it must have its essential properties in order for it to exist. On this view, objects' essential properties are absolute, i.e., are not determined by contexts of describing (or thinking, etc.) about the object, and truths about such properties are absolute truths. Shallow essentialists oppose deep essentialists: they reject the view that objects can be said to have essential properties independently of contexts of description or evaluation, and so substitute context-dependent truths for the deep essentialist's context-independent ones. (2006: 333)

So, for example, let's agree that it is part of my essence that I am human (let's say): *I could not have existed without being human*. By contrast, having long hair is not part of my essence, since I could still have existed (and once did exist) without having long hair. According to the deep essentialist, the former fact about my essence in no way depends on how I am described or the context within which my essence is being discussed. According to the shallow essentialist, by contrast, there are no absolute, context-independent facts about essences. David Lewis is a prime example of a shallow essentialist: for Lewis, '*a* has property *F* essentially' amounts to '*a* has property *F* in all possible worlds in which *a* exists', which in turn amounts to 'all of *a*'s counterparts have *F*'. So far, we don't have anything that a deep essentialist need disagree with (though of course some do, e.g. because they reject counterpart theory). The crucial move is the further claim that the counterpart relation—what makes an inhabitant of another possible world a counterpart of *me*, say—is context-dependent. Lewis asks whether there is a 'settled answer, fixed once and for all, about what is true concerning a certain individual according to a certain (genuine or ersatz) world' (1986: 198). And his answer is an emphatic 'no':

> there is a great range of cases in which there is no determinate right answer to questions about representations *de re*, and therefore no right answer to questions about modality or counterfactuals *de re*. Could Hubert Humphrey have been an angel? A human born to different parents? A robot? A clever donkey that talks? An ordinary donkey? A poached egg? Given some contextual guidance, these questions should have sensible answers. There are ways of representing whereby some worlds represent him as an angel, there are ways of representing whereby none do. (1986: 251)

Shallow essentialism is 'shallow', then, because it regards essence claims as entirely legitimate—it takes objects to *have* essences—while denying that they have essences in any 'absolute, context-independent sense' (Paul 2006: 345). We can agree, in ordinary conversational contexts, that I am essentially human, but that is not a 'deep' fact about me: in a different context, where the bar for counterparthood is set lower, I am only accidentally human (I might have been a robot, say, or an angel). So while the shallow essentialist agrees with the deep essentialist that (in ordinary contexts) *I* could not have existed without being human, this is not really a very interesting fact about me: it does not reveal a deep metaphysical truth about the conditions for my existence, since we can change the essential facts merely by switching context.

What is important about shallow essentialism for present purposes is that it is 'essentialism' in a very innocuous sense. It is 'nontrivial' in Salmon's sense because it is a version of the view that the accidental/essential distinction is 'independent of the language in which the thing is referred to'. Lewis's view, for example, is not that whether some non-human in another possible world is a counterpart of me is determined by how I am referred to. In ordinary contexts referring to me as 'the object, part of which is currently in contact with the "a" key on the laptop' doesn't make it the case that I am only accidentally human; the question whether *I* am essentially human is a *de re* modal question about *me*, and not a *de dicto* question about the necessity or contingency of the sentence 'the object partly in contact with the "a" key is human'.[9] Nonetheless, Lewis's essentialism is 'shallow' because this *de re* question about me cannot be settled independently of context: it will only have a 'sensible answer' given 'some contextual guidance'.

For the purposes of this chapter, the important question is whether, consistent with KP, we can import something like the shallow/deep distinction into the case of natural kinds. If we can do this, and if shallow essentialism is consistent with KP, then it will turn out that KP is consistent with metaphysical views that only just barely deserve to be called 'essentialist'. It will thus become clear that the kinds of metaphysical work that the authors discussed in Section 2 claim on behalf of KP cannot, in fact, be done by KP just by itself.[10] If that work is to be done at all, it must be done by independent metaphysical assumptions that need to be argued for on independent grounds.

In relation to Salmon, the basic point is this. Salmon is right that if we are to generate necessary a posteriori truths such as 'water is H_2O', 'nontrivial essentialism' must be assumed. So KP does indeed enshrine an independent metaphysical assumption. But that assumption is, by the lights of most contemporary metaphysicians, still pretty trivial; in other words, it is compatible with shallow essentialism—although we will not be in a position to see exactly what 'shallowness' amounts to until Section 8.

4 Carving nature across its joints

Natural kinds, as is often remarked, are supposed to 'carve nature at its joints'. It is not always very clear what 'carving nature at its joints' is supposed to amount to, but I take it

---

[9] I take it Salmon's view is that 'Venus is essentially identical to Phosphorus' is also a *de re* modal fact but is 'innocuous' because being identical to Phosphorus doesn't count as a genuine *attribute*.

[10] As Lewis himself says: 'The true-hearted essentialist might well think me a false friend, a Quinean sceptic in essentialist's clothing' (1983a: 42).

the basic idea is that there is one, unique way to carve out the natural kinds. Thus, first, artificial or gerrymandered kinds (*emerose*, say, or *football*, or *thing bigger than the average car*) 'crosscut' nature's joints, a bit like a bad butcher hacking through the carcass of a cow and ending up with thin rib plus a bit of brisket, or most of the rump and a bit of sirloin. Second, higher-level kinds that crosscut each other are ruled out, so that (for example) if two chemical substances are of the same higher-level kind (e.g. chlorine and iodine are both halogens), there is no *other* higher-level kind that has one as a member but not the other. Stretching the analogy somewhat, the top and bottom sirloin are both sirloin cuts, but there is no cut that has one but not both of these lower-level cuts as a part (say, top sirloin plus rump). Third, *which* way the joints are 'correctly' carved is *absolute*. There isn't (let's suppose) the 'right' way to carve up a cow carcass for the French, and another for the British, and so on, with no fact of the matter about which way *really* carves it up 'correctly'. Similarly, there isn't a 'right' way to carve up nature from the perspective of Newtonian physics (or one 'species concept' in biology) and a 'right' way to carve it up from the perspective of relativistic physics (or a different species concept), with no fact of the matter about which way *really* carves it up 'correctly'.

In view of the fact that natural kinds are commonly supposed to carve nature at its joints, one might hold that the thesis that there is one unique way in which to carve it up is an a priori constraint on any theory of natural kinds, properly so-called. But, as we shall see, some apparently entirely legitimate kind terms of the sciences *do* crosscut. In response to this fact, one might dig one's heels in and insist that a *truly* natural kind obeys the hierarchy thesis. Or one might (as Ian Hacking (2007) does) cite the existence of crosscutting kinds (in the second sense above) as one reason to abandon talk of natural kinds all together. The dominant view, however, is that, however unruly talk of natural kinds may have become in recent years, there is, at the very least, an intuitive distinction in nature between arbitrary and gerrymandered kinds on the one hand and kinds such as *electron, tiger*, and *oxygen* on the other; and that, however strongly participants in the debate may disagree on the extension of 'natural kind', the notion of a natural kind is still worth holding on to. So we should not start out—or at least not without good reason—with the assumption that any natural kind worthy of the name will not crosscut in *any* of the above senses.

As we saw in Section 2, defenders and enemies of KP alike have claimed that KP rules out crosscutting of one or other of the types just identified. In other words, they claim that, if KP holds, we *do* have good reason to hold that natural kinds do not crosscut, in at least one sense of 'crosscut'. Thus Dupré takes KP to be incompatible with species pluralism, and both Putnam and LaPorte take it to rule out Kuhnian relativism. These claims, I shall argue, are mistaken.

In the rest of this section, I shall distinguish between four different ways in which someone might hold that natural kinds can crosscut (building on Tobin 2010, which distinguishes between 'intrataxonomic' and 'intertaxonomic' crosscutting), as follows:

Artificial crosscutting: Artificial kinds are, of course, easy to come by (*house, blue car, lampshade*); and, one might think, equally easy to dismiss as candidates for natural kinds.

I shall not attempt to argue that KP fails to rule out even artificial crosscutting, though it should be noted that Putnam himself argues that kinds such as *pencil* and *paediatrician* count as 'natural kinds'—for example, he argues that it is necessary a posteriori that pencils are artefacts (1975: 242–3). If Putnam is right that KP is consistent with the necessary a posteriori status of 'pencils are artefacts', then of course any account of the naturalness of truly natural kinds (i.e. kinds that do not include *pencil*) is going to have to deploy independent metaphysical assumptions to get the job done.

Intrataxonomic crosscutting is crosscutting within a single classificatory framework (hence 'intra'), and is incompatible with the hierarchy thesis. There are, in fact, several different versions of 'the' hierarchy thesis (see Tobin 2010: 180–5). One might hold that for any two natural kinds K_1 and K_2, if any object or substance o is a member of both kinds, then either K_1 is a sub-kind of K_2, or vice versa. Ellis subscribes to a weaker thesis: he requires only that 'if anything belongs to two different natural kinds, these natural kinds must both be species of some common genus' (2001: 20) (a requirement he takes to be 'satisfied trivially if one of the two kinds is a species of the other' (ibid.)).

Emma Tobin argues that *enzyme* and *protein* constitute a clear example of intrataxonomic crosscutting (2010, Section 3; see also Khalidi 1998 and Hacking 2007: 214). This is a (putative) case of intrataxonomic crosscutting because there is no disagreement within chemistry about what it takes for something to be an enzyme or a protein; rather, these kinds crosscut in the sense that they fail to fit either the stronger or the weaker hierarchical theses described above. The categories *enzyme* and *protein* crosscut in that not all enzymes are proteins and not all proteins are enzymes. This is incompatible with both the stronger hierarchy thesis (since *enzyme* is not a sub-kind of *protein*, and nor is *protein* a sub-kind of *enzyme*) and the weaker one (since there is no chemical genus of which both *enzyme* and *protein* are species).

It may seem obvious that KP does not entail the hierarchy thesis, taken in either of the above senses. In fact, however, in the case of biological kinds a hierarchy thesis is typically built into some ways of specifying the biological-kind analogue of premise (3) in the *OK*-mechanism, as we shall see in Section 5.

Intertaxonomic crosscutting, as Tobin defines it, is cutting across different classificatory frameworks—the rough equivalent of the French vs British schools of butchery, if we imagine that the French and the British carve up their carcasses differently and that (as seems plausible in our imagined scenario) there is no fact of the matter about who carves them up correctly. The case Tobin has in mind is species pluralism. There is a smorgasbord of different 'species concepts' from which to choose—in particular, morphological (based on shared characteristics), biological (based on reproductive isolation), and phylogenetic (based on genealogy). Dupré, following Kitcher (1984), argues for a 'radically pluralistic conception of species' (1993: 50): 'both historical (evolutionary) and structural (or functional) inquiries should be accorded equal weight in biology, and . . . they may require different classificatory schemes' (1993: 50–1). To accept species pluralism is thus to endorse intertaxonomic crosscutting. As we have seen, Dupré takes species pluralism (and so, presumably, intertaxonomic crosscutting generally) to be incompatible with KP.

Interparadigm crosscutting: Let's define interparadigm crosscutting as the thesis that the theoretical terms of successive scientific paradigms are incommensurable, so that there is no fact of the matter about which of the incommensurable classificatory systems carves nature up 'correctly'. '[A]fter discovering oxygen Lavoisier worked in a different world', Kuhn says (1970: 118); more generally, the paradigm one adopts determines the 'correct' classificatory scheme, rather than attempting to get closer to theory-independent joints in nature than did its predecessor.[11] As we've seen, LaPorte explicitly takes KP to rule out interparadigm crosscutting.

In Sections 5–7, I shall argue that intrataxonomic (Section 5), intertaxonomic (Section 6), and interparadigm crosscutting (Section 7) are all compatible with KP, even granted its nontrivial essentialist premise.

5   Intrataxonomic crosscutting

Intrataxonomic crosscutting is crosscutting that is enshrined within a single theoretical framework (as with—according to Tobin—*enzyme* and *protein*). I'll argue for the compatibility of intrataxonomic crosscutting with KP via a slightly circuitous route, and begin by recalling premise (3) of the *OK*-mechanism.

Let's start, then, with what Putnam calls the '*same-liquid* relation' or, more broadly but similarly, the *same-substance* relation. In what does this relation consist? Salmon's answer, on behalf of defenders of KP, is: having the same chemical structure (as in (3)); and defenders of KP do indeed endorse (3), or something similar. Thus Putnam himself says: 'we can understand the relation $same_L$ ... as a cross-world relation by understanding it so that a liquid in world W_1 which has the same important physical properties (in W_1) that a liquid in W_2 possesses (in W_2) bears $same_L$ to the latter liquid' (1975: 232). And he takes these 'important physical properties' to be 'the microstructure of water' (ibid.). Kripke is rather less forthcoming, saying only that 'science attempts, by investigating basic structural traits, to find the nature, and thus the essence (in the philosophical sense) of the kind' (1980: 138); so for Kripke the *same substance* relation is determined by shared 'basic structural traits'.

Relatedly, Scott Soames says:

The term 'water' is to designate the unique substance of which (nearly) all members of the class of its paradigmatic samples are instances. Substances are explanatory kinds instances of which

---

[11]   In fact, 'crosscutting' is perhaps a little misleading, because it suggests that there is such a thing as 'nature' that is differently carved by different theories, when Kuhn's stated position—at least in the above quotation and some other places—is that there is no such thing. On the other hand, he later describes his view as 'a sort of post-Darwinian Kantianism' (1990: 12), which makes 'crosscutting' seem a little more appropriate, in that it suggests that there is indeed *something*—namely the noumenal realm—that incommensurable theories carve up in different ways.

share the same basic physical constitution, which in turn explains their most salient characteristics—in the case of *water*-samples, the fact that they boil and freeze at certain temperatures, that they are clear, potable, and necessary to life, etc. Hence, the predicate 'is water' will apply (at a world-state) to precisely those quantities that have the physical constitution which, at the actual world-state, explains the salient features of (nearly) all paradigmatic *water*-samples. (2007: 330)

For Soames, then, the *same-substance* relation is determined by a shared 'basic physical constitution' that explains the 'most salient characteristics' of samples of the liquid or substance.

The problem I want to raise is best seen by considering a dispute between LaPorte and Alexander Bird over the issue of whether or not, prior to scientific investigation, the reference of 'water' was indeterminate, as LaPorte claims. LaPorte presents a thought experiment involving 'Deuterium Earth' (2004: 104–8). We are asked to imagine that inhabitants of a distant planet (DE) invite Earthlings for a visit, and Earthlings discover that, while the stuff flowing in the rivers and lakes of DE is a lot like water (it is certainly watery stuff), it has many different properties. For example, it is poisonous to animals brought to DE by the Earthlings, it melts and boils at different temperatures, and has been used by Deuterium Earthlings to create a powerful explosive weapon. As you might have guessed, the mysterious substance turns out to be D_2O. (Deuterium is an isotope of hydrogen, so D_2O is a species of H_2O.) In the light of the many differences between D_2O and the watery stuff here on Earth, the Earthling scientists come to the view that D_2O is not water. LaPorte argues that our imaginary Earthling scientists have not made any *mistake* in refusing to classify D_2O as water, and hence that *actual* scientists might, without error, have counted D_2O as falling outside the extension of 'water'. Hence 'water is H_2O', while necessary, is not *discovered* to be true but *stipulated* to be true, and so is not a posteriori.

In a later paper, LaPorte notes that 'D_2O is a form of H_2O with certain salient properties, that distinguish it from ordinary H_2O: drinking it will not sustain our biological processes, for example. D_2O behaves differently than ordinary H_2O in nuclear reactions, its ability to absorb radiation…, and across a range of other matters' (2010: 107). Hence—again—scientists might, without error, have counted D_2O as falling outside the extension of 'water'. Bird responds to LaPorte by appealing to the 'division of linguistic labour among scientists, such that it is the job of a particular subset of scientists to determine the facts concerning particular sorts of natural kinds … in the light of this, it will be chemical facts that determine the identity of substances' (2010: 127). And he claims that the relevant 'chemical facts' (structure, reactions, qualitative chemical properties, and so on) 'class D_2O with other kinds of H_2O' (ibid.). He is unmoved by the fact that, for example, pure D_2O is poisonous for many organisms and can be used in making powerful explosives, since 'these reasons [for not classifying D_2O as water] come from outside chemistry' and so 'are not pertinent to the science whose job it is to investigate the nature of and to classify water' (2010: 128).

Since my aim is to uncover the consequences of KP and not to question its truth, let's grant that Bird's response succeeds. It turns, in effect, on the claim that it is the specific job of chemists to determine the nature of the *same substance* relation. Indeed, Bird quotes Linus Pauling here: 'The different kinds of matter are called *substances*. Chemistry is the science of substances—their structure, their properties, and the reactions that change them into other substances' (Pauling 1970: 1).The problem is that Bird's response, if it is to succeed, makes the determination of the *same-NK* relation (here the *same-substance* relation) hostage to one of the very kinds of crosscutting that one might have hoped that KP would rule out, namely intrataxonomic crosscutting, as exemplified by chemical kinds such as *protein* and *enzyme*.There are, of course, no 'folk' terms associated with these kinds. Nonetheless, the terms were coined by scientists (in the 18th and 19th centuries) well before their 'essences' were discovered; correspondingly, experts could (fallibly) distinguish a protein from a non-protein, and an enzyme from a non-enzyme. Hence the terms 'protein' and 'enzyme' would seem ripe for delivering necessary a posteriori theoretical identities of the form 'a protein is . . . and 'an enzyme is . . .'; in which case, we have intrataxonomic crosscutting, consistent with KP.

One might object that the kind *enzyme* fails to satisfy the requirements of the *same-NK* relation. Enzymes are characterized in terms of the role they play in chemical reactions (they are catalysts), and do not have any unified underlying nature: most are globular proteins, but some are RNA molecules. But now the question is: why should we think that members of chemical kinds *must* share an underlying nature, in a way that would rule out *enzyme* from counting as a natural chemical kind? If, as Bird claims, the division of linguistic labour requires us to defer to chemists to work out what the essence of a natural kind is, and if chemists recognize *enzyme* as a legitimate kind (which they do), on what grounds could we rule out *enzyme* as counting as a genuine, crosscutting chemical kind? Of course, as we have seen, many natural kind essentialists claim that the *same-NK* relation—or at any rate the *same-substance* relation—is a matter of sameness of structure or constitution. But this—as the case of enzymes makes clear—is not a requirement that is delivered by chemistry itself.

It might be objected that I have here slipped from talking about the *same-substance* relation to talking about the *same chemical kind* relation, and that there is an important distinction between the two: albumin and the hairpin ribozyme are both enzymes, but they are not the same *substance*. So if we are concerned with the *same-substance* relation, as Bird is, we do not have a counter-example to the hierarchy requirement that bans intrataxonomic crosscutting.Well, grant that there is an ordinary, common-sense notion of 'substance', according to which albumin and the hairpin ribozyme are not the same substance. Nonetheless, there is *a* chemical kind of which they are both members, namely, *enzyme*. And if KP is to be extended in such a way as to deliver the natural kinds recognized by the sciences, then it simply cannot be restricted a priori to just those kinds that we pre-theoretically recognize as *substance* kinds. In other words, if we restrict our *categories*—the 'NK' in 'same NK'—to the vernacular (*substance, fruit, liquid*, and so on), KP will deliver only a tiny fraction of the necessary a posteriori theoretical identities required by natural kind essentialism.

This last point is important because it raises the issue with which the rest of this chapter will be concerned. Recall premise (1) of the *OK*-mechanism: 'It is necessarily the case that: something is a sample of water if and only if it is a sample of *dthat* (the same substance as *this* is a sample of)'. (1) thus appeals to the *same-substance* relation in its formulation. Putnam notes, in the cases of *same-liquid*, *same-fruit*, and so on, that '*liquid*' and '*fruit*' are 'markers' that 'may be explicit or implicit' (1975: 229). In the case of albumin and the hairpin ribozyme, what will the relevant 'marker' be?

We have a choice here. We could say that it is still the *same-substance* relation, where 'substance' is now no longer the pre-theoretical notion but a term of art from chemistry (though of course we would then have to distinguish different notions of 'substance' in order to distinguish those substances such as water and gold, for which (3) is true, and those 'substances' such as enzymes and proteins, for which some suitable substitute for (3) is true). Or we could keep the pre-theoretical notion of 'substance' and admit that it doesn't capture all the chemical kinds. In that case, we will in addition need to recognize not only the kinds *enzyme* and *protein*, but also something like *same-chemical-kind* in order to get KP off the ground for enzymes and proteins. Thus, for example, a suitable candidate for an analogue of (1) might be: 'It is necessarily the case that: something is an *enzyme* if and only if it is *of the same chemical kind* as *this* is a sample of'.

Either way, we will have to accept that deference to the taxonomy of chemistry is required in order to generate premise (1), for what *counts* as a chemical kind is, of course, a matter for chemistry to determine: it is simply not open to us, pre-theoretically, to determine what does and does not count as a chemical kind. This point will, I hope, become clearer in the next section.

6   Intertaxonomic crosscutting

Let's move on to intertaxonomic crosscutting, as exemplified by species pluralism. Here we have to move away from the *same-substance* relation, since of course biological kinds are not kinds of substance. What should we replace it with in the biological version of the OK-mechanism? As we have seen, Putnam takes the relevant relation to be the *same-animal* relation. We can think of *same-animal* as on a par with *same-substance*, in that the concept of an animal is a common-sense, pre-theoretical concept. Of course, Putnam says that the *same-liquid* relation is a '*theoretical* relation: whether something is or is not the same liquid as *this* may take an indeterminate amount of scientific investigation to determine' (1975: 225). Presumably he takes the same to hold for *same-animal* too. But that is not incompatible with saying that 'animal' is a pre-theoretical concept; someone with no knowledge of biology can point to two pigs and reasonably say 'this is the same animal as that' without having any idea what the *same-animal* relation consists in.

Well, since *same-animal* is allegedly a theoretical relation, in Putnam's sense, what, according to a biologist, does it consist in? The answer will surely be a shrug of the shoulders, since the question is simply not framed in a way that makes it answerable from the perspective of biological classification. Take elephants, for example. Is *this* (African) elephant the *same animal* as *that* (Asian) elephant? Well, the African and Asian elephants are members of different genera (*Loxodonta* and *Elephas*) of the same family (*Elephanti-dae*). So if by 'same animal' we mean 'same species' or 'same genus', the answer to the question, 'is this the same animal as that?' is 'no'; but if we mean 'same family', the answer is yes. It's pretty obvious that on our pre-theoretical understanding of 'same animal', whatever that is, it does not *mean* either of those things. So biology must do more than merely determine whether something is or is not the same animal as *this*; it must also, if KP is to have any connection with the natural kinds recognized by biology, supply the categories that fill in the 'NK' in 'same NK': not, as it turns out, *same animal*, but *same sub-species, same species, same genus*, and so on.

In fact, this point is implicit in more recent attempts to get KP off the ground for bio-logical kinds; in particular, both Soames and Salmon replace the *same-animal* relation with the *same-species* relation. Thus Soames says:

The term 'tiger' is to designate the species of animal of which (nearly) all members of the class of its paradigmatic samples are instances. Hence, the predicate 'is a tiger' will apply (at a world-state) to precisely those individuals that are members of the species of which (nearly) all para-digmatic *tiger*-samples are actually members. (2007: 330)

Note that Soames does not tell us what the *same-species* relation consists in; while he is happy to assert that 'substances are explanatory kinds instances of which share the same basic physical constitution, which in turn explains their most salient characteristics' (2007: 330), he says nothing at all about what sameness of species might amount to.

Salmon's own version of the *OK*-mechanism for tigers, on behalf of the defender of KP, runs as follows:

(1′) It is necessarily the case that: something is a *tiger* if and only if it is a member of *dthat* (the same species that *this* is a member of).
(2′) *This* has the biological class property of *being a mammal*.
(3′) Being a member of the same species as something consists (in part) in being a member of the same biological class.

Therefore,

(4′) It is necessarily the case that: all tigers are mammals.

So Salmon, like Soames, fixes on the *same-species* relation. Unlike Soames, he does say *something* about the necessary conditions for the relation to hold, namely, in effect, that species are part of a hierarchical taxonomic structure: in order for two animals to be members of the same species, they must both equally be members of the same higher-level biological class—in the case of tigers, this is *Mammalia*.

Now, Salmon's primary interest is in whether or not (3′) (or rather, the inter-world version thereof) can be known wholly a posteriori; and his conclusion is that it cannot, roughly because it is unclear how empirical investigation might deliver knowledge of inter-world *same-NK* relations, even if it delivers knowledge of *intra*-world *same-NK* relations. My interest is different: my claim is that (3′)—and indeed (1′)—cannot so much as be *stated* without deploying the (or a) classificatory framework of biology. We need to appeal to that framework in order to have at our disposal the appropriate 'marker' or category *NK* in 'the same *NK* that *this* is a member of'. In other words, biological science, and the classificatory framework(s) it deploys, is needed not merely to tell us what the *same-species* relation *consists* in (or has as a necessary condition); it is needed to provide us with the very concept of *species* required for the *OK*-mechanism to get off the ground. Or at least it does if KP is to work out for the natural kind terms recognized by biology.

Why is this so? Simply because *species* is not (at least not in the sense required for the KP to do the work it is supposed to do) a pre-theoretical notion. The pre-theoretical notion of a species is simply the notion of a *kind* (or perhaps the notion of a sub-kind, as in '*x* is a species of *y*', where *y* is a higher-order kind of which *x* is a sub-kind); and that, as we saw in the case of *same-animal*, is not good enough. For we need a substitute for '*NK*' in '*same NK*'—that is, we need a category—that is sufficiently fine-grained to yield a determinate answer to the question, 'is *this* the same *NK* as *that*?' Without that, no determinate kind has been identified, such that the essence of that kind can be established. And the notion of *species* that is sufficiently fine-grained to play that role is not the ordinary, pre-theoretic concept of *species*, but the biological concept of *species*, which occupies a determinate level (between *genus* and *subspecies*) in biological taxonomy. Moreover, *species* will not deliver all the required necessary a posteriori truths we need. We need also to be able to run the *OK*-mechanism for elephants, for example, so that our elephant version of the *OK*-mechanism runs: 'It is necessarily the case that: something is an *elephant* if and only if it is a member of *dthat* (the same . . . that *this* is a member of)', where the blank can only be filled in by 'family'. So, again, we need to appeal to the classificatory framework of biology in order to get KP off the ground.

We are now in a position to see that KP and species pluralism are compatible, and hence that KP is compatible with intertaxonomic crosscutting. By way of a foil, consider why someone might be inclined to think that the two are *not* compatible. In order to deliver necessary a posteriori theoretical identities of the form 'substance *S* is . . .' ('gold is the element with atomic number 79'), or 'all *T*s are . . .' ('all tigers are . . .', where the blanks are filled in with a specification of the essence of, or a necessary condition on, tigerhood), where '*S*' and '*T*' are vernacular kind terms, it must surely be the case that the vernacular term designates *one* substance or species or whatever: a single natural kind. For recall premise (1′) of the *OK*-mechanism that generates the necessary a posteriority of 'all tigers are mammals': it is necessarily true that: something is a *tiger* if and only if it is a member of *the* same species that *this* is a member of. But if species pluralism were true, there would be no such thing as *the*, unique, *same species* relation. Rather there would be, say, the *same species*$_M$ relation, the *same species*$_B$ relation, and the *same species*$_P$ relation, corresponding to the morphological, biological, and phylogenetic conceptions of species respectively. Hence, one might argue, 'something is a *tiger* if and only if it is a member of the same species that *this* is a member of' would, if species pluralism were true, simply be indeterminate in truth-value (or perhaps false), and so would not be necessarily true. Hence (1′) would be false and the *OK*-mechanism couldn't get off the ground.

Unfortunately, this defence of the claim that species pluralism is incompatible with KP fails in the face of the claim defended above, that appeal to the classificatory framework of biology is required in order to furnish us with the categories that can replace '*NK*' in '*same NK*'. If that claim is right, then the correct way to run the *OK*-mechanism is not to start out with (1′) itself, since this deploys the vernacular or near-vernacular term, 'same species'. Rather, we must fill in the blank in 'same . . . as this is a member of' by appealing to the appropriate category, as enshrined in the 'correct' classificatory framework for biology. Species pluralism, if true, entails that there is not just one *same species* relation, for example, but several: *same species$_M$*, *same species$_B$*, and *same species$_P$*, say. This generates three distinct versions of (1′): 'it is necessarily true that: something is a *tiger* if and only if it is a member of the same species$_M$ that *this* is a member of' is one; replacing 'species$_M$' with 'species$_B$' and 'species$_P$' delivers the other two versions of (1′). And now we can run the *OK*-mechanism and end up with our necessary a posteriori truth.

My conclusion, then, is that—*pace* Dupré—KP is compatible with species pluralism. In case this seems implausible from the perspective of KP, it is worth reiterating that the kind of line defended above is required by KP in any case, even if species pluralism is false, if KP is to apply to biological kinds at all. *Subspecies, species, genus*, and so on are no part of pre-theoretical common-sense classification. Pre-theoretical classification arguably does involve some degree of hierarchy: we might recognize, for instance, that a tabby cat and a Manx cat are both kinds of domestic moggy, and that the domestic moggy, tigers, and lions are all kinds of cat. But we have no pre-theoretic grasp of where the levels of biological classification lie: no pre-theoretical grasp of whether, say, *tabby* and *Manx* are species or subspecies, or whether *elephant* is a genus of a family. It is not currently known, even by biologists, whether the African forest elephant is a subspecies of the African elephant, or whether the African forest and bush elephants are distinct species. So the defender of KP must in any case take it that we defer to biologists to determine *which* biological kind (species, genus, etc.) is to replace the placeholder '*NK*' in '*same NK*'.

7 Interparadigm crosscutting

Finally, let's consider the most radical kind of crosscutting: interparadigm crosscutting. As I noted earlier, Putnam (1975) explicitly takes his version of KP to undercut Kuhnian relativism by securing stability of reference across theory change. As we have seen, LaPorte (2004, 2010) agrees, but seeks to undermine KP: he argues that a broadly causal story about reference-fixing is consistent with a degree of 'vagueness' of reference at the pre-scientific stage at which reference (of, say, 'water' or 'gold') is fixed by the folk; the meaning of the term is then precisified by scientists at the point at which a decision needs to be made. Hence scientists do not *discover* the essence of (say) water, but rather stipulate a new meaning.

LaPorte's basic claim, then, is that a broadly causal theory of reference need not deliver necessary a posteriori theoretical identities: according to LaPorte, in effect, premise (3) in the *OK*-mechanism is secured by stipulation rather than discovery.[12] In contrast to LaPorte, I want to argue that, even if we grant the necessary a posteriori status of theoretical identities, we do not necessarily secure referential stability: nothing in KP, just by itself, rules out interparadigm crosscutting, which I defined in Section 4 as the thesis that the theoretical terms of successive scientific paradigms are incommensurable, so that there is no fact of the matter about which of the incommensurable classificatory systems carves nature up 'correctly'.

Putnam's basic thought is that referential stability is secured by semantic externalism. If we abandon the view that the reference of 'gold' is fixed by a description, then the change in description that goes along with a change in theory need not amount to any change in reference. When we move from thinking of gold as (say) a yellow, malleable metal to being the element with atomic number 79, there is no shift in meaning of the term 'gold', since the meaning of 'gold' is just its reference, and that remains constant: we're still referring to the same *substance*, we just take a different view of what it's like. More precisely, in this case we move from not knowing the essence of gold but only knowing some criteria by which gold can reasonably reliably be distinguished from non-gold to knowing its essence (or at least having a reasonable but nonetheless fallible belief about its essence).

It might seem *obvious* that all this is incompatible with interparadigm crosscutting. After all, if the meaning of 'gold' is just its reference, then of course changes in theory cannot change the reference of 'gold': gold remains the same substance, whatever our theories happen to say about it. But recall the basic point developed so far. If the semantic category of natural kind terms is to have any systematic connection with the kinds recognized by the sciences, deference to science cannot amount merely to the discovery of what it is to stand in the *same-NK* relation, where '*NK*' is some pre-scientific category (*substance, animal*, etc.). Instead, science must also be deferred to when it comes to specifying the value of '*NK*': scientific enquiry reveals that the relevant relations are not merely *same substance, same animal*, and so on, but also *same kind of subatomic particle, same chemical kind, same genus*, and so on—and, if species pluralism is true, also *same species$_M$*, *same species$_B$*, and *same species$_P$*, or whatever.

The problem now is that, with this degree of linguistic deference to science on the table, it is far from obvious that the resources of KP, just by themselves, are sufficient to ward off the threat of relativism. Putnam's anti-relativist move depends on the assumption that gold in 1973 is the *same substance* as gold in 437 BC; all that's changed is the

<hr />

[12] Robin Hendry (2010) argues that LaPorte's claim about 'water' doesn't generalize, and that whether a given term fits the model of KP must be decided on a case-by-case basis; in particular, he argues that 'oxygen' *does* fit the KP model.

extent of our knowledge of its nature. In other words, it depends on the claim that there is a theory-neutral sense of *same substance*, such that changes in theory are powerless to change what it *is* for one thing to be the same substance as another. We can grant that there is indeed a set of pre-theoretical categories (*substance, liquid, animal, fruit*) that resist referential instability. But, as we have seen, such categories on their own will not get the defender of KP what they need, in the context of marrying up the semantic category of natural kind terms with the natural kinds recognized by science. For that, we need distinctively theoretical categories. And of course such categories are apt to change as the theories within which they are categories are replaced by different theories with different taxonomic structures.

The defender of Kuhnian relativism can, I claim, hold that such changes deliver genuine changes in reference of the kind terms involved, *consistent with KP*. Take chemistry. As things currently stand, in a period of what Kuhn calls 'normal science', let's suppose that KP works out as normal. Some new kind of stuff is discovered, given a name, and its essence is then revealed by chemical analysis, delivering us a necessary a posteriori theoretical identity. All well and good. But this presupposes a classificatory framework that comes from chemistry itself: *same element, same chemical kind, same organic compound*, and so on. Without that classificatory framework, there is no way to fill the placeholder '*NK*' in '*same-NK*' that can make sense of the vast range of natural kinds that chemistry tells us there are.

Now imagine some seismic change in the classificatory framework of chemistry. The new framework, let us imagine, simply does not recognize the categories *element, catalyst, organic compound*, and so on at all, and replaces them with new categories that carve up the terrain in very different ways. More generally, the category *chemical kind* now incorporates very different subspecies. So, for example, we can no longer say truthfully, pointing at two samples of proteins, that they are *of the same chemical kind*, because the new framework recognizes no kind of which both our samples are members. But we can still, from within the new framework, perfectly happily go about the business of identifying substances or objects and discovering the essences of the kinds to which they belong (although of course this project will not be fully distinct from the project of discovering which kinds they belong to).

The Kuhnian relativist will characterize this situation as one in which the natural kinds have *changed*: it is not that the *same* kind of substance or entity has been discovered to have different essence to the one we thought it had; rather, the old kind has genuinely ceased to exist, and has been replaced with another kind. After all, if it is the *same* kind of substance or entity, *which* kind of substance or entity, exactly, would that be? Not the same *chemical* kind, because the old chemical kinds are no longer a part of the classificatory framework of chemistry. Albumin and rennin would not both be enzymes, and hydrogen and deuterium would not both be isotopes of the same element, because such categories, we are imagining, have ceased to apply.

My claim here is not that Kuhnian relativism is a defensible position. It is rather that relativism—which is to say, interparadigm crosscutting—is *consistent* with KP: we simply relativize the *same-NK* relations to the classificatory framework enshrined by a given paradigm. Hence KP, on its own, does not have the resources to defeat relativism.

It might be thought that such a conception of *same-NK* relations is incompatible with semantic externalism in general, and so *must* be incompatible with KP in particular. For surely the very basis of semantic externalism is the thought that the meaning of a natural kind term is *just* its referent: a mind-independent object or substance whose existence and nature is independent of our theoretical claims *about* it. But the existence of such fully mind-independent entities is in no way *secured* by the casual theory of reference. All that the causal theory of reference requires is that reference is secured via causal interaction rather than by description; and so far as I can tell there is nothing in Kuhnian relativism that is incompatible with that claim.[13] Of course, we might add to KP a healthy dose of metaphysical realism, and insist that the causal interactions that underpin reference to natural kinds are interactions with fully theory-independent objects and substances. But that would be to make an independent metaphysical assumption—one that is in no way entailed by KP just by itself.

8 Nontrivial essentialism revisited

In Section 3 I raised the question: how nontrivial is nontrivial essentialism? My answer was 'not very'—at least by the lights of contemporary metaphysics, where *de re* modality is virtually *de rigueur*. I also suggested an analogy with Paul's distinction between 'deep' and 'shallow' essentialism about individuals. In the light of the discussion above, we might define 'shallow' essentialism for natural kinds as the view, not that natural kind essences are relative to context (this is Lewis's shallow essentialist position when it comes to the essences of individuals), but that they are relative to the taxonomic hierarchy enshrined within a particular scientific theory.

KP is entirely consistent with 'shallow' essentialism thus defined. Thus, for example, the question of what birds essentially are—where *bird* is a natural kind—might depend on which taxonomic structure we presuppose: there may turn out to be no uniquely best or correct taxonomic structure that provides a single, correct answer to that question. Nothing in KP, I have argued, rules this out. Similarly, there may be no unique, theory-independent answer to whether *this* substance is of the same (natural) chemical kind as *that* one, since, consistent with KP, what constitutes sameness of chemical kind will, if Kuhnian relativism is true, be relative to the taxonomy of a particular paradigm.

I turn, finally, to Brian Ellis's scientific essentialism. As we saw in Section 2, Ellis claims that '[m]etaphysically necessary propositions... are true in virtue of the essential natures of things' (2001: 235)—and that the mark of metaphysical necessity is that it is not 'grounded in... descriptive language' (ibid.), so that the necessity of 'water is H_2O' 'survives' when we replace 'water' with 'this stuff'. If the argument of this chapter is correct,

---

[13] Note in this regard that the Putnam of *Reason, Truth and History* (1981) abandons metaphysical realism but not the causal theory of reference.

however, Ellis has no grounds for thinking that 'non-descriptive' necessity is the mark of necessity that is *grounded* in 'the essential natures of things'. Consider again shallow essentialism, as applied to individuals. On that view—or at least on Lewis's version of it—while of course a proposition that expresses the essence of some object (Humphrey, say) will be metaphysically necessary, there is no substantive metaphysical sense in which the necessity is 'grounded in' Humphrey's essential nature. For his essential nature is grounded in the obtaining of the appropriate counterpart relation, and this in turn is a context-relative matter. There is nothing about *Humphrey*, considered in himself in isolation from his counterparts, that grounds any metaphysical necessity whatever.

The same point applies to shallow essentialism about natural kinds—which, I have argued, is entirely compatible with KP. On a shallow conception of natural kind essences, the natural kinds that *have* those essences are relativized to the taxonomic structures within which the relevant kind terms play a role: there is no theory-independent *same-kind* relation, and so there are no theory-independent 'essential natures', that might serve as the grounds for metaphysical necessity. Scientific theories do not, on the shallow conception of kind essences, latch onto fully mind-independent essences any more than do claims about *Humphrey's* essence on the shallow, Lewisian view of individual essences. To put the point another way, KP—and the a posteriori necessity that it delivers—does not entail that kind essences are mind- or language-independent *simpliciter*, which is the result Ellis needs. It entails only that what is metaphysically necessary and what is epistemically necessary can come apart in the case of natural kinds. But, as Lewis's shallow essentialism so clearly demonstrates, metaphysical necessity may itself fail to be a fully mind- and language-independent matter. Contrary to what Ellis claims, analyticity is not the only way for necessary truths to depend on us: KP does not, just by itself, deliver the mind- and language-independence of natural kind essences.[14]

This is not, of course, to say that KP *demands* only a shallow kind of essentialism, for of course KP is also entirely compatible with deeper forms of essentialism that are often—mistakenly, I have argued—taken to be a consequence of it. One might, for example, hold that the truly natural kinds obey the hierarchy requirement, or one might ward off the threat of Kuhnian relativism by presupposing metaphysical realism. My claim is only that these deeper forms of essentialism about natural kinds enshrine metaphysical assumptions that are independent of KP. Thus those who wish to embrace intrataxonomic crosscutting, or species pluralism, or even Kuhnian relativism do not need to take a stand against KP; they merely need to challenge the relevant additional metaphysical assumptions.

---

[14] Nor, according to some authors, is *a posteriority* required for 'real' necessity, in Ellis's sense that necessity is grounded in essence rather than vice versa; see for example Fine 1994 and Oderberg 2007.

8

Are natural kinds and natural properties distinct?

Emma Tobin

Introduction

What is it for a set of objects to form a kind, beyond sharing natural properties? To say that a kind is *natural* is to say that it corresponds to a grouping that is independent of human classifications. This grouping reflects a natural division in nature. Likewise, to say that properties are natural is to say that there are entirely mind-independent similarities between things. If we grant some distinction between natural and non-natural properties, is a supplementary distinction between natural properties and natural kinds required?[1] In other words, is there any more to natural kind classification than mind-independent similarities between things?

On the one hand, one might argue that natural kinds and natural properties are not distinct; namely, some account of natural kinds can be given solely in terms of natural properties. In other words, natural kinds do not require a distinct ontological category because an ontology of properties is sufficient. For example, a Lewisian account of natural kinds might be extrapolated, where natural kinds are identified with the perfectly natural properties (Lewis 1999). Alternatively, natural kinds might be considered reducible to properties (or at least to property conjuncts), where properties are construed as universals (Armstrong 1978, 1997, 1999). Yet another way would be to consider natural kinds to be the extensions of properties. For example, natural kinds might be understood as sets (Quine 1969). On any of these views, I will argue that an ontological account of properties suffices for natural kind classification.

---

[1] Katherine Hawley, in her keynote paper, a talk entitled 'Natural Kinds and Natural Properties', proposed this very question at the AHRC Metaphysics of Science Conference in Nottingham on 13 September 2009.

'Suppose we accept a distinction between natural and nonnatural properties, or at least a scale from more to less natural properties. Do we also need natural kinds?' (Handout)

The question is subsequently addressed in Hawley and Bird (2011).

On the other hand, one might argue that natural kinds and natural properties are distinct. In other words, natural kinds require a distinct ontological category over and above the category of properties. For example, natural kinds could be considered as a *sui generis* type of entity. One way of arguing for this view is to claim that natural kinds themselves have essences or relatedly, natural kinds require a distinct kind of universal, substantival universal, or sortal (e.g. Ellis 2001; Lowe 2006; Strawson 1997). Yet another way of claiming that natural kinds themselves require a category is to say that the properties themselves form natural kind groupings; in virtue of causal mechanisms (Boyd 1999b; Machamer et al. 2000). An example is homeostatic property cluster theory; the view that natural kinds form real property clusters in virtue of homeostatic mechanisms (Boyd 1999a).

This chapter examines each of these views in turn. Section 1 provides a preliminary introduction to natural kinds and properties. Section 2 addresses the claim that natural kinds and natural properties are not distinct. Three views are considered: (.1) natural kinds are the perfectly natural properties, (.2) natural kinds are reducible to property universals, and (.3) natural kinds are the extensions of properties (e.g. sets).

Section 3 examines the claim that natural kinds and natural properties are distinct. In this context, the view that natural kinds are a *sui generis* type of entity is considered. The most accepted way of arguing for this view is to claim that natural kinds have essences. Section 3.1 examines three metaphysical accounts of the essence of natural kinds; namely, the view expressed in Section 3.1.1, that the essences of natural kind are universals, and second, in Section 3.1.2, that natural kind essences are sortals. Third, in Section 3.1.3 the view that natural kinds are causal essences (e.g. property clusters) is considered. In the final analysis, this chapter argues that classification into natural kinds can reflect real differences between natural groups, without the supplementary ontological distinction between properties and kinds. Thus, an ontological distinction between natural kinds and properties is not required.

1 Natural kinds and natural properties

1.1 What are natural kinds?

Natural kind classifications are considered to be *natural* classifications or as is often claimed in Plato's terminology, natural kinds 'carve nature at its joints' (*Phaedrus*, 265d–266a).[2] The naturalness of kinds makes them projectible; the observation of some instance of a natural kind *Ka*, licenses the inference that any future instance of *K* will be similar to *Ka* and gives credence to the belief that any future *K* will be similar to *Ka*.

---

[2] In *Phaedrus*, 265d–266a, Plato compares the task of defining a universal to the job of being a butcher. The inexperienced butcher just cuts the meat up however he sees fit, but the expert butcher slices the animal at its natural joints, those distinct segments already objectively existing in each member of the species involved. This realist view of taxonomizing species is one that is often rejected in modern discussions of the species problem. This will be briefly discussed in the next subsection.

One reason for thinking that natural kinds support induction is the intuition that if kind predicates do pick out natural divisions (kinds), then this fact guarantees that past instances will successfully guide our inference towards future ones. Thus, the postulated existence of natural kinds lies at the very core of our scientific inferences and practices.[3]

Most famously, the issue of natural kinds was brought to the fore as a question regarding the reference of natural kind terms. Conventionalists argue that there is no theory neutral way of classifying natural kinds. Kuhn (1970), for example claimed that the term 'mass' as it occurs in Newtonian mechanics has a different referent to the term 'mass' as it occurs in relativistic mechanics because Newtonian mass is conserved, whereas Einsteinian is convertible with energy. They are classified relative to the background paradigm.

This relies on an empiricist conception of the referential semantics of scientific terms; namely, *descriptivism*: the referent of a term is picked out by a description (Frege 1892; Russell 1905). According to descriptivist theories of reference, the speaker grasps the sense of a term internally and the sense determines the reference. For Kuhn, the description gives a definition for the scientific term, within the context of a background theoretical paradigm. The definition of a scientific term is given by the laws, which contain the term in the scientific theory.

In contrast, theories of reference originating with Kripke (1972) and Putnam (1973, 1975) argued for an externalist semantics for natural kind terms, where the meaning of terms is not just a matter of being in a certain psychological state. Putnam's (1975) famous slogan 'meanings just ain't in the head' signified a referential turn. The twin earth thought experiment presented a case where two senses, though considered the same, did not determine one and the same referent. The reference of 'water' on Earth is H_2O, but the reference of 'water' on twin earth is XYZ. So, XYZ satisfies all the descriptions we associate with the *meaning* of 'water' as used on Earth and thus, it has the same sense as our term water on earth. Yet, the reference of the term on Earth excludes XYZ. Putnam concludes that XYZ is not water. We can only discover the meaning of 'water' by a posteriori means. Thus, the meaning of scientific terms does not come from our concepts or our descriptions, but rather from the causal structure of the world.

Kripke and Putnam's semantic theories also *seem* to imply a metaphysical thesis about natural kinds; namely, the referents of our terms are determined externally, because natural kinds have the properties that they do.[4] In the case of natural kinds, a natural kind

---

[3] Bird (2009) argues that natural kind classifications cannot merely be those that permit inductions, because we can make inductions about natural properties (e.g. objects with the property of electric charge). Bird claims that natural kinds are the richest source of inductive knowledge. He states that natural kinds are: 'marked by the confluence of several natural properties, such that membership of the kind can be inductively inferred from knowledge that a particular possesses some subset of those properties, which in turn permits an inductive inference to the remainder of the properties associated with the kind.' (Bird 2009: 6)

[4] The relationship between the semantics of natural kind terms and the essentialist metaphysics of the kinds themselves has been contested by Salmon (Salmon 1979, 1982). See Bird and Tobin (2008) for a more elaborate discussion.

term will be linked to a kind in virtue of a causal link to some *instance* of that kind. It would seem that in order for the term to link to further members of the kind, there must be something that those members have in common. In other words, the best explanation for why kind terms continue to successfully refer is because every instance of a given natural kind has properties that are essential to it. These properties constitute the essence of the kind. Thus, some philosophers (e.g. Wilkerson 1995 and Ellis 2001) have extrapolated an essentialist metaphysics for natural kinds from the Kripke/Putnam semantics.

1.2 Natural kinds and scientific kinds

Despite the later metaphysical turn, the relationship between natural kinds and proper-ties is made problematic by considering examples of putative scientific kinds from natural science. There has been much discussion of the issue of natural kinds in philosophy of biology, where the view that biological species are natural kinds has been largely rejected (Ghiselin 1974; Hull 1965). Indeed, even those theorists who accept that there are natural kinds in other domains (e.g. chemistry and physics) often argue that the division between biological species is ultimately arbitrary:

If evolution occurs in the gradual way that Darwin supposed, or if small changes in genetic constitution can be brought about artificially, then the distinctions between adjacent species— living, dead or yet to be created—must ultimately be arbitrary. (Ellis 2001: 169)

The empirical fact of evolution alone is not the only reason for scepticism about bio-logical natural kinds. Another compelling reason is the fact that biological species are divided up differently by different taxonomic systems in biology. This makes it even more difficult to divide biological species simply into natural kinds, since biological spe-cies are divided into kinds in virtue of whatever properties are deemed appropriate by whichever taxonomic system is being used. For example, morphological properties are of chief importance when applying the morphological species concept, but the capacity to interbreed is more important when applying the interbreeding species concept. Thus, there appears to be no fact of the matter concerning which taxonomic system is the most natural; namely, which system delineates the real biological species.

Nevertheless and in contrast, at the level of microbiology and biochemistry natural kinds are considered less controversial, according to Ellis. Ellis (2001), while rejecting the view that species are natural kinds, nevertheless insists for example that biomolecules are natural kinds. He states:

Most of the processes described by biochemists and microbiologists are processes belonging to natural kinds. [...] The cells and cell structures are natural kinds of things. (Ellis 2001: 168)

Similarly, the putative scientific natural kinds in chemistry and physics are considered to be the least controversial. Consider, for example, the chemical natural kind, calcium. Calcium is a naturally occurring element—a major material for example in bones and shells. It has certain superficial properties, for example it is a soft, grey, metallic element.

It also has microstructural properties; it has the atomic number 20 and an atomic mass of 40.078 amu. Additionally, it has dispositional properties; it has a high reactivity with water and air, and high electrical conductivity.

Nevertheless, even in this case a natural question arises from these considerations concerning the properties of calcium: is there something additional to classification of the natural kind calcium, than a simple grouping together of these salient properties? Moreover, since it is the property of atomic number which individuates the chemical elements *qua* natural kind, because the atomic number is considered necessary and sufficient for chemical kind membership, then why is it not the property of atomic number that is considered fundamental for chemical classification? Hence, is chemical kind classification required over and above the property of atomic number?

Moreover, *pace* Ellis, the relationship between chemical kinds and their properties is even more difficult to assess at higher levels of chemical composition; namely compounds, mixtures, and macromolecules, where the composing parts are often used up in the chemical reactions which result in chemical synthesis. This makes the precise relationship between complex kinds and their composing parts less straightforward.[5] Thus, a proper analysis of the relationship between chemical kinds and their properties is required.

Furthermore, the distinction between kinds and properties can even be questioned where fundamental physics is considered. Take as an example one of the fundamental particles, the fermions. Fermions are fundamental particles, which obey the Pauli exclusion principle: two fermions cannot occupy the same quantum state as each other. The Pauli principle *only* applies to fermions, because they form anti-symmetric quantum states and have a half-integer spin. Thus, given a complete understanding of the property of spin and the restrictions imposed by the Pauli exclusion principle, do we need to categorize the fermions as natural kinds over and above these facts? In other words, an ontology composed of laws and properties would seem to suffice for a thorough categorization of the fermions.[6]

Other considerations from physics may lead to further scepticism about requiring a natural kind category. For example, the well-known two-slit experiment in quantum mechanics suggests that we must accept both that Schrödinger waves are real on the one hand and that they do not behave as waves on the other (they act locally and behave like classical particles).[7] Thus, to construe Schrödinger waves as natural kinds of classical particle would be a misleading oversimplification.

A glimpse at candidate natural kinds from the natural sciences suggests that the precise relationship between natural kinds and properties requires a proper analysis. Indeed,

[5] See Hendry (2006) and Tobin (2010) for a discussion. For example, any sample of water can survive the destruction of any of the individual H_2O molecules that compose it.
[6] The issue of whether Pauli's exclusion principle should be considered a law of nature goes beyond the scope of this chapter.
[7] See Ellis (2009 ch. 4) for a discussion.

an examination of the relationship between natural kinds and their properties is required to understand even those often considered as the least controversial examples of natural kinds; namely the chemical elements and the fundamental particles.

In the literature, the debate about natural kinds has often been discussed as though it is orthogonal to the corresponding ontological debate about properties. A closer consideration of properties, however, reveals that in fact the two debates should be considered in tandem. Thus, it is worth exploring the possible relationship between natural kinds and properties in more detail. This is what I propose to do in the remainder of the chapter. Before discussing this relationship, the next subsection will introduce the ontological debate regarding properties.

1.3 What are properties?

Properties include the attributes, qualities, features, and characteristics of things. Of course, philosophers disagree greatly about which properties exist. Most theorists will agree for example that my chair now has the property of having a certain mass and that this property is a mind-independent feature of the object, while properties like *being a chair* are more controversial. But, it is a feature of properties that they are *general* and so can be instantiated by more than one individual and thus, philosophers have been interested in properties that are repeatedly instantiated. Thus, being a chair can be instantiated by more than one individual over time. The traditional realism versus nominalism debate about properties is an ontological debate over whether in order to account for properties (e.g. being a chair), we need to invoke an additional category of entity, namely universals. Realism about properties considers properties to be mind-independent.

There is an additional debate on whether realism is justified in relation to all kinds of properties. Lewis (1986a) for example, insists upon a distinction between natural and non-natural properties. In his terminology, the distinction is between sparse and abundant properties (Lewis 1986a). There is an ontological difference between abundant properties and sparse properties. Abundant properties are not genuine entities at all. The abundant properties merely reflect our predicates and should not be construed as natural in the proper sense. He states:

The abundant properties may be as extrinsic, as gruesomely gerrymandered, as miscellaneously disjunctive as you please. They pay no heed to the qualitative joints, but carve things up every which way. Sharing of them has nothing to do with qualitative similarity. (Lewis 1986a: 59)

On the other hand, sparse properties must be qualitatively similar parts of the world.

Sharing of them makes for qualitative similarity, they carve at the joints, they are intrinsic, they are highly specific, the sets of their instances are *ipso facto* not entirely miscellaneous, there are only just enough of them to characterise things completely and without redundancy. (Lewis 1986a: 59)

A natural question arises from this distinction: if sparse properties also 'carve natures at their joints' because of qualitative similarity, then how are they different to natural kinds?

Or putting it the other way around, are the natural kinds just the same as the subset of properties that we call the sparse properties? Clearly, the debates about natural kinds and natural properties are inextricably linked.

Schaffer (2004) has posed an interesting additional question regarding sparse properties; namely, are sparse properties drawn from all of the levels of nature or just the fundamental level? He distinguishes two conceptions; the first is the scientific conception of the sparse properties, which allows any property at any level, which is delineated by our scientific understanding of the world, to be a sparse property. On the other hand, he distinguishes the fundamental conception, where the sparse properties are only those properties that are delineated by our most fundamental level of scientific understanding: namely, fundamental physics. In Schaffer's terminology, should the fundamentalist conception of sparse properties override our scientific one? If we answer yes, then it would seem that some properties are *more* natural than others; namely, the fundamental sparse properties are the most natural of the broader category of scientific sparse properties.

So then if we take it as primitive that some properties are natural regardless of your preferred ontology (e.g. universals/tropes etc.) and we also accept that some properties are more natural/fundamental than others, then the natural kinds, for example, might be considered as a subclass of properties: the *natural sparse* properties. Thinking about natural kinds in this way will lead to the claim that natural kinds and natural properties should not be considered as ontologically distinct.

2 Natural kinds and natural properties are not distinct

2.1 Natural kinds are the perfectly natural properties

Lewis (1999) reasons in precisely this way, carving nature at its joints is a matter of discovering the perfectly natural properties. From the claim that some natural properties are considered more natural than others, Lewis argues that naturalness permits of degrees. In other words, there is a scale of naturalness for properties. On this view, some natural properties (e.g. fundamental physical properties) are more elite than others; namely, the perfectly natural properties. In addition to positing the perfectly natural properties, Lewis posits a relation of more and less natural on properties. The perfectly natural properties are those whose members all resemble one another, less natural properties are classes of properties whose members do not all resemble one another. He states:

physics discovers which things and classes are the most elite of all; but others are elite also, though to a lesser degree. The less elite are so because they are connected to the most elite by chains of definability. Long chains, by the time we reach the moderately elite classes of cats and pencils and puddles; but the chains required to reach the utterly ineligible would be far longer still. (Lewis 1999: 66)

For Lewis, the elite class are the sparse properties, those delineated primarily he says by fundamental physics. Thus, for Lewis the perfectly natural properties are primitive, and the naturalness of all other properties can be defined in terms of them.

A natural question that might be raised then is whether natural kinds too can be defined in terms of the naturalness of perfectly natural properties. In other words, can the kind electron be defined in terms of the perfectly natural property of negative charge? The relationship between kinds and properties on this view can be defined in the following way:

(1) **Two objects are members of the same kind *iff* they have the same perfectly natural properties.**

Furthermore, this Lewisian framework provides a perfectly legitimate reductive analysis of kinds in terms of their constituent properties.

Among all the countless things and classes that there are, most are miscellaneous, gerrymandered, ill-demarcated. Only an elite minority are carved at the joints, so that their boundaries are established by objective sameness and difference in nature. Only these elite things and classes are eligible to serve as referents. (Lewis 1984: 227)

Natural properties then are those grounded in objective sameness and difference in nature. These are the elite minority that carve nature at its joints; namely, the sparse properties.

On this view, naturalness is derived. Any property connected to one of the most elite sparse properties by a chain of definability, derives its naturalness from it. Yet, many (perhaps most?) scientific kinds are conjunctive properties. Take for example, the much-discussed example of H_2O, a paradigmatic example of a natural kind in the Kripke/Putnam tradition. Any H_2O molecule is composed of hydrogen and oxygen in the ratio 2:1. Each of the chemical components can themselves be divided into their component parts. The naturalness of any of these chemical kinds must be derived from the naturalness of their fundamental physical properties, even if in practice, it is difficult to give an exhaustive account of the quantum properties of chemical elements.[8]

An additional problem arises in that even some fundamental particles are themselves conjunctive in that they have more than one property. Consider for example elementary particles. Mesons are composed of one quark and one antiquark, for example. But, if such kinds are defined purely in terms of their perfectly natural properties, then the *naturalness* of conjunctive properties is derived from the naturalness of the properties

---

[8] This is even more problematic when we consider the classification of molecules as natural kinds. Recent discussions in the philosophy of chemistry have revealed how problematic it is to map molecular shape to quantum chemistry. For example, a molecule is described within quantum mechanics in terms of its Schrödinger equation. The problem is that this description at the quantum level involves a massive idealization, in that the only forces considered relevant are electrostatic forces. Now the problem is that this idealization presents Coloumbic Hamiltonians as symmetric, but molecules have an asymmetric charge distribution. Thus, relating molecules to Hamiltonians is not simple, since the classification of their properties at the quantum level differs to the classification of their core properties at the molecular level.

that compose them. If this is the case, then it is not their naturalness *qua* kinds that makes natural kinds natural, but rather the naturalness of their composing properties. Thus, the Lewisian framework reduces kinds to properties.

This view has the rather odd consequence that some natural kinds should be considered as more natural than others. Admitting degrees of naturalness means that naturalness is a relative notion. But, it certainly appears odd to think that some natural kinds are *more* natural than others. Are bosons *more* natural than water molecules? As we saw earlier, since antiquity the popular intuition regarding natural kinds is that kinds carve nature at the joints. Allowing naturalness to admit of degrees also means that natural kinds must admit of degrees. Thus, natural kindhood appears to become a matter of degree, insofar as some natural kinds must be considered as more natural than others.

Moreover, the lack of a common objective criterion for determining what counts as a natural kind entails that there are no significant criteria for distinguishing between the natural and the non-natural kinds. On what grounds could one maintain that whilst water molecules are more natural than bosons, both are natural kinds, whereas a kind such as 'multiple personality sufferers' does not delineate a natural kind?

To the reductionist, however, this kind of criticism is not worrisome. The reductionist will admit that bosons are indeed to be considered more natural than water molecules. The naturalness of kinds is derived from the naturalness of conjunctive properties, which is in turn derived from the naturalness of the conjuncts. Cutting nature at its joints is a matter of finding the *most* perfectly natural properties. In the final analysis, only the kinds in physics will count as *REAL* natural kinds (e.g. the fundamental particles delineated by the standard model such as the electron, tau neutrino, charm quark, and so on).

If we accept this, then we have to accept that most of the putative scientific kinds that are presently postulated by science (e.g. the chemical elements, molecules and macromolecules, planets, species, and so on) are not *REAL* natural kinds. Carving nature at its joints is a matter of discovering their microstructural properties. In principle, as we have seen above, this reductive analysis might even occur within the context of physics itself, so for example broader categories like lepton and quark and higher kinds (like fermion and boson) would have to be considered less natural than tau neutrinos and charm quarks. Clearly then, on this view, the distinction between kinds and properties is irrelevant, because there is nothing to being a natural kind over and above being a perfectly natural property. Thus, the Lewisian framework must be seen as a thoroughly reductive analysis of natural kinds in favour of an ontology solely consisting of properties.

There is another pervasive assumption in this line of reasoning; namely, that there is some fundamental physical level where the boundaries are established by objective sameness in nature. Schaffer (2003) and Brown and Ladyman (2009) have argued persuasively for agnosticism about the ontological *assumption* that there is one fundamental level, composed of real entities, while any remaining contingent entities are at best derivative. It is certainly an open question, whether in fact this assumption is warranted. Schaffer states:

The claim that a complete microphysics must be a theory of particles, much less of discrete entities at all is just an article of faith. [...] Indeed, considerations of renormalization in quantum field theory have led physicist Howard Georgi to suggest that effective quantum field theories might form an infinite tower. (Schaffer 2003: 505)

Thus, there is at least an open empirical possibility that there is not a fundamental physical level, or at the very least that there is no bedrock, which might be considered to be constitutive of it. This would pose serious difficulties for the Lewisian framework. There is an assumption that there is some elite minority of natural properties that carve nature at its joints. If it should turn out that there is an infinite regress of layers without end, then determining the naturalness of natural properties in Lewisian terms would become very problematic. It would only be possible to state that some properties are more natural than others, but it would be difficult to delineate any properties to constitute Lewis's elite minority. If the minority is to be composed just of any kind once it is a physical kind, then some independent argument for why kinds in physics are perfectly natural is required. Otherwise, the perfectly naturalness of physical properties is purely dogmatic.

2.2 Natural kinds are property universals

A second possibility for thinking about the relationship between natural kinds and properties is to treat natural kinds as reducible to a particular kind of property; namely, kinds supervene on property universals. According to the thesis of Humean supervenience, everything supervenes on intrinsic properties of point-sized entities and spatio-temporal relations. Likewise, according to Armstrong (1999), kinds supervene on more simple monadic properties.

It is of course a great fact about the world that it contains kinds of things [...] The kinds mark true joints in nature. But it is not clear that we require an independent and irreducible category of universal to accommodate the kinds. [...]. All the kinds of thing that there are, supervene. And if they supervene they are not an ontological addition to their base. (Armstrong 1999: 67–8)

According to this view, natural kinds supervene upon conjunctive universals. The relationship between kinds and properties on this view can be defined in the following way:

(2) Two objects are members of the same natural kind *iff* they supervene upon the same conjunctive property universal.

The naturalness of kinds is derived from the naturalness of the conjunctive property universals. For example, CO_2 is composed of two oxygen atoms covalently bonded to a single carbon atom. The kind CO_2 supervenes on oxygen, which has the property of having eight protons in its outer shell and carbon, which has the property of having six protons in its outer shell. A distinct kind of substantival universal is not required to account for the natural kind CO_2. Similarly, an electron is composed of the properties of its mass, charge, and the absolute value of the spin. These properties are identical for all electrons. Conjunctive properties are not properties over and above their conjuncts. All higher-level properties are reducible to their constitutive properties.

Mellor (1991: 178–80) pointed out there are nevertheless, independent logical worries about the relationship between conjunctive universals and their constituents. Conjunctive universals cannot be straightforwardly composed out of their constituents and would be better eliminated in favour of their constituents altogether. This involves the same reductionist move that was seen in the earlier Lewisian framework; where because the real natural properties are, in the end, the fundamental microstructural constituents, rather than the conjunctive universals, it is these microstructural constituents that serve as nature's joints. The reductive analysis of natural kinds in terms of properties has the consequence that kinds do not require any fundamental place in ontology. The natural kind categories serve at most as heuristic devices that guide us to the more fundamental natural properties.

2.3 Natural kinds are the extensions of properties (e.g. sets)

There is a final way of characterizing the relationship between properties and kinds, which is to claim that natural kinds are the extensions of properties. The *extension* of a concept or expression is the set of things it extends to. The relationship between kinds and properties could be construed in a similar way; namely, a natural kind is a set of properties (e.g. Quine 1969).

For example, take again the kind calcium. Call it C. C = (soft, grey, metallic element, the atomic number 2, an atomic mass of 40.078 amu, a high reactivity with water and air and high electrical conductivity…). Any coherent classificatory principle will determine a set of things whether natural or artificial. Not all sets are natural kinds, but on this view any set whose members share a *natural property* is a natural kind. The relationship between kinds and properties on this view can be defined in the following way:

(3) **Members of the same natural kind belong to a set whose members share a natural property.**

Since any coherent classificatory principle will determine a *set* of things, whether it is a natural or an artificial set, then treating natural kinds as sets does not of itself explain there being natural kinds anyway. If natural kinds are just sets, then there is no criteria for distinguishing natural and artificial kinds. On this view, it is sharing a natural property that counts for qualitative similarity in the set. Membership of a natural set, just is sharing a natural property.

Indeed, Quine concedes this point when he argues that mature science will not require the *kind* category at all. Once a science reaches the requisite level of maturity, the business of that science becomes the discovery and classification of natural properties. He states:

In general, we take it as a very special mark of the maturity of a branch of science, that it no longer needs an irreducible notion of similarity or kind. (Quine 1969: 170)

Thus, natural properties and their instances will in the end do all the work traditionally associated with natural kinds and their instances. In mature science, properties will replace natural kinds altogether. Just like in the Lewisian and Armstrongian framework, only the very elite fundamental physical properties will support our inductive practices and inferences. Only the very elite fundamental physical properties will count as natural kinds. But, at this level the distinction between kinds and properties is difficult to maintain. Moreover, it relies, as does its counterparts, on the claim that there is a level of fundamental properties that are discoverable by our best physical theories.

This section has examined three accounts of natural kinds: (1) that natural kinds are the perfectly natural properties, (2) that natural kinds are reducible to property universals, and (3) natural kinds are the extensions of properties (e.g. sets). On all three views, natural kinds and natural properties are not distinct. A deeper analysis of these views shows that natural kinds are a superfluous ontological addition. An ontology of properties alone will suffice to determine natural classifications.

3 Natural kinds and natural properties are distinct

Nevertheless, there is a strong intuition that when we divide the world into kinds we pick out natural boundaries between things, that we taxonomize real kinds of stuff. In other words, that categorizing things into natural kinds is categorizing according to the real nature of substances. Some theorists go further still and argue that the distinctions between different kinds of substances exist because they belong a priori to distinct ontological categories.

Pieces of stuff and living organisms are objects belonging to two quite distinct ontological categories – and this is something we know a priori, quite independently of any empirically ascertainable facts concerning the changes which may befall any objects. (Lowe 1998: 178–9)

Reasoning in this way leads to the claim that natural kinds should be considered as a *sui generis* type of entity. This entails that natural kinds and properties should be considered as ontologically distinct. The most accepted way of arguing for this view is to claim that natural kinds have essences. The next section, 3.1, will examine three metaphysical accounts of the essence of natural kinds. Section 3.1.1 will examine the view that the essences of natural kind are universals. Second, Section 3.1.2 will examine the view that natural kind essences are sortals. Third, Section 3.1.3 will examine the view that natural kinds are causal essences (e.g. property clusters).

3.1 Natural kinds have essences

Natural kinds are distinguished from non-natural kinds because they have essences. This view can be characterized in the following way:

(4) For each kind K there is some property p of kinds such that it is essential to K that $p(K)$ and $p(K)$ constitutes the essence of K.

These are essences that can only be known a posteriori. Once the essence is discovered, then the natural kind is identified with its essence (e.g. electron = negative charge). Individual members of a kind all share a type identical kind-essence in virtue of their possession of a common set of fundamental intrinsic properties.

However, the essentialist account is subject to the following criticism: if natural kind essences are type identical to a set of fundamental intrinsic properties, then are natural kinds just intrinsic properties? Once the set of fundamental intrinsic properties are discovered a posteriori the role of the kind category is surely obviated in favour of the intrinsic essential properties. But if natural kinds are identical with their essences, then natural kind categories are only required as long as we are waiting to discover their essences.

One reply that the essentialist can make is to say, as Lowe (1998, 2006) does, that even our ability to judge the microstructural divisions between kinds can only be done against a background framework of ontological categories. For example, Lowe (1998: 177–9) compares our classificatory practices in relation to the following two natural processes: natural radioactive decay (e.g. when a lump of uranium changes into lead) and metamorphosis (e.g. the transformation of a tadpole into a frog). In the first, we accept a change of kind from uranium to lead, but in the second we make the judgment that there is no change of kind. Lowe argues that the only way of explaining the difference in adjudicating between these two situations is that we have an a priori background ontological framework into which our a posteriori empirical taxonomies are placed. Living things are fundamentally different in ontological terms from pieces of stuff.

Second, the essentialist can simply reply that kinds are not identifiable with one simple essential property. Many natural kinds involve complex essences. Thinking of natural kinds as distinct entities provides the only rationale for the unity of these complex essences. The kind category provides the unity; it is that entity in virtue of which these properties cluster together. This issue has recently been raised in Dumsday (2010: 619):

Natural-kind essentialism faces an important but neglected difficulty: the problem of complex essences (PCE). This is the question of how to account for the unity of an instantiated kind-essence when that essence consists of multiple distinct properties, some of which lack an inherent necessary connection between them.

Interestingly, this response can even be raised for more simple fundamental properties; namely, even for those properties which would be considered the fundamental sparse properties in Lewis's sense. For example, an electron has the properties of negative charge and a precise resting mass of 9.109×10^{-18}. Positrons have the same resting mass as an electron, but are positively charged. It would be difficult to explain why positrons and electrons constitute different groups of properties given an ontology of properties alone. Thus, natural kinds are required because a kind is the thing in virtue of which these properties are grouped together.

This will certainly be even more complex in the case of biological and chemical kinds (e.g. H_2O, proteins, enzymes), because the properties associated with these kinds are even more complex. However, merely stating that natural kinds account for the unity for complex essences does not account for *how* natural kinds unify complex essences. Answering this question would provide a real rationale for keeping the distinction between kinds and essential properties.

3.1.1 Natural kind essences are universals One way of accounting for the unity of complex essences is to claim that complex essences are themselves universals. Ellis (2001) argues for this position when he claims that natural kinds exist in nested hierarchies of complexity. Take the example that was mentioned above. CO_2 is a natural kind essentially composed of the complex essence—two oxygen atoms covalently bonded to a single carbon atom. Ellis argues, *pace* Armstrong, that property universals are insufficient to account for this complex essence.

Ellis argues that natural kinds should be understood in a looser way: not merely in terms of substantial universals (e.g. quarks, leptons, inert gases, and molecules), but also as property universals (e.g. mass, charge, spin, spatiotemporal interval, and field strength) and dynamic universals (e.g. energy transfer, photon emission, and ionizations). The kind category is a more general one, which includes *any* kind of universal including properties, relations, and substances. So, property universals are merely one subclass of natural kinds. Thus, Ellis's ontology makes natural kinds the most basic of all. Properties are a subset of the broader category of natural kinds. Thus, Ellis would argue that kinds are more ontologically fundamental than properties.[9] The conflation of kinds and properties seen in the views explored in the last section is because properties are a real subset of the natural kinds. Ellis provides the following justification for the expansion of his ontology: the fact that natural kinds exist literally and at all levels of hierarchical arrangement provides the best ontology for current science and the best explanation for the laws of nature at each level.[10]

However, one might question whether expanding the ontology results in too many natural kinds. For example, should the repulsion between two magnets be taken as a literal natural kind? It certainly appears more intuitive to think that repulsion is the result of Maxwell's laws together with the charge properties of the two magnets.[11] An ontology of laws and properties is certainly more parsimonious than reifying properties at all

---

[9] Natural kind then is a broader disjunctive category, which includes substances, properties, and processes. However, for Ellis the natural kind category is still more basic than these disjuncts. This is because for Ellis the direction of existential entailment is identical to the direction of ontological dependence. Determinables in every category are ontologically more fundamental than any of their species (see Ellis 2001: 63–7).

[10] I have argued elsewhere, there are certainly scientific motivations for rejecting the claim that natural kinds exist in hierarchies (Tobin 2010).

[11] In Ellis (2009, ch. 3), a more parsimonious ontology is presented to accommodate this kind of worry.

levels of organization, so the essentialist needs to do more to justify the requirement for an independent natural kind category.

Moreover, the essences that are constitutive of higher-level natural kinds are conjunctive universals, whose conjuncts are the essences of lower-level kinds. We saw above that Mellor (1991) expressed some logical concerns about the conjuncts in conjunctive universals. Ellis's hierarchical framework is supposed to get around this difficulty because the conjuncts of any conjunctive universal are related to the higher-level conjunctive universal as species to genus. Wherever there is an overlap between two species, insofar as both species seem to share members, then the species can be subsumed under the higher-level genus. Thus, the unity of complex essences comes from the fact that there is a hierarchy of natural kinds. Complex essences are irreducible to the essences of their conjuncts, because for Ellis, the essences of generic kinds existentially entail the essences of their infimic species.

But, this is clearly circular, since conjunctive universals are introduced to explain how natural kinds unify their essential properties. Armstrong and Mellor simply deny that conjunctive universals are required and also claim that introducing them brings with it a host of logical problems. So, it appears that to avoid these problems associated with conjunctive universals, a hierarchical world of natural kinds, with complex essences, must be already assumed.

3.1.2 Natural kind essences are sortals One way of trying to justify the requirement for an independent natural kind category is to claim that natural kinds play a specific sortal role. Theorists understand sortals differently, some as predicates (e.g. Quine 1960), others as concepts (Wiggins 1980, 2001), and still others as universals (Strawson 1997; Lowe 2006). But, since for the purposes of this discussion, an ontological account of natural kinds is what is required to underwrite the distinction between kinds and properties, then we require an ontological account of sortals that captures the distinction between natural and non-natural kinds. One possibility is sortal essentialism, which claims that sortals are universals (Lowe 2006; Strawson 1997). This view applied to natural kinds is the claim that it is metaphysically necessary that a sortal essence be possessed by all and only members of a natural kind. Thus, each natural kind possesses a sortal essence intrinsically.

Construing natural kinds as sortals captures the intuition that kinds play more than a classificatory role. Natural kinds require a distinct category, because they also play a distinct *individuating* role. To classify something as a natural kind does more than merely specify the essential properties of a kind. It provides a criterion of identity for that kind. It also provides a criterion for the continued existence of a sample and thus permits induction. Importantly, it also provides a counting role: a criterion for counting the items of that kind which does not apply to the parts or constituents of things of that kind (e.g. any one of the essential properties).

However, it is the last characteristic which is problematic. An expression is a sortal if and only if it takes numerical modifiers (e.g. two tigers). But many natural kinds are mass terms, e.g. 'water', and so are not sortals; we ask for 'two glasses of water' and 'two molecules of H_2O'. If the essence of natural kinds has to be a sortal, then we end up with the odd scenario that 'tiger' is a natural kind, but water and H_2O are not. Thus, a problem arises in the case of natural kinds when distinguishing between sortal universals and non-sortal universals. Some kind candidates are sortal universals (e.g. tiger, electron) and others appear to be non-sortal universals (e.g. H_2O and gold). Thus, if our best ontology is supposed to capture scientific kinds, then construing kinds as sortals does not appear to get the distinction between natural and non-natural kinds right.

Equally, the category is too wide and captures some non-natural kinds (e.g. seminar group). The sortal essentialist may reject this criticism by claiming that non-natural kinds, like *the seminar group*, may very well be sortals, but nonetheless these sortals are not universals. Natural kinds are distinguished from non-natural kinds by the fact that the essence of a natural kind is a sortal universal, whereas the putative essence of a non-natural kind may be a sortal, but is nevertheless, not a universal.[12]

However, this line of response does not help with the fact that some excellent candidates for natural kinds are not sortals at all (e.g. H_2O and gold). Since not all natural kinds are sortals (e.g. H_2O and gold) and not all sortals are natural kinds (e.g. seminar group), it appears that it is the essence *qua* universal, rather than *qua* sortal, that is doing the real classificatory work. But, if it is not the sortal that is doing the work, then we no longer have the justification for characterizing complex essences as natural kinds, on the basis that they play a distinct sortal role (e.g. not just a classificatory, but a distinct individuating and counting role). Thus, we still need an independent justification for claiming that complex essences are not reducible to or supervenient upon the property universals of which they are composed.

3.1.3 Natural kind essences are causal essences The two essentialist accounts of essence that have just been examined concur that essence causally explains the other properties associated with a natural kind. According to both of these essentialist views, a kind's essence is a universal. According to Ellis's essentialism, necessarily all members of a natural kind possess the same intrinsic essence, which is a universal (be it a property, substance, or relation). Likewise, according to the sortal version of essentialism, it is metaphysically necessary that all members of a natural kind possess a sortal essence intrinsically.

However, there is another way of understanding complex essences; namely as causal essences. Causal essences need not all be intrinsic and need not even be possessed by all members of the kind. Indeed, it may not be a matter of metaphysical necessity at all that all members possess the kind essence. It may be merely a matter of nomological necessity or indeed, even weaker, it may be just a matter of physical necessity. For all natural kinds, there may be borderline cases, which possess some, but not all the properties that

---

[12] See Grandy (2007) for an excellent discussion of sortals.

are constitutive of the kind, and over time the properties associated with kind membership may change.

An example of this less stringent view of essences is Boyd's (1991, 1999a) homeostatic property cluster theory. Many advocates of the HPC theory are philosophers of biology and psychology, who object to essentialist accounts of essence on the grounds that there is too much natural variability among biological and psychological individuals. This natural variability means that essences are not always intrinsic and certainly cannot be specified with necessary and sufficient conditions. Nevertheless, they reject the move made by others which rejects talk of natural kinds altogether in favour of an ontology of individuals.

According to HPC theory, a natural kind is a cluster of properties that regularly occur together. However, not just any group of properties clustering together will be a natural kind. Kinds cluster together in virtue of some regulating mechanism. This mechanism explains why the properties occur together and ensures that they continue to do so. Thus, we can reply upon homeostatic property clusters for inductive and classificatory purposes. Homeostatic mechanisms can be *intrinsic* (e.g. gene exchange within a specific species population) or *extrinsic* (e.g. a species' evolutionary habitat providing common selective advantages or disadvantages). The co-occurrence of properties in a natural kind cluster is maintained by these homeostatic mechanisms. The property cluster must also have causal import: namely, it must figure in important causal generalizations; and any refinement of the definition of the kind either introduces causally and inductively irrelevant distinctions or glosses over causally and inductively relevant similarities.

However, this view is subject to the same criticism that we saw earlier. It is less clear why a distinct ontology of natural kinds (properties + HPC mechanisms) is required, once some a posteriori story about property clustering can be provided. A more parsimonious ontology of properties together with the a posteriori story about extrinsic contextual determinants would provide just as rich a picture of how natural property clusters are maintained.

One possible argument for claiming that causal essences are sufficient for introducing a distinct kind category is that many of the property clusters identified by discovering such causal essences are multiply realizable. For example, all members of the natural kind metals are good conductors of both heat and electricity. But, how precisely they do this depends on the behaviour of the atoms of the different elements. Thus, there is no possibility for a simple reduction of these kinds to their constituent properties. Indeed, Boyd's HPC theory (1991, 1999a) is motivated by the idea that there are natural kinds in the special sciences, even though these kinds are multiply realizable. However, multiply realized causal essences could surely themselves be construed as properties, rather than kinds.[13] Thus, some independent argument would still be required to justify the supplementary category of natural kind.

An alternative way to argue that causal essences are sufficient for introducing a distinct kind category would be to claim that mechanisms should themselves be reified.

---

[13] Indeed, in the original multiple realizability debate in the philosophy of mind the discussion involved a relation between properties rather than natural kinds.

Machamer et al. (2000) postulate a dualistic ontology for mechanisms, where both kinds and properties are reified components of mechanisms. They claim that the activities of entities cannot be reduced to their properties and their transitions. They criticize those theorists who portray too close a relationship between kinds and properties:

Substantivalists appropriately focus attention upon the entities and properties in mechanisms, e.g., the neurotransmitter, the receptor, and their charge configurations or DNA bases and their weak polarities. It is the entities that engage in activities, and they do so by virtue of certain of their properties. (Machamer et al. 2000: 6)

Instead, entities and their activities should be reified as real functions. Functions are the activities by virtue of which entities contribute to the workings of a mechanism. Thus, the causal essence of a natural kind is the functional role that it plays in the context of its place in the overall system/organism. They state:

entities having certain kinds of properties are necessary for the possibility of acting in certain specific ways, and certain kinds of activities are only possible when there are entities having certain kinds of properties. Entities and activities are correlatives. They are interdependent. An ontically adequate description of a mechanism includes both. (Machamer et al. 2000: 6)

Thus, if mechanisms are construed realistically, then there would be a real and irreducible functional role for natural kinds.

But, by this line of reasoning, we would need not two ontological categories but three: properties, kinds, and mechanisms. Even if mechanisms should be reified, then there is certainly room for a more parsimonious account involving only properties and mechanisms. Once an a posteriori story can be told about how properties cluster into functional groups by virtue of mechanisms, then why should such natural groups require a distinct ontological category?

Moreover, classification into functional kinds can reflect natural divisions (e.g. property clusters), without a supplementary ontological distinction between kinds and properties. A perfectly consistent a posteriori story about how properties cluster together into functional groups can be provided purely by an examination of the causal structure of the world; namely, by finding those mechanisms in virtue of which properties are clustered together.

But, these functional groups can be given a naturalist classification, without requiring a distinct ontological category. Thus, for example, a weak realist like Quine could consistently say that functional groups are sets of real natural properties, maintained by extrinsic causal mechanisms, and yet, consistently hold that ontologically speaking there is only one ontological category: the properties. Thus, once we reject essentialism, and the unity of complex essences becomes something extrinsic, then the unity is not something that needs to be explained by an ontological category; it may be just a contingent physical fact about the causal structure of the world. Alternatively, it may be something that is the result of nomological necessity. Indeed, this is how a theorist like Armstrong would respond: he would argue that an ontology of laws and properties will suffice for giving a complete explanation of properties clustering together in virtue of mechanisms.

In this section, the view that natural kinds and natural properties are distinct was considered. But, if natural kinds are to be considered as a *sui generis* kind of entity, then some independent justification for introducing a distinct ontological category for natural kinds is required on all of the views of essence that were considered (universals, sortals, and causal essences). Naturalism about natural kind classifications is perfectly consistent with any of the views examined in Section 2, where natural properties and natural kinds are not distinct. Classification into kinds can reflect real divisions (e.g. property clusters), without an ontological distinction between kinds and properties.

4 Conclusion

The original question at the outset of the chapter asked: if some distinction between natural and non-natural properties is taken for granted, is an independent distinction required between the natural properties and the natural kinds? Classification into natural kinds can reflect real differences between natural groups, without a supplementary ontological distinction between properties and kinds. An ontological distinction between natural kinds and properties is not required.

9

Realism about structure and kinds

L. A. Paul

In 1976 Hilary Putnam set forth his model-theoretic argument, claiming that it showed that the semantic realist's programme[1] was 'unintelligible', since it implied, *contra* the realist view, that reference is radically indeterminate.[2] The response, for the most part, was unsympathetic. Semantic realists argued that the only reason Putnam's argument gave us the wildly implausible conclusion that reference is radically indeterminate was because the model-theoretic argument's representation of the realist view was fatally flawed. Putnam failed to represent a crucial part of their view, claimed the realists: that the world itself constrains the reference of terms in theories. Different sorts of semantic realists characterized the constraint differently. 'Pure' causal theorists of reference argued that terms are endowed with (moderately) determinate reference in virtue of baptism ceremonies, while semantic realists of a descriptivist bent argued that interpretations for terms in the language of a theory must respect the natural kinds or properties of the world. The additional constraint, argued both kinds of realists, refuted Putnam's claims by securing the (moderate) determinacy of reference.

Although I find the conclusion that reference is indeterminate unattractive, I shall argue that the descriptivist position needs to be supplemented with a premise about the sorts of kinds, that is, the sort of *structure*, that our world includes. The need for this premise gives a counterintuitive result: the descriptivist account of reference makes the very possibility of determinate reference contingent upon the sorts of kinds that make up the world. The need for this premise can pave the way towards a new kind of scepticism about what we may and may not assume about the nature of the world.

For those who are inclined to accept Putnam's conclusions, my arguments may be sufficient to motivate the adoption of a pragmatic or coherentist theory of truth. But for those who cannot accept the idea that reference is radically indeterminate, the lesson

---

[1] The realist that Putnam calls a 'metaphysical realist' is who I am calling the 'semantic realist'.

[2] Putnam claimed that semantic realism was 'unintelligible' because it implied that any ideal theory was true. It followed from his argument that reference was radically indeterminate; the argument and its conclusions are discussed in Section 2.

will be that, under the descriptivist view, if we wish to preserve realist intuitions about truth we will have to embrace a characterization of reference that violates a strong intuition about how our words refer.

1 Semantic realism

Define the semantic realist as one who believes that an account of truth relies in part upon there being a reference relation that holds between the words we use and the things in the world. This is intended to be a somewhat loose definition: to be this sort of realist one need not adopt a fancy or detailed correspondence theory of truth; one need only think that in order to have true theories about the world there needs to be a fairly determinate way in which the terms in the theories refer to parts of the external world.[3] Under this view, we are able to utter true sentences and think true thoughts if there is a fairly determinate reference relation that holds between objects in the world and the words in the sentences that we use to describe them. (If there is moderate indeterminacy, this could interfere with some, but not most, of the things that we say.) For the semantic realist, since terms of our theories determinately refer, the theorems of our theories about the world can be evaluated as objectively true or false.

Now, this sort of semantic realism seems to be a fundamental assumption, accepted by many philosophers, and implicitly relied upon by many other realist views, as it provides an account of truth and reference that applies to all theories. Anyone who holds that the sentences of her favourite theory are (approximately) true in a way that does not involve a construal of truth that is pragmatic or coherentist, or is not inconsistent with a correspondence theory of truth in some other way, should subscribe to semantic realism. If the scientific, mathematical, or moral realist thinks that the reason the sentences of her favourite theory are true is because the terms in the theory actually refer to properties, relations, and objects in the world, then she (implicitly) adopts semantic realism by adopting her version of scientific, mathematical, or moral realism.

But to make semantic realism a respectable doctrine, especially if we want to make it respectable for those who propound naturalism, we should provide an account of how determinate reference is possible and why we think the terms in our theories determinately refer. If realists are unable to give such an account, it does not prove their theories false, but seriously weakens their case against antirealists. If the semantic realist has naturalist leanings, the concession that one is simply assuming determinate reference is particularly galling.

---

[3] Perfect determinacy may be too much to ask. The reasonable realist may be willing to accept a small amount of indeterminacy, such as the sort of indeterminacy that arises with the vagueness of predicates like 'is bald'. Moreover, as David Lewis (1984: 228) argues, we might reasonably accept the idea that 'rabbit' refers indeterminately to rabbits, undetached rabbit parts, rabbit-fusion, etc. Other kinds of moderate indeterminacy, however, are less palatable than these: I discuss this point in Section 4.

Attempts to give constitutive accounts of determinate reference have been presented by realists. Pure causal theorists of reference argue that reference obtains between words and things in the world in virtue of a causal relation established by a baptism ceremony, which fixes the reference in the original cases, and is then passed along from speaker to speaker. Pure causal theorists reject descriptions as reference-fixing. This theory runs into trouble in accounting for how we can refer to objects that we cannot perceive directly, such as numbers, moral properties, and unobservable objects. Descriptivists argue that reference obtains in virtue of descriptions of a thing in the world that associate a word with an object, property, etc. Causal descriptivism, the view I find most promising, holds that the reference-fixing descriptions are couched in causal terms.

Perhaps the most plausible account of reference would be one that cobbles together some form of casual descriptivism with the pure casual theory of reference. The pure causal theory of reference seems to provide an adequate account of how we endow many proper names with referents, while causal descriptivism seems to provide a good account of how theoretical terms in scientific theories,[4] as well as most other kinds of terms, get their reference. Neither theory is adequate by itself; the pure causal theory in particular faces many counterexamples.[5] Since my interest is with theories that include a description of the world in terms of its fundamental physical properties, I shall focus on causal descriptivism,[6] which seems to provide the best account of how the terms in fundamental physical theory get their reference, and as such is an essential part of the hybrid view suggested above.[7] If the terms of fundamental physics fail to refer (moderately) determinately, then our project of coming up with a suitable theory of the world already has more trouble than we can handle.

2 Putnam's 'model-theoretic' argument

Putnam and the proponents of his model-theoretic argument attack the thesis that the semantic realists' programme implies that our words have determinate reference. Putnam does not argue against the individual theories of descriptivism and the causal theory of reference; his is a general argument that (he claims) shows that the very idea of having determinate reference for the terms of our theories under the realist programme is a chimera.

In his argument, Putnam says that we can take a theory T that is 'ideal' from the point of view of operational utility, is consistent, has maximal inner beauty and elegance,

---

[4] Lewis (1970) provides such an account.

[5] For some very nice examples, see Peter Unger (1983).

[6] Although my preference is for causal descriptivism, my conclusions hold for other sorts of descriptivism as well. For this reason, I will not distinguish between causal descriptivism and other forms of descriptivism in what follows, since the differences between the varieties will in no way affect the argument.

[7] Moreover, I find the response that the causal theorist of reference must give to Putnam unappealing. The causal theorist of reference must claim that the causal theory of reference is true (and gives us enough determinacy), whether or not it can be *proved* that it is true. See footnote 9, below.

'plausibility', simplicity, 'conservatism', etc., and correctly predicts all observation sentences. We stipulate, after excluding the property a realist would call 'objective truth' for the purposes of the argument, that theory T has all the other 'best properties' a theory should have. Now, a realist, on Putnam's view, argues that such a theory could nevertheless be false (Putnam 1977: 484). Putnam maintains that such a theory would have to come out true. This is because he thinks that we can pick a model of T that is the same cardinality as the world, then map the individuals taken as satisfying the predicates 1-to-1 directly into the world. The individuals of the model can be mapped into the world in *any way we please*. So the mapping defines relations of the model directly in the world, i.e. relations between individuals in the model are constructed in the world. We may say that the structure of the model is reflected in the world by the mapping, or that the structure of the model is isomorphic to a structure of the world. Since there are countlessly many ways to map the model into the world, and countlessly many ways to interpret the terms of the theory T, there are countlessly many ways for terms in T to denote. What this means, in effect, is that in each possible mapping, different arbitrary classes of objects in the world are set up as the referents of terms or predicates in the language L, and thus reference is radically indeterminate.

For example, the set of all rabbits might be the extension of the predicate 'is an R' in one interpretation for an ideal theory, but the set of all cherries might be the extension of the same predicate in another interpretation.[8] For Putnam, both interpretations can serve equally well, as long as the claims of the theory are satisfied. Worse yet, a set made up of rabbits *and* cherries could instantiate the predicate 'is an R' in yet another interpretation. If all these interpretations can assign referents to the terms in the theory such that the claims of the theory are satisfied, then according to Putnam, all of them give us a true theory, and so each interpretation (and thus each way of assigning referents) is equally good.

Putnam argues that all of these interpretations must give us a true theory, because the result of mapping the model of the theory into the world is the definition of a satisfaction relation which gives us a correspondence between the terms of the language of the theory (as interpreted by the model) and sets of pieces of the world. His claim is that this correspondence relation is as good as any other; for him, truth just amounts to there being such a correspondence. Since there are many different ways of setting up this correspondence relation, there are many different interpretations of the language of a theory such that the theory comes out 'true'. If the theory is ideal, then for Putnam we have all we need to call the theory 'true'. In effect,

...Putnam's argument retraces the model-theoretic proof that given any consistent theory demanding a universe of cardinality c, and given any set of cardinality c, there will exist a model of the theory whose universe is that set. In virtue of this model which establishes a correspondence between the language of the theory and the set in question, the theory is true of that set (under the given correspondence). (Merrill 1980: 70)

---

[8]   Cardinalities of the sets permitting.

Now, the realist will reject this notion as a notion of truth, and argue that not just any interpretation could be the correct interpretation; i.e. not just any interpretation *I* that satisfies the claims of the theory is such that truth under *I* is truth *simpliciter*. Indeed, the realist will argue, we may be so unlucky that we will have no correct interpretation, and be left with a theory that meets all of our pragmatic desiderata, conforms to all observations, yet nevertheless is false. Putnam's response to the realist is to maintain that it is ridiculous to try to privilege any of these ways of mapping the model into the world. He thinks that the realist has no legitimate way to define particular interpretations as 'intended'. For Putnam, any attempt by the realist to impose a constraint on the eligibility of interpretations to satisfy the theory would require a theory of the constraint, but this theory would be subject to the same indeterminacy as the original theory, since the model-theoretic argument applies equally well to the new addition. Putnam employs this argument against realists who respond to his argument by defending the causal theory of reference, arguing that '[h]ow "causes" can uniquely refer is as much of a puzzle as how "cat" can on the [semantic] realist picture' (Putnam 1977: 486).

3 The descriptivist response

Unsurprisingly, realists reject Putnam's view, arguing that there is one more thing aside from theoretical constraints constraining the choice of interpretations for theories—the world itself. David Lewis (1983a, 1984) is the foremost proponent of such a view; his response draws on Gary Merrill's (1980) argument that the descriptivist can rebut Putnam by arguing that the world has a unique structure.[9] We see a contemporary version of the Lewisian view in Sider's (2012) defence of a world with objective structure.

Lewis's response to Putnam is simple and elegant: there are objective samenesses and differences in nature; in other words, there exist objectively natural properties. This stipulation, claims Lewis, is sufficient to give us (fairly) determinate reference. To see the beauty of this response, view Putnam's model-theoretic argument in terms of different ways of carving up the objects in the world into classes. Putnam's claim is that one way of carving up the world is as good as any other, and thus any way of grouping objects into classes is acceptable for the purposes of assigning extensions to predicates. Thus, the class of all grue things is just as legitimate a class to serve as the referent of a predicate as the class of all green things. So, for Putnam, an interpretation that assigns predicates the

---

[9] Realists who are sanguine about the prospects of the causal theory of reference as a complete account for the reference of the terms of our theories could follow Michael Devitt instead, who argues that the causal theory of reference is still the correct theory, whether or not we can establish it in a theory-independent way. So, in response to Putnam's argument that the causal theory of reference just adds more theory to the whole that must be interpreted, Devitt bites the bullet, and argues that the causal theory of reference is true (and gives us enough determinacy to eliminate errant interpretations), whether or not it can be *proved* that it is true. Although Devitt's response is sufficient to rebut Putnam, I think it could be counted as a violation of the naturalist methodology of which Devitt, like most who argue for the causal theory of reference, is a proponent.

extensions grue and bleen is just as good as an interpretation that assigns predicates blue and green. (For the uninitiated: define 'grue' as a predicate that applies to all things examined before the year 2013 just in case they are green but to other things just in case they are blue. Define 'bleen' as a predicate that applies to all things examined before the year 2013 just in case they are blue but to other things just in case they are green.)

Lewis disagrees, and argues that there exist objective distinctions among ways in which objects of the world may be grouped into classes, and that the world imposes a requirement upon interpretations: they must respect these objective groupings. Among all the countless things and classes that there are, most are miscellaneous, gerrymandered, ill-demarcated. Only an elite minority are carved at the joints, so that their boundaries are established by objective sameness and difference in nature (Lewis 1984: 227; Sider 2012). In other words, out of the countless number of different sets that can be created out of the parts of the world, only some of these classes reflect the objective way the world is broken up. The realist thinks these classes are the only eligible referents for terms in the language of a theory. Thus, some ways of carving the beast of reality are objectively correct ways.

In the simplest case, suppose that the interpretation of the logical vocabulary somehow takes care of itself, to reveal a standard first-order language whose nonlogical vocabulary consists entirely of predicates. The parts of the world comprise a domain; and sets, sets of pairs, ..., from this domain are potential extensions for the predicates. Now suppose we have an all-or-nothing division of properties into natural and unnatural. To have a property is to be a member of a class. Say that a set from the domain is *eligible* to be the extension of a 1-place predicate iff its members are just those things in the domain that share some natural property; and likewise for many-place predicates and natural relations. An eligible interpretation is one that assigns none but eligible extensions to the predicates. A so-called intended interpretation is an eligible interpretation that satisfies the ideal theory' (Lewis 1983a: 371–2)[10]

The extent to which the interpretation respects the elite or natural classes of the world is the extent to which the interpretation can be taken as correct or intended. According to Lewis, if the class of green things is natural and the class of grue things is not, then the class of green things can serve as the extension of a predicate and the class of grue things cannot. So Lewis believes that there is a constraint upon eligible interpretations: the constraint that a property or relation should be assigned by the model to a predicate when its image under the mapping m is *really* one of the properties and relations among objects in the world. This constraint is imposed by the world, not by us, so it is not subject to Putnam's 'just more theory' argument. A realist is one who believes that the world has natural properties, and that any interpretation of a theory of the world must respect these objectively existing classes if it is to make the theory true. There are countlessly many interpretations which satisfy a consistent theory T: T is 'true' with respect to each

---

[10] One of Sider's interesting contributions to this discussion is to *not* assume that the first-order vocabulary 'takes care of itself'. Instead, Sider argues that we need a preferred interpretation for the quantifiers as well.

of these interpretations, but what realists want is truth under an *eligible* interpretation, not truth under some interpretation or other.

Now, I've been talking as if naturalness and eligibility are all-or-nothing affairs, but this is an oversimplification. Ultimately, Lewis's claim about eligibility of referents makes eligibility a matter of degree, and correct or 'intended' interpretations are defined as those which strike the best balance between eligibility and making the claims of the theory come out true. In this way, we may distinguish interpretations which satisfy the claims of a theory: those that maximize naturalness in their assignments of extensions to predicates are better than those which do not. All else being equal, the more natural the extensions of the predicates assigned by the interpretation, the better the interpretation.

So Lewis has managed to defuse Putnam's bomb quite effectively. If we accept the claim that eligibility of interpretations depends upon naturalness, then the number of eligible interpretations for the language of a theory is greatly reduced. It is again possible for an ideal theory to be false, and Putnam's claim that 'any interpretation which satisfies an ideal theory makes it true' is refuted.

Many semantic realists who accept natural kinds take Lewis to have successfully provided a constitutive account of determinate reference and a decisive refutation of Putnam's model-theoretic argument. The account has been taken as the foundation for several different descriptivist programmes, such as analyses of causation, analyses of moral properties, functionalism, objective structure, and various other metaphysical projects.[11] Even realists who are less comfortable with kinds accept Lewis's argument as a refutation and grant that his account of determinate reference seems moderately plausible. But as we shall see, the story is not yet complete.

4 Permutability

Recall that part of the realist's task was to provide an account of moderately determinate reference that could underlie a theory of truth.[12] He has an account of how an ideal theory can still be false. But does this account guarantee us moderately determinate reference? Unfortunately, it does not. There are two ways in which indeterminacy can remain; the lesser of the two is one which the realist might reasonably accept, but the greater of the two is unpalatable to even the most entrenched.

---

[11] For example, Menzies (1999), Jackson (1998), Jackson and Pettit (1995, 1996), Jackson (1992), Braddon-Mitchell and Jackson (1996). Worrall's (1989) structural realism also seems to depend, implicitly, on the success of the sort of programme that Lewis advocates. Further, any philosopher who assumes that we have (fairly) determinate reference and that some form of descriptivism plays a role in establishing reference is relying indirectly on this sort of semantic programme; see for example, Sider (2012).

[12] Since my focus here is on descriptions rather than the causal theory of reference, from this point onwards (unless otherwise specified) I will use the terms 'realist', 'semantic realist', and 'descriptivist' interchangeably to refer to the descriptivist who thinks that our terms have (moderately) determinate reference.

Moderate indeterminacy, of the sort noticed by Quine, is a familiar bugbear of the descriptivist programme. Since eligibility is a matter of degree, we may on occasion assign fairly poor referents if such an assignment allows us to maximize the eligibility of referents overall or the truth to falsity ratio of the theory's sentences. Lewis (1984: 229) notes that we might have to accept as eligible interpretations that assign rabbit stages, undetached rabbit parts, and a rabbit-fusion as referents. This is not too troubling. But the indeterminacy is not as innocuous as all that, for along with accepting that 'rabbit' might refer to rabbit-stages, we might also have to accept grue and bleen things as referents for, say, 'green' and 'blue'. This sort of moderate indeterminacy, while not as upsetting as radical indeterminacy, is a step beyond accepting rabbit stages as referents, and will make many realists uncomfortable.

For example, suppose we have an interpretation *I* for our best theory that assigns the predicate 'is green' to all grue things, 'is blue' to all bleen things, and does an adequate job of mapping the rest of the individuals in the domain of the model to moderately eligible parts of the world while satisfying all or most of the sentences of our theory. Now suppose there is no better interpretation, i.e. no interpretation that assigns more eligible referents can satisfy any of the sentences of the theory. Then the realists would have to accept a somewhat unpleasant consequence: 'green' refers to the property grue and 'blue' refers to the property bleen. This might make realists uncomfortable. But this is, of course, not a refutation of the realist view, since if the realist can allow that the difference between referring to green things and referring to grue things is not too obnoxious, such mild cases of indeterminacy can be consistent with a moderate realist lifestyle.[13] Such a consequence, the realist might argue, is better than the alternative of radically indeterminate reference.

It may seem as though the issue has been settled: we may have a moderate amount of indeterminacy but nothing too outrageous, so the sensible realist may go on as before, undeterred in his philosophical pursuits. But even after he accepts moderate indeterminacy, and accepts naturalness as a condition for eligibility of interpretations, the realist is still in trouble. Without an additional constraint upon interpretations, he is still faced with the prospect of having to accept a large amount of indeterminacy, an indeterminacy so radical that he may not be able to distinguish between referring to rabbits and referring to cherries, or between referring to green things and referring to spherical things. Even though by assuming that natural kinds exist he can refute Putnam's claim that nearly any empirically ideal theory is true of the world, this assumption is not sufficient to refute the thesis that reference is radically, not just moderately, indeterminate. This spells trouble.

The worry surfaces when we realize that although linking naturalness to acceptability of interpretations is enough to avoid Putnam's claim that nearly any interpretation of

---

[13] Lewis was prepared to accept this much indeterminacy, just as he is prepared, if need be, to accept the sort of indeterminacy we have with respect to rabbits versus rabbit stages, etc. It is not a conclusion he welcomed. I myself find it objectionable.

an ideal theory will make it true, it does not eliminate the possibility that more than one radically different interpretation of the language of an ideal theory could receive the title 'most eligible'. If we had two or more interpretations that maximized naturalness while making the claims of the theory come out true (as our grue and green cases did above), yet the way in which the interpretations assigned referents were very different, we could be faced with indeterminacy that is far more radical than that of rabbit versus rabbit stages.

Recall that Lewis circumvented Putnam by claiming that the world has a structure. But if there exist two or more very different interpretations for a theory that preserve the structure we have attributed to the world, then we are still in trouble. How could such a thing be the case? It could be the case if, for some interpretation that maximizes both naturalness and satisfaction of the claims of the theory, there exists a permutation of the natural properties of the world into itself which also maximizes both desiderata. In other words, there could be an alternative, equally good, mapping of terms in the language of the theory to natural properties. This would give us more than one (potentially) radically different interpretation for our best theory.

One familiar way that radical indeterminacy could occur arises with the possibility of isomorphic models for the same (syntactic) theory.[14] We have isomorphic models for a theory when there is a way of pairing the objects of the domain of one model with the objects of the domain of the second model in such a way that relations which hold between objects in the first model correspond to relations that hold between objects in the second model. If it is possible to state a rule by which the elements of the system $\Sigma 1$ are paired in a mutually unique manner with the elements of the system $\Sigma 2$, so that elements in $\Sigma 1$ between which R (or R', ...) holds correspond to elements in $\Sigma 2$ between which the relation Q (or Q', ... respectively) holds, so that R is correlated with Q, and R' is correlated with Q', etc., even though the Rs and Qs may mean entirely different things, then the two domains are isomorphic (i.e. they share the same structure). A simple example is the progression of the odd natural numbers, which is isomorphic to the progression of the even natural numbers when we set up a correspondence whereby 1 corresponds to 2, 3 to 4, etc.

Now, we might have an interpretation $I\star$ that assigned the predicate 'is a G' to green things, and 'is an R' to rabbits. In addition, we might have an interpretation $J\star$ that assigns 'is a G' to cherries, and 'is an R' to meteors. (Of course, many referents of other predicates in the two interpretations would also differ. But assume that we are able to assign the rest of the referents in some satisfactory way.) Both interpretations map predicates to natural kinds. Since both interpretations assign eligible referents to their predicates, if both turn out to give us the same balance between eligible kinds and satisfying the claims of the theory, then both are equally eligible interpretations. If they are the best available interpretations, and the theory is ideal in other respects, we should, if we follow

---

[14] Of course, the unsurprising fact that there exist identity transformations is not relevant here.

realist doctrine, accept both of them. However, this means that we must also accept a significant amount of indeterminacy with respect to the referents of the predicates 'is a G' and 'is an R', indeterminacy far more radical than most realists would feel comfortable with.[15] And note that the interpretations of predicates for relations such as 'counterfactually depends', 'causes', and 'is earlier (or later) than' are also up for grabs.[16]

When evaluating interpretations for our best theory of the world, we could end up with two interpretations such that the objects referred to by predicates in both interpretations were natural kinds, and the relations which obtained between the properties in one model were as natural as those which obtained in the second model. This means that we would end up with two 'best' or maximally natural interpretations.[17] If these models were isomorphs of one another, so that one interpretation mapped into the other, then they would be elementarily equivalent models, i.e. the same sentences would be made true by both interpretations. But note that isomorphism isn't a requirement, merely a sufficient condition: even if we can't construct isomorphs that maximize naturalness, we might still be able to permute the natural properties in the domain of a model for the theory so as to get 'approximate' isomorphisms: alternative interpretations that do an approximately equal job of maximizing naturalness and satisfying the claims of the theory.[18] If we assume that the same natural properties in the world are subsets of each of the domains (or subsets of sets of pairs, triples, etc. of the domains) of competing models for the theory, then the models are automorphs, not just isomorphs, of one another. It is possible that an interpretation for our best theory of the world that maximized naturalness might be one that would admit of such permutations, automorphic, isomorphic, or otherwise.[19]

For a physicalist or materialist, the most elite properties and relations are most likely things like counterfactual dependence, or having mass, charge, and quark flavour. Less elite properties such as 'is a cherry' could be supposed to be connected to these fundamental ones by long chains of definability.[20] The problem with interpretations would arise most vividly at the level of the assignation of fundamental properties and relations. Thus quark flavour, quark colour, and protons might be assigned to the predicates A, B, and C in one interpretation that maximizes naturalness, and mass, charge, and electrons

[15] Michael Smith (1994: 48–54) has a good example of local permutability, based on the (supposed) symmetry of the colour wheel, that shows how permutations can confound uniqueness claims.

[16] And if the interpretation for the fundamental quantifier is up for grabs, then things get even crazier. This is relevant to the arguments in Sider (2012).

[17] If the structure of the world exhibits enough symmetry, we will certainly have alternative competing interpretations.

[18] Since naturalness and satisfaction of claims of the theory are both matters of degree, and the realist holds that these two desiderata may need to be balanced against one another.

[19] Moreover, I've been assuming so far that the language of first-order logic has a fixed interpretation. Putnam seems to assume this, although I see no reason for it. But if we do not assume, as Sider (2012) does not (and as I do not), that the language of first-order logic has a fixed interpretation any more than the rest of our language has a fixed interpretation, then the possibility of competing radical interpretations is significantly increased.

[20] Lewis (1984: 228).

to A, B, and C in another, equally eligible interpretation. Or, since maximizing natural-ness and the satisfaction of claims of the theory involves balancing matters of degree, we might have the interpretation that assigns quark flavour, quark colour, and protons to the predicates A, B, and C (respectively) competing with an equally eligible interpreta-tion that assigns quark flavour and some protons to the predicate A, quark colour and some protons to the predicate B, and the rest of the protons to the predicate C. Such variance at the fundamental level would most likely give us extreme variance at the macro-level of cherries and rabbits, as in the example given earlier, given that the funda-mental properties are used to define these less elite properties.

John Winnie (1967: 226–7) gives an example that shows how the existence of two (or more) competing interpretations is not implausible. Imagine a theory with one inter-pretation, K, that assigns what we now call neutrons to the predicate N and electrons to the predicate E. Then imagine another interpretation, $K^\star$, that assigns all neutrons but one to the predicate N and all the electrons plus one neutron to the predicate E. We may then assign other referents so as to satisfy the claims of the theory. We are left with a measure of indeterminacy at the micro-level and perhaps much more radical indeter-minacy at the macro-level, depending upon the chains of definability in which the neutron is involved.[21] Of course, we can come up with many more such models in which only a small switch is made. Now, in this simple case, we know that K is a better interpretation than $K^\star$, but that is because we are assuming they do equally well with respect to satisfaction. But since naturalness and satisfaction are matters of degree, the existence of competing interpretations like K and $K^\star$, but where $K^\star$ does a bit better with satisfaction while K does a bit better with respect to eligibility may not be too far-fetched. For a (more far-fetched) case where only perfectly natural kinds are referred to, imagine an interpretation $I^{\star\star}$ that assigned the property of having positive charge to the predicate POS and the property of having negative charge to the predicate NEG. Then imagine an alternative interpretation $J^{\star\star}$ that assigned the property of having positive charge to the predicate NEG and the property of having negative charge to the predi-cate POS. If the world exhibited enough global symmetry, then both these interpreta-tions could do an equal job of maximizing naturalness and satisfaction of claims—so by the realist's own lights, the predicates POS and NEG would refer indeterminately.

If our world is one in which the natural kinds actually are permutable in any of the ways I have specified, that is, if the world exhibits the right sorts of deep-level sym-metries, then the existence of competing interpretations is physically possible. If the world admits more than one interpretation as eligible, then *contra* the realist programme,

---

[21] Winnie's proof is relevant in the event that so-called observational predicates do not have a fixed inter-pretation in sentences that contain both observational and theoretical predicates, as is the case here, with discussions about what Lewis (1984) calls 'global descriptivism'. His argument does not refute Lewis (1970), since Lewis takes as a premise that the interpretations of observational (or 'old') predicates remain fixed in 'mixed' sentences containing the old predicates and new (theoretical) predicates.

we would still have radical indeterminacy of reference, where the indeterminacy involves reference to objects or kinds that are very dissimilar to one another.

5 Realist responses

There might be a way out for the semantic realist who hopes for a constitutive account of determinate reference: deny that our actual world is one in which the natural kinds are permutable. The realist could agree that an alternative interpretation that permutes the kinds that the predicates of our best theory are to apply to while preserving empirical virtues is possible, but not in our world. This amounts to a claim about the sort of structure that our world has.

Such a claim makes sense, the semantic realist might argue, given what we know about the world. Science tells us about the world, and its main business is to try to discover natural kinds and talk about them in its theories. The referents of so-called theoretical and observational terms are the natural kinds of the world. Science tells us what the natural kinds are, such as the natural kind of being an electron and the natural kind of being a quark, and these, at least *prima facie*, don't seem to allow us to construct competing 'most natural' interpretations. However, the realist might argue, surely part of the language of our theory of fundamental physics will be indexical, and our use of 'here' and 'now', combined with assertions about our use of predicates about change, location, and the direction of time,[22] will eliminate alternative interpretations. Although competing interpretations are logically possible, we don't have to worry about them because it doesn't seem like the kinds we have *are* permutable in a way that would maximize naturalness.[23] The realist could then try to use this argument to refute the examples in the previous section which suggested that the existence of competing interpretations was not implausible.

Now, this argument deserves close examination. The first objection to make to it is to point out that the indexical properties and fundamental relations described by our ideal theory are as open to interpretation as any of the other terms—we're talking *global descriptivism* here—and so the possibility of permutation still exists.[24] Recall that all we are working with is a set of existentially generalized sentences. Hereness and nowness, along with 'depends upon', 'causes', and 'is earlier than' are just more natural kinds that enter into the equation when we balance naturalness and satisfaction of claims.

But perhaps a very strong version of scientific realism could imply that the kinds are not permutable. The realist could argue that science tells us the natural kinds, and that it does not seem that an interpretation that respected these kinds would be permutable.

---

[22] Assuming, of course, that the realist accepts the thesis that temporal or other relevant fundamental relations are asymmetric.
[23] Lewis (1997) takes this line in response to worries about uniqueness with respect to the referents of colour terms.
[24] And does the realist really want to assume that, e.g., the property of hereness is a natural property?

Thus, the semantic realist assumes that the kinds science tells us about are really all and only the kinds that there are. Since (via science) we know what all and only the kinds of the world are, claims the semantic realist, we can judge that they are not permutable and therefore that reference is (moderately) determinate.

This seems, *prima facie*, to be a plausible line of defence for the realist. After all, most scientific realists think that we have fairly strong reasons to think that our theoretical desiderata lead us to the truth. In other words, the semantic realist seems to be assuming something fairly reasonable for a scientific realist to assume—that our scientific theories are (approximately) true claims about the world (including the world's unobservable realms). The realist who accepts a version of scientific realism that tells her what the kinds are and implies that they are not permutable would seem to have a reasonable response to permutation worries.[25]

If we grant the semantic realist the assumption that we know, via science, that the kinds of our world are not permutable and that this ensures (fairly) determinate reference, three conclusions follow immediately.[26] First, the semantic realist must assume that science will not discover any new natural kinds, kinds which would allow for permutations involving the predicates of current theory. Second, in order for one to be a semantic realist, one must first embrace strong scientific realist views such as the view that our current theory is reasonably close to what our ideal theory will be. These two results show us that a rather optimistic realist view of science is called for, one which places great faith in today's science (and rejects the idea that the world has deep or fundamental unbreakable symmetries).[27]

If the realist is right, we must now base semantic realism upon scientific realism, reversing the more usual view that realism about scientific theories is bolstered by semantic realism. But there is more: the realist must now claim that determinate reference is contingent (in a surprising new way). Determinate reference, according to the realist view, is dependent upon the nature of the natural kinds that make up a world. If a world has the wrong sort of kinds, then determinate reference might not be possible. We've granted to the semantic realist who holds a strong version of scientific realism that our world has the right sort of kinds so as to avoid permutability, but surely there are many other worlds where the kinds *are* permutable. So even if we grant the realist the claim that science tells us what the kinds are and that these kinds are not permutable, the realist conception of reference makes reference contingent—not only in the trivial sense that it is a contingent matter how languages and theories are constructed, but contingent upon the world having the right sort of structure. If we had lived in a world with different fundamental structure, we might not be able to refer determinately.

---

[25] I'm assuming here that most semantic realists would accept abductive inferences as reasonable and as fairly likely to be (objectively) true.

[26] Among other things, this implies the view that science tells us that the world is asymmetric (overall).

[27] For a discussion of how a local symmetry of colour properties can be broken by taking a more global perspective, see Lewis (1997).

Now, here's the rub: the realist can't argue that he knows that his strong (or optimistic?) version of scientific realism is true simply because current theory seems to do a fairly good job of meeting our empirical and theoretical desiderata, since he has already argued against Putnam that such a theory can be false.[28] So he can't *argue* that scientific theory must be true. Instead, within the context of his rejoinder to Putnam, the realist must assume, based on his *faith* that scientific theory is true, that the kinds of our world are not permutable.

But although the strong scientific realist can make this assumption about the kinds, the antirealist about science will not be so sanguine. She will reject the assumption as unjustified, and argue that therefore no satisfactory account of determinate reference is available. Scepticism about the existence of natural kinds is familiar; we may add to this scepticism about contingent properties of kinds.

More importantly, semantic realists who prefer moderate scientific realism will be caught in a bind, for *they* cannot use their version of scientific realism to claim that the kinds are not permutable.[29] Unless she is exceedingly optimistic about the status of current scientific theory, the moderate scientific realist who thinks descriptivism can give us moderately determinate reference will also have to make an additional assumption (without scientific justification) about the contingent structure of the physical world.

We come then to a sort of scepticism. In order to provide an adequate account of how reference is determinate, the realist must make the assumption that the world has structure. But in order to secure the sufficiency of this account, the realist who accepts only moderate scientific realism must make an additional substantial ontological commitment: she must assume that the structure of the world is such that it does not permit the possibility of multiple, radically different, 'most natural' interpretations for our best theory. Realists already tend to take the thesis that kinds exist as a primitive assumption about the world; now, unless they are exceedingly optimistic about current science, they must assume, without independent evidence, that the structure of the world is non-permutable.

Providing ways to motivate acceptance of such an assumption will not be easy. The semantic realist who is not comfortable with assuming strong metaphysical theses to ensure determinate reference may well find the burden of accepting yet another controversial metaphysical claim too much to bear. Perhaps she thought, when she accepted the semantic realist view, that accepting natural kinds was sufficient to refute Putnam's

---

[28] We can see how this debate drops into a debate in the philosophy of science: the realist maintains that science is about discovering the real, i.e. natural, properties of the world, whereas the antirealist argues that the properties that science discovers and defines are based on pragmatic (human) desiderata. See van Fraassen (1989, 1995, 1997) and Elgin (1995).

[29] By 'moderate scientific realist' I mean a scientific realist who thinks that we have good reason to believe that our theories of fundamental physics are approximately true, but doesn't want to rule out the possibility that there might be significant revisions made to these theories, or a realist who thinks that part but not all of fundamental physics should be held to be approximately true, or a realist who doesn't want to rule out the possibility that we might discover new natural kinds that would allow for permutations involving the predicates of current fundamental physical theory.

sceptical arguments. Perhaps she thought, when she accepted the semantic realist view, that even though accepting the idea that there exist natural kinds was somewhat repugnant, that such an assumption—just barely—outweighed the consequences. After all, accepting the existence of natural kinds, even a much weaker version than Lewis's, helps to solve other philosophical problems. Moreover, there is a clear reason why the assumption that natural kinds exist is acceptable to realists: it conforms to our intuitions about truth and reference that interpretations for theories whose terms refer and whose theorems are true do so in virtue of the fact that they respect the actual, real differences and samenesses between objects in the world. Using the assumption that natural kinds exist to refute Putnam reflects traditional realist values; as Lewis puts it, 'the realism that recognizes a nontrivial enterprise of discovering the truth about the world needs the traditional realism that recognizes objective sameness and difference, joints in the world, discriminatory classifications not of our own making' (Lewis 1984: 228).

But while there is support for the idea that the world has some structure, there is no such support for the stronger idea of non-permutability—the realist does not have a story about the intuitions captured by denying deep structural symmetry. Yet, she must attribute non-permutability to the structure of the world. This is a problem for the realist. The attribution seems ad hoc, and the fact that it must be accepted on faith sounds more like a layman's argument for the existence of God than an argument for a respectable naturalist philosophy of reference and truth.[30] The moderate scientific realist may well feel that the need to accept the additional assumptions about structure, coupled with the counterintuitive result that determinate reference is contingent upon the properties of the kinds, tips the balance towards a view of semantics that construes reference differently from its construal under the descriptivist view.

6 Conclusion

At the start of this chapter, I argued that a descriptivist theory of reference seemed to do the best job of capturing our views about how reference for theoretical and other terms in our language is established. A pure causal theory of reference might be suitable as an account of how proper names get their reference, but it isn't going to give us all the reference we want or need. For these reasons, a descriptivist theory seems to be the best theory of reference that we have (for many of the terms of our language). In the face of Putnam's model-theoretic argument, Lewis and other realists have marshalled elegant

---

[30] There may be another option (for which I am indebted to David Lewis): reject the assumption that the kinds are permutable and instead accept the thesis that a term has determinate reference if it refers to the same entity under all eligible interpretations. However, this means accepting the possibility that truth may be much gappier than is normally thought to be the case. Moreover, if we do not assume within the context of the model-theoretic argument that the language of first-order logic has determinate reference (and I don't think we ought to assume this—see footnote 19), some cherished truths (such as logical or mathematical truths) may go by the wayside.

and interesting theses that embellish descriptivism so as to refute Putnam's claim that their views allow for radical indeterminacy of reference.

But the problem of permutability shows us that, according to the realist's constitutive account of reference, the possibility of determinate reference is contingent upon the properties of the kinds that make up our world. The semantic realist who is willing to accept strong scientific realism on faith must accept this conclusion; the semantic realist who is a moderate scientific realist must accept this conclusion *and* make the additional assumption that the kinds of the world are not permutable (in a way that jeopardizes determinate reference). I find this new contingency of determinate reference quite counterintuitive, even apart from the need to hold a strong version of scientific realism or to make assumptions about the properties of worldly structure in order to bolster the view. We knew, as per the realist view, that reference depends on the external world in the sense that if we were living on twin earth, our tokens of 'water' should refer to XYZ instead of H_2O. But the permutation problem shows us something new: reference also depends on contingent properties of the structure of the world. In other words, using tokens of 'water' on our world in the way that we do is not enough to secure moderately determinate reference to H_2O; our world must also be one where the kinds are not per-mutable. Similarly on twin earth: tokens of 'water' on twin earth refer to XYZ, but might also refer to vastly different things if XYZ is permutable with the other kinds of twin earth. According to the realist view of reference, if we are unlucky and the structure of the world admits the possibility of permutability, then *nothing we can do or say* will secure us even moderately determinate reference. Such a consequence is grounds for rejecting the descriptivist view as an adequate characterization of the reference of the terms in our theories.

PART IV

Emergence

10

Nonlinearity and metaphysical emergence

Jessica Wilson

Introduction

The nonlinearity of a composite system or 'entity', whereby certain of its features (including associated powers and behaviours) cannot be seen as linear or other broadly additive combinations of features of the system's composing entities, has been often taken to be a telling mark of metaphysical emergence, coupling a composite system's *dependence* on an underlying system of composing entities, with the composite system's having some degree of ontological *autonomy* from this underlying system.[1] But why think that nonlinearity is a mark of emergence, and moreover, of metaphysical rather than merely epistemological emergence? Are there diverse ways in which nonlinearity might enter into an account of properly metaphysical emergence? And what are the prospects for there actually being phenomena that are metaphysically emergent in any of these ways?

Here I will explore the mutual bearing of nonlinearity and metaphysical emergence, with an eye towards answering these and related questions. Given considerations of space I cannot hope to be comprehensive, but by focusing on a representative range of relevant accounts of emergence, and associated paradigm cases of nonlinearity, fairly robust results can, I think, be achieved.

I'll start, in Section 1, by considering how nonlinearity entered into the British Emergentist account of 'strong' metaphysical emergence, as involving the presence of new fundamental powers, forces/interactions, or laws; the emergence here is 'strong' in being of the sort that, were the base entities to be physical or physically acceptable, would falsify physicalism (or 'mechanism') were it to exist.[2] In particular, British Emergentists typically

---

[1] It is additionally typically supposed that the ontological autonomy at issue will bring some degree of causal autonomy in its wake: epiphenomenalist views are not to the point here.

[2] The question of how best to characterize the physical, hence physicalism, is controversial, but nothing in what follows will turn on the specific characterization of the base entities at issue. Most commonly, the physical entities are taken to be those treated more or less directly by (ideal, or at least approximately accurate) fundamental physics; physically acceptable entities are entities that are supposed to be, one way or another 'nothing over and above' the physical entities—e.g. by being lower-level aggregates of physical particulars standing in physical relations, or by being weakly emergent from such aggregates, as the case may be (see Wilson 2005).

supposed that non-linearity of composite features and associated powers or behaviours was a sufficient indication of strong metaphysical emergence of the features, hence systems, involved. As we'll see, this supposition (properly understood as involving a broad notion of additivity, involving not just intrinsic but also certain lower-level relational features of composing entities as 'summands') was plausible enough at the time. It was shown to be incorrect, however, by the discovery and creation of nonlinear complex systems (e.g. turbulent fluids, populations reproducing under conditions of finite resources, the Game of Life) clearly failing to involve new fundamental interactions or laws; indeed, awareness of such complex systems provides another reason, besides the advent of quantum mechanical explanations of chemical phenomena noted in McLaughlin 1992, for the 'fall' of British Emergentism. That said, it remains a live if somewhat outside possibility that some complex phenomena involve new fundamental interactions, and (drawing on Wilson 2002) I identify a better, scientifically supported criterion of the presence of a new fundamental interaction, in which a recognizable descendant of nonlinearity as indicative of strong metaphysical emergence is present in the form of seeming violations of conservation laws.

In Section 2 I consider a representative variety of accounts of 'weak' emergence of the sort supposed to be compatible with physicalism (the idea being that weakly emergent entities are physically acceptable if their base entities are), which typically take as their starting point one or other variety of nonlinear system. Some such accounts—e.g. Newman's (1996) account of features such as *being in the basin of a strange attractor* as identical, though inaccessibly so, to lower-level features—cannot be seen as characterizing emergence in other than merely epistemological terms. Others, including Bedau's (1997, 2002) account of features such as *being a glider gun* in the Game of Life as explanatorily or algorithmically 'incompressible', and Batterman's (1998) account of phase transitions as involving asymptotic universality, aim (or can be seen as aiming) to characterize emergence in genuinely metaphysical terms. As I argue, however, incompressibility and universality are compatible with the ontological reducibility of nonlinear systems and associated features; hence these criteria do not in themselves succeed in establishing that any nonlinear systems are even weakly emergent in a properly metaphysical sense.

In Section 3 I turn to an account of weak emergence that does successfully combine physical acceptability with ontological autonomy, based in the notion of *degrees of freedom* (DOF)—parameters needed to specify the states relevant to the law-governed properties and behaviour of a given entity or system. I first motivate and summarize the key features of the DOF-based account (presented in detail in Wilson 2010), according to which it suffices for a composite entity E's being metaphysically weakly emergent from the system of its composing entities e_i that E has DOF some of which are eliminated relative to the comparatively unconstrained system of e_i. I then argue that various paradigmatic nonlinear systems are plausibly seen as having DOF some of which are eliminated relative to entities in their composing base system, hence as being weakly metaphysically emergent.

1 Nonlinearity and strong metaphysical emergence

1.1 Nonlinearity in the British Emergentist tradition

Mill (in 'On the Composition of Causes', 1843/1973) distinguished two types of effects of joint or composite causes. 'Homopathic' effects conform to 'the principle of composition of causes' in being (in some sense) mere sums of the effects of the component causes when acting in relative isolation, as when the weight of two massy objects on a scale is the scalar sum of their individual weights, or when the joint operation of two forces conforms to vector addition in bringing an object to the same place it would have ended up, had the forces operated sequentially. 'Heteropathic' effects, by way of contrast, violate the principle in *not* being mere sums in any clear sense. What is most crucial for Mill about this distinction is that the advent of heteropathic effects is taken to be indicative of the operation of new laws. Mill says:

> This difference between the case in which the joint effect of causes is the sum of their separate effects, and the case in which it is heterogeneous to them; between laws which work together without alteration, and laws which, when called upon to work together, cease and give place to others; is one of the fundamental distinctions in nature. (1843/1973: 408–9)

And he offers chemical compounds and living bodies as entities that are capable of producing heteropathic effects.

   Mill did not use the term 'emergence' (evidently Lewes 1875 first did so), and his discussion appears to target a diachronic notion of emergence rather than the broadly synchronic emergence typically at issue in debates over whether some 'higher-level' goings-on are properly seen as emergent from some 'lower-level' goings-on. But given the reciprocal connection between powers and effects, it is straightforward to translate between the two approaches: to say that an effect of a feature of a composite entity is non-additive, relative to effects of features of the parts acting separately, is just to say that the higher-level feature has a power not had by the lower-level base features when in additive combination.[3] Mill himself moves seamlessly from talk of heteropathic effects to talk of new properties of and laws governing entities capable of causing such effects:

---

[3] A background issue here concerns whether lower-level features 'in additive combination' are to be understood as features of a relational entity, consisting in lower-level entities standing in lower-level relations (as well as Boolean and mereological combinations) or not; this question is related to the question of whether realization should be understood as a one-one or many-one relation (see Gillett 2002). *Contra* Gillett, I don't think anything of importance hangs on this issue, since it's clear that both the one-one and the many-one approaches to characterizing lower-level (i.e. physically acceptable) base features target the same phenomena. To wit: on the non-relational approach we consider the nature of the dependence (as involving either emergence or realization) of higher-level features on features of comparatively non-relational lower-level entities given certain allowable combinatorial principles, whereas on the relational approach we consider the nature of the dependence of higher-level features on features of a relational lower-level entity understood as 'put together' by the allowable combinatorial principles. In my view, it's more perspicuous to take the one-one approach, as reflecting or encoding the sorts of features of lower-level aggregates that all parties agree would not give rise to emergence. But to gloss over this issue I will typically speak of the composing base 'system', leaving open whether the system is comprised by many lower-level entities or a single lower-level relational entity.

[W]here the principle of Composition of Causes [...] fails [...] the concurrence of causes is such as to determine a change in the properties of the body generally, and render it subject to new laws, more or less dissimilar to those to which it conformed in its previous state. (Mill 1843/1973: 435)

Both Mill's reference to 'new laws' and his taking such cases to contrast with 'the extensive and important class of phenomena commonly called mechanical' indicate that Mill's appeal to non-additivity of effects is aimed at identifying a criterion for a higher-level feature's having a new fundamental power, enabling it (or its possessing 'body') to override the usual composition laws in the production of certain effects. As McLaughlin (1992) notes, 'Mill holds that collocations of agents can possess fundamental force-giving properties' (65). Hence it is that Mill's conception is appropriately seen as a variety of 'strong' metaphysical emergence, of the sort that, were it to exist, would falsify physicalism ('mechanism').

Other British Emergentists followed Mill in characterizing strong metaphysical emergence in terms of nonlinearity, as involving violations of broadly additive composition laws, including Alexander (1920), who characterized emergent properties as having powers to produce heteropathic effects; Morgan (1923), who contrasted resultant with emergent features as being 'additive and subtractive only'; and Broad (1925), who offered scalar and vector addition as paradigms of the compositional principles whose violation was characteristic of emergence.[4]

As in Mill's case, these appeals to nonlinearity are best seen as attempts to provide substantive metaphysical criteria of the operation of new fundamental powers, forces, or laws that come into play only at certain complex levels of existence, as when Broad (1925) says, '[T]he law connecting the properties of silver-chloride with those of silver and of chlorine and with the structure of the compound is, so far as we know, an unique and ultimate law' (64–5). As such, McLaughlin accurately characterizes British Emergentism as:

[...] the doctrine that there are fundamental powers to influence motion associated with types of structures of particles [...] In a framework of forces, the view implies that there are what we may call 'configurational forces': fundamental forces that can be exerted only by certain types of configurations of particles [...].[5] (1992: 52)

1.2 Is nonlinearity a mark of fundamentality?

Were the British Emergentists right, or at least reasonable, to take nonlinearity as a mark of emergent fundamentality? In answering this question we need first to address a clear

---

[4] Lewes's (1875) was an exception to this rule, in characterizing emergence as involving any failure of 'general mathematizability'. Lewes's characterization is faulty, however: since one can always construct a broadly mathematical function from base to higher-level features, such a characterization will rule out any features as being emergent.

[5] McLaughlin goes on to note that some British Emergentists were suspicious of forces per se, and to claim that the thesis could be preserved just as a thesis about new fundamental powers. For reasons that I'll get to in Section 1.3, I think the appeal to forces/interactions is essential to making out the position, but nothing in this subsection turns on this specific issue.

objection to the sufficiency claim, arising from taking the contrasting understanding of linearity to require that every feature (or associated power, etc.) of a composite entity be a linear combination of *intrinsic* features (powers, etc.) of its composing entities, or as it is sometimes put, a linear combination of features of its composing entities when these are 'in relative isolation'. Consider, for example, the shape of a molecule composed of some atoms.[6] The molecule's shape (and associated powers, etc.) is clearly not the product of any new fundamental interactions; but on the other hand this shape is clearly not a function (linear or otherwise) of *just* the shapes of the atoms when in relative isolation, but also of the bonding relations between the atoms holding these at some distance from each other.

British Emergentists were aware of this concern, and the most sophisticated and careful of them—that is, Broad—included pairwise and other relatively non-complex relations between the composing entities (or states of affairs consisting of lower-level entities standing in relatively non-complex lower-level relations) as among the physically acceptable 'summands' apt to be combined in broadly additive or mereological fashion, and against which a given claim of emergent nonlinearity was to be assessed. Hence it was that Broad characterized 'pure mechanism' as involving broadly additive deducibility of all higher-level features from features of lower-level entities 'either individually or in pairwise combination', and couched his official formulation of emergence in terms of failures of in-principle deducibility of composite features from features of composing entities both 'in isolation' and 'in other wholes'. The notion of linearity in these construals clearly adverts to lower-level relational as well as intrinsic features of composing entities, hence can accommodate the physical acceptability of, e.g., the shape of a molecule, as a broadly additive combination of shapes associated with atoms in pairwise or other relatively non-complex combination. Note that the broadly linear deducibility here can help itself to vector addition of forces exerted by atoms standing in bonding relations.

Given an appropriately sophisticated understanding of the notion of linearity at issue, then, it was quite reasonable for the British Emergentists to take nonlinearity to be a mark of emergent fundamentality. To start, various paradigm cases of non-emergent features of composite entities are simple scalar sums of features of their composing entities, as when the mass of a composite entity is the sum of the masses of its composing entities. More generally and more importantly, at the time it was common to suppose that effects ultimately involve the exertion of various fundamental forces, including gravity and electromagnetism, operating either singly or together. Moreover, as Mill's discussion makes especially clear, the combination of fundamental forces was taken to proceed in accord with linear composition laws—that is, by means of vector rather than scalar addition. As such, and again recalling the correspondence between powers and effects, linearity looked to provide a general handle on when the features of composite

---

[6] I assume here that molecules (or larger entities, such as tables) and atoms have fairly contained shapes.

entities did *not* involve or invoke any new fundamental powers, forces, or laws. Failures of features or behaviours of composite systems to be subject to linear analysis would thus have been reasonably interpreted as indicating that some additional fundamental force—a force not operative at lower, less complex levels of natural reality—was now on the scene.

Though reasonable at the time, the Emergentist supposition that nonlinearity is sufficient indication of strong metaphysical emergence is no longer plausible. For one thing, the picture of causal relations as constituted by the operation of additive combinations of fundamental push–pull forces is now seen as largely heuristic, or in any case not generalizable; it is fundamental interactions, involving particle exchanges, or yet more abstract accounts of the existence and evolution of natural phenomena, that provide the ultimate story as regards the 'go' of events, and to the extent that broadly Newtonian forces can be seen as real (as they arguably can be; see Wilson 2007), they are now assumed to be non-fundamental (as, e.g., constituted by fundamental interactions). For another, 20th-century investigations into a wide range of complex systems revealed not just that nonlinearity was rampant, but that in many of these cases the nonlinearity was generated simply as a result of complexity, without any need to posit additional fundamental interactions.

The recognition of many complex composite systems as genuinely nonlinear proceeded along several fronts. Even as early as the late 1880s, there were difficulties in seeing complex systems of the sort associated with turbulence in fluids and gases, and phase transitions in general, as linear. Attempts were made to explain away failures of linear prediction in these cases as due to noise or imprecision in measurement; but in a nice recapitulation of the move from a Ptolemaic to a Copernican system of astronomy, the anomalies and epicycles associated with the supposition of linearity eventually gave way to an understanding of chaotic complex systems as having genuinely nonlinear dynamics. This is not to say, of course, that failures in prediction were thereby (always) overcome; rather, such failures were alternatively explained as reflecting, most saliently, the highly sensitive dependence of the associated nonlinear functions on initial conditions (a.k.a. 'the butterfly effect').

That the predictive anomalies in some complex systems could not generally be put down just to noise or imprecision was confirmed by attention to natural and artificial nonlinear systems for which the relevant initial conditions could be specified with complete accuracy. Population growth, for example, is straightforwardly modelled by the nonlinear logistic map:

$$x_n + 1 = ax_n - a(x_n)^* 2$$

Here *a* is a parameter representing birth and death rates, and is different for different systems. The behaviour of a given system is strongly dependent on *a*. For most values of *a*, the system evolves to a fixed point; as *a* approaches 4, the system's behaviour becomes periodic, and subject to increasingly rapid bifurcation; for *a* = 4, the system's behaviour becomes chaotic, with very small differences in initial conditions x_1, associated with distant decimal places, eventually leading to wildly different trajectories. The discovery of natural nonlinear systems encouraged attention to nonlinear systems in general, and with the advent of computers in the latter half of the 20th century much attention focused on artificial complex systems such as cellular automata, where, as in Conway's 'Game of Life' (see Section 2.2 below), the stipulated dynamics are nonlinear.

What is the bearing of such genuinely nonlinear systems on the British Emergentist supposition that nonlinearity is sufficient for strong metaphysical emergence? Most obviously, the sufficiency claim is undermined, in that at least some cases of nonlinear complex systems—e.g. that associated with population growth or cellular automata— clearly do not involve any additional fundamental forces/interactions, etc. (in the case of automata, as a matter of explicit stipulation).

More generally, it is often taken for granted that strong metaphysical emergence, of the sort, again, whose existence would falsify physicalism (mechanism), is not at issue in any cases of nonlinear systems along lines of those mentioned above. Hence Bedau says:

An innocent form of emergence—what I call 'weak emergence'—is now a commonplace in a thriving interdisciplinary nexus of scientific activity [...] that includes connectionist modeling, non-linear dynamics (popularly known as 'chaos' theory), and artificial life. (Bedau 1997: 375)

It is worth noting, however, that stated reasons for thinking that nonlinear systems *in general* are physically acceptable aren't good. Newman (1996) cites the fact that complex systems are 'strictly deterministic' in support; but nothing prevents emergent features from entering, both as regards their emergence and their subsequent evolution, into a deterministic nomological net.[7] Nor does the fact that features of nonlinear systems are 'derivable' from nonlinear equations and initial (or boundary) conditions establish physical acceptability, since—as the British Emergentist tradition makes explicit—unlike linear combinations, that nonlinear combinations of physically acceptable features are themselves physically acceptable is not obvious. Bedau (1997) claims that features of nonlinear systems are physically acceptable because 'structural'—that is: are features of a relational system consisting in composing entities standing in lower-level relations; but given that the features of such a relational entity do not consist solely in additive combinations of features of the parts, that such features are *merely* structural (as with, e.g., the shape of a molecule), in a sense that would entail physical acceptability, is again not obvious. One might aim to support the general claim via an argument by analogy, maintaining that insofar as various surprising features associated with nonlinearity (period doubling, extreme sensitivity to initial conditions) can be modelled in comparatively

---

[7] Cf. Broad's (1925) claim that emergent features are 'completely determined' by lower-level features, in that 'whenever you have a whole composed of these [...] elements in certain proportions and relations you have something with the [compound's] characteristic properties' (64).

simple and artificial systems for which no fundamental novelty is at issue, there is no reason to suppose that more complex natural nonlinear systems involve fundamental novelty, either. But this argument by analogy fails, for precisely what is at issue is whether, in the more complex natural cases, the nonlinearity at issue has a physically acceptable source.

Indeed, there is in-principle room for maintaining that strong metaphysical emergence is at issue in at least some cases of nonlinearity. Consider, for example, cases where the non-linear phenomena involves feedback between the micro-entities constituting the base, associated with strange attractors and other dynamic phenomena. As Silberstein and McGeever (1999) note, non-linearity might be taken to involve a kind of system-level holism:

What is the causal story behind the dynamics of strange attractors, or behind dynamical auton-omy? The answer, it seems to us, must be the non-linearity found in chaotic systems. [...] But why is non-linearity so central? [...] Non-linear relations may be an example of what Teller calls 'relational holism' [...]. (1999:197)

Silberstein and McGeever go on to suggest that relational holism of this sort might reflect emergent features' possessing fundamentally new powers ('irreducible causal capacities'). It has also been suggested (or interpreted as being suggested) that the singularities standardly associated with thermodynamic phase transitions are indicative of strong emergence. Hence Callender and Menon (forthcoming) interpret Batterman's claim that 'thermodynamics is correct to characterize phase transitions as real physical discontinuities and it is correct to represent them mathematically as singularities' (Batterman 2005: 234) as signalling Batterman's commitment to phase transitions' being emergent along British Emergentist lines. Whether Teller and Batterman would agree that relational holism or thermodynamic singularities should be understood as involving new fundamental powers/interactions/laws is disputable (see in particular my upcoming discussion of Batterman's view). Still, for present purposes the crucial point is that one *could* maintain strong emergence as underlying some features associated with complex natural nonlinear systems.

Let's sum up the results so far.

First, whether or not all nonlinear systems are physically acceptable, in any case there's no doubt that *some* are. The general moral to be drawn from the identification of straight-forwardly mechanistic and artificial nonlinear systems is that, contra Mill and the other British Emergentists, nonlinearity is not sufficient indication of fundamental higher-level powers/interactions/laws. This result represents a second salient reason for the fall of British Emergentism, besides the advent of quantum mechanical explanations of chemical phenomena noted in McLaughlin (1992).

Second, though many nonlinear systems clearly do not involve strong metaphysical emergence, stated reasons for generalizing this result to all nonlinear systems do not go through, and the general claim, as it stands, appears to be something of an article of faith. It would be nice if, given that nonlinearity *itself* can no longer be seen as criterial of strong metaphysical emergence, there was an alternative criterion which could distinguish physically acceptable from physically unacceptable cases of nonlinearity (assuming any of the latter exist). I turn now to identifying such a criterion, as entering into a somewhat refined account of strong metaphysical emergence.

1.3 Nonlinearity's descendant

In Wilson (2002) I offered an account of strong metaphysical emergence along British Emergentist lines, as explicitly (as opposed to implicitly, as on Broad's characterization in terms of 'in-principle failure of deducibility') involving a new fundamental force/ interaction. As above, at the heart of the Emergentist position is that an emergent composite system has features bestowing new powers, grounded in new fundamental forces or interactions, to produce effects that the composing system can't enter into producing.[8] McLaughlin claimed (see note 3) that those suspicious of forces (and presumably also of interactions) could dispense with this aspect of the view, retaining only the appeal to new powers; but as I argued in my (2002), this claim is likely incorrect, for on a wide variety of accounts of which powers are bestowed by a given feature, the powers of features of a composite system are inherited by the features of the composing system, simply in virtue of the latter features' being nomologically necessary preconditions for the former. Without a more fine-grained way of assigning powers to features, the possibility of strong metaphysical emergence threatens to be ruled out of court—a bad result, since surely the truth of some version of physicalism is not that easy to establish. I considered various ways of getting around this problem—by appeal, e.g., to a distinction between 'direct' and 'indirect' bestowing of a power, or by appeal to different systems of laws— but concluded that the most straightforward and metaphysically illuminating solution to the problem proceeds by recognizing that powers are typically grounded in specific fundamental forces/interactions, and incorporating this dependence into the operative account of strong metaphysical emergence.

That powers are grounded in distinct fundamental forces/interactions is, I take it, scientifically uncontroversial. The power of being able to bond with an electron, in circumstances where one is in the vicinity of a free electron, is grounded in the electromagnetic (or electroweak) force/interaction, as opposed to the strong nuclear or gravitational forces/interactions. The power of being able to fall when dropped, in circumstances where one is poised above Earth's surface, is grounded in the gravitational force, as opposed to the other fundamental forces in operation. The power of being able to bond with other atomic nuclei in a stable configuration is grounded in the strong nuclear force/interaction, as opposed to the electromagnetic, weak, or gravitational forces/interactions. The power of being able to sit on a chair without falling through it is grounded (at least) in the gravitational and the electromagnetic forces/interactions. In

---

[8] The notion of 'power' here serves in the first instance as a metaphysically neutral way of registering what effects an entity may enter into causing, when in certain circumstances. Nothing in my use of this notion depends on controversial assumptions.

grounding the powers bestowed by properties, fundamental forces/interactions explain, organize, and unify vast ranges of natural phenomena. More could and eventually should be said about the details of the grounding relation at issue, but for present purposes it will suffice to note that we appear to be within our rights to speak of a feature's bestowing (or not bestowing) a power, *relative to* a given set of fundamental interactions.

But are there philosophical problems with positing fundamental forces or interactions— in particular, should we be suspicious of such entities on metaphysical grounds? One thing to say here is that, as above, Newtonian forces, understood as pushes and pulls having magnitudes and directions, have been replaced in fundamental theorizing by fundamental interactions, involving particle and energy exchanges; as such, one might maintain that Newtonian forces are no longer directly relevant to the characterization of strong emergence. That said, the primary reason for rejecting Newtonian forces— namely, that their posit is redundant, since the properties giving rise to the purported forces are sufficient unto the task of explaining causal relations—might also be supposed to apply to fundamental interactions. It is thus worth noting that ways of responding to this concern about forces (set out in Wilson 2007) also serve to vindicate the posit of fundamental interactions. Fundamental interactions are thus both scientific and metaphysical posits in good standing; hence it is reasonable to appeal to them in characterizing the strong emergence of broadly scientific entities.

My suggestion, then, is that strong emergence (and also its 'complement', realization) should be understood as a *relative* notion—relative, that is, to a specified set of fundamental interactions $\{F\}$. Let us assume, as per usual, that every feature of a composite entity E is (at least) nomologically necessitated by a feature of the system of its composing entities e_i.[9] Schematically expressed, the account is as follows:

Interaction-relative Strong Emergence: Feature P of composite entity E is strongly emergent from feature Q of the system of composing entities e_i, relative to $\{F\}$, if (i) Q nomologically necessitates P, and (ii) P is associated with at least one power that is *not* identical with any power of Q that is grounded only in fundamental interactions in $\{F\}$.[10]

The British Emergentist's account of strong emergence is then accommodated by taking the fundamental interactions in $\{F\}$ to be the fundamental physical interactions— that is, those coming into play at or below the atomic level of organization.[11] And British Emergentism would then be the thesis (contrasting with any version of physicalism), that at least one feature of at least one composite entity is strongly emergent in having at least one power that is not grounded *only* in fundamental physical interactions.

---

[9] Recall that in my talk of a 'system' of composing entities I am remaining neutral between the one-one and one-many characterizations of the system; see note 1.

[10] This account can be extended to apply to cases of non-composite emergence (e.g. emergence of melded 'fusions' as discussed in Humphreys 1997).

[11] See Wilson 2005 for discussion of how to characterize the physical entities (including interactions) so as to avoid concerns stemming from 'Hempel's dilemma'.

As prefigured, *Interaction-relative Strong Emergence* makes room for there to be strong metaphysical emergence: even if, taking *all* fundamental interactions into account, features of the composing system inherit all the powers of any features they nomologically necessitate, it remains that composite features may be associated with powers that are relevantly 'new', in not being grounded only in the set of physical fundamental interactions.

Interaction-relative Strong Emergence also has three features relevant to investigating the mutual bearing of nonlinearity on strong emergence.

First, the account nicely accommodates the supposition that features of a composite entity that *can* be analysed as broadly additive combinations of physically acceptable features of the composing entities will *not* be strongly emergent. For whatever the precise account of how powers are grounded in fundamental interactions, in any case it is clear—to go back to Mill's original discussion—that every power of a feature that is a broadly additive combination of physically acceptable features will be grounded only in fundamental physical interactions, hence fail to be strongly emergent.

Second, the account suggests an alternative criterion for strong emergence, that not only survives the advent of physically acceptable nonlinear systems, but moreover provides the means of distinguishing, at least in principle, between cases of nonlinearity that *do* and cases that *don't* involve strong emergence. On the interaction-relative account, strong emergence explicitly involves the coming into play of a new fundamental interaction; hence in determining whether there is any such emergence we can adopt whatever scientific methods are available for tracking such fundamental novelty. Here it is especially useful to attend to the discovery of the weak nuclear interaction, since this interaction occurs at a lower-level but still configurational level. This discovery was motivated by its seeming to be that certain nuclear processes, involving alpha radiation in particular, violated well-entrenched conservation laws of mass-energy and momentum. Rather than reject the associated conservation laws, the books were balanced by positing an additional fundamental interaction. A similar strategy makes in-principle empirical room for testing whether or not the unusual features associated with complex natural nonlinear systems are due to configurational fundamental interactions, by comparing the values of relevant conserved quantities predicted by fundamental physical theory as attaching to composite entities, with the actually observed values of these quantities. If there's less (or more) energy coming out than going in, for example, we might well be inclined to conclude, following accepted scientific procedure and as per the strong emergentist thesis, that a new configurational force/interaction is in operation.

Third, in the appeal to apparent violations of conservation laws as a sufficient criterion of strong emergence, we have, it seems to me, a recognizable descendant of the British Emergentist appeal to apparent violations of linearity as such a criterion. For in both cases, the apparent violations serve to flag that the whole is more than the mere sum of its parts; and that additional fundamental entities must be posited, if the sum—of forces, of conserved quantities—is to come out right.

All this said, I take it that there is not much motivation for thinking that any complex natural nonlinear systems involve new fundamental interactions. Still, it is useful to observe, first, that strong metaphysical emergence understood in interaction-relative terms is conceptually viable, and second, that (unlike bare appeals to relational holism or representational mismatch, whose status as criterial for new fundamental interactions is controversial) such an account suggests a criterion for strong emergence upon which all parties are likely to agree, and which could, in principle, be tested for.

2 Nonlinearity and weak metaphysical emergence

I now want to turn to the role nonlinearity has played in a representative range of accounts of weak metaphysical emergence (of the sort, again, whose occurrence is supposed to be compatible with physicalism) intended to apply to three different kinds of nonlinear systems. As above, accounts of properly metaphysical emergence aim to combine the *dependence* of a composite system E on the system of its composing base entities e_i with E's ontological (and also causal) autonomy from the composing e_i; and in cases of weak emergence the autonomy is supposed to be compatible with the composite system and its features' being physically acceptable. But as I'll argue, (a representative range of) accounts of weak emergence are compatible with the ontological (hence causal) reducibility of the nonlinear systems at issue, and hence establish, at best, that such systems are epistemologically or representationally emergent. I'll establish this, in turn, for Newman's account of emergence as a matter of epistemologically inaccessible identity between composite and base features, applied to properties such as *being in the basin of a strange attractor*; Bedau's account of weak emergence as involving algorithmic or explanatory incompressibility, applied to properties such as *being a glider gun* in the Game of Life; and Batterman's account of emergence as involving asymptotic universality, as applied to thermodynamic systems undergoing phase transitions.[12] I'll then present my (2010) account of weak metaphysical emergence as involving an *elimination in degrees of freedom* associated with the composite entity as compared to the unconstrained system of its composing base entities, and argue that at least some nonlinear systems are weakly emergent, by lights of the DOF-based account.

2.1 Newman's inaccessible-identity-based emergence

Newman's focus (1996) is on chaotic nonlinear systems, characteristically exhibiting (among other interesting features) extreme sensitivity to initial conditions (as per the 'butterfly effect'). Such systems are, he notes, associated with 'strange attractors':

[12] As we'll see, there's good reason to think that Batterman doesn't really have any sort of metaphysical account of emergence in mind. Still, asymptotic universality runs through his work and it is worth considering whether this (or the related notion of stability under permutation) could serve as a basis for weak metaphysical emergence. Another feature of the sort of systems Batterman discusses receives a thoroughly metaphysical treatment in my own account of weak emergence (Section 3).

A strange attractor is a non-periodic trajectory in the state space that exhibits sensitive dependence on initial conditions. This means that as the state of a chaotic system evolves toward the
attractor in its state space, it will never be in exactly the same state twice, and any two nearby
points in the state space will diverge exponentially under the dynamical evolution of the system.
(1996: 254)

Typically, for certain parameters of a given non-linear dynamical equation, a system
governed by the equation will evolve towards a strange attractor A in its state space, no
matter what its initial state; such a system is said to be 'in the basin' of strange attractor A.
So, for example, in the case of the logistic map, the onset of chaos occurs for $a = 4$.

Chaotic nonlinear systems exhibit two epistemological characteristics. First, due to
the sensitive dependence on initial conditions we are unable to predict the future trajectory of a chaotic non-linear system:

[F]or any chaotic system, since the measurements that we can make of its state are less than
perfect [...] the future states of that system are impossible to predict. [...] The kind of unpre-
dictability introduced by chaotic systems is a kind of epistemic impossibility rather than a metaphysical impossibility. (Newman 1996: 254)

Second, difficulties in measurement also mean that it is epistemically 'impossible to
determine exactly which chaotic system we are dealing with'. These characteristics
enter into Newman's account of weak emergence, on which emergent features of composite systems are, while identical to some lower-level feature of the composing system,
such that it is epistemically impossible to make the identification, as follows:

A property designated by a predicate P in an ideal theory T is emergent [from T'] if
and only if the following conditions are met:

(i) T describes a class of systems which are structured aggregates of entities
described by T'.

(ii) T' is an ideal theory of those entities, and the entities described by T strongly
supervene on those described by T'[13]

(iii) Occurrences of the property designated by P are epistemically impossible to
identify with occurrences of any property finitely describable in T'

(iv) Each occurrence of the property designated by P is an occurrence of one of a
set of properties PC, which is modelled by T'. Each member of PC is epistemically indistinguishable in T' from some other member of PC.

Newman argues that the property of *being in the basin of a strange attractor* is such an
emergent property of nonlinear systems. Nonlinear chaotic systems (described by the
relevant higher-level science T) are structured aggregates of lower-level physically
acceptable entities (ultimately described by fundamental physical theory), as per (i);

---

[13] This clause is intended to characterize emergent dependence as physically acceptable, though as it happens there are good reasons to think that even the strongest varieties of supervenience do not guarantee
transmission of physical acceptability; see, e.g., Horgan 1993, Wilson 2005.

nonlinear chaotic systems, Newman assumes, strongly supervene on entities described in fundamental physical theory, as per (ii); moreover, every occurrence of a property of a chaotic nonlinear system is, Newman assumes, identical to the occurrence of a lower-level physically acceptable property, as per (iv); but given that occurrences of the higher-level property are so extremely sensitive to initial conditions, the precise values of which are epistemically inaccessible to us, we are never in position to specify the relevant identities, as per (iii).

Newman's account is straightforwardly epistemological, and indeed in supposing that every property of a nonlinear dynamic system is identical with some lower-level physically acceptable property, he is clear that he thinks the former are ontologically, hence causally, reducible to the latter. I mention Newman's account as representative of perhaps the most common approach to the weak emergence of nonlinear systems—namely, one on which the 'emergence' of such systems is cashed in terms of one or other epistemological feature commonly associated with such systems (see also Popper and Eccles 1977; Klee 1984; Rueger 2001). However illuminating such accounts may be as regards why we find the features and behaviour of such systems interesting, novel, or unpredictable, they go no distance towards establishing nonlinearity as a mark of weak *metaphysical* emergence. The accounts to be next considered aim (or can be seen as aiming) to do better.

2.2 Bedau's incompressibility-based emergence

Bedau's focus is on a feature of nonlinear systems shared by both chaotic and non-chaotic nonlinear systems; namely, that such systems typically fail to admit of analytic or 'closed' solutions. The absence of analytic or otherwise 'compressible' means of predicting the evolution of such systems means that the only way to find out what this behaviour will be is by 'going through the motions': set up the system, let it roll, and see what happens. It is this feature—namely, *algorithmic incompressibility*—that serves as the basis for Bedau's account of weak emergence, as follows:

Where system S is composed of micro-level entities having associated micro-states, and where microdynamic D governs the time evolution of S's microstates:

Macrostate P of S with microdynamic D is weakly emergent iff P can be derived from D and S's external conditions but only by simulation. (1997: 378)

Derivation of a system's macrostate 'by simulation' involves iterating the system's micro-dynamic, taking initial and any relevant external conditions as input. The broadly equivalent conception in Bedau's (2002) takes weak emergence to involve 'explanatory incompressibility', where there is no 'short-cut' explanation of certain features of a composite system. In being derivable by simulation from a micro-physical dynamic, associated macrostates are understood to be physically acceptable; as Bedau (1997) says, such systems indicate 'that emergence is consistent with reasonable forms of materialism' (376).

By way of illustration, Bedau focuses on Conway's Game of Life, an example of a non-chaotic nonlinear map. The game consists in a set of simple rules, applied simultaneously and repeatedly to every cell in a lattice of 'live' and 'dead' cells.[14] Here there is no problem of sensitivity to initial conditions, since these conditions consist just in the discrete 'seeding' of the lattice. Still, Bedau argues that the property of *being a glider gun* in the Game of Life is weakly emergent, in his sense. That this property (involving a gun-like shape that moves across the grid, emitting 'bullets') does not involve any strong emergence is clear, since for cellular automata the long-term behaviour of the system is completely determined by ('derived from') the lower-level 'rules' applying to cells in the grid. But that a given system will evolve in such a way as to generate a glider gun can typically not be predicted from knowledge of initial conditions (seeding) and these rules.

On the face of it Bedau's account, like Newman's, does not characterize a genuinely metaphysical account of weak emergence, an impression seemingly confirmed when Bedau says that 'weakly emergent phenomena are autonomous in the sense that they can be derived only in a certain non-trivial way' (Bedau 2002: 6). Indeed, Bedau is explicit that he takes weakly emergent features of composite systems to be both ontologically and causally reducible to features of their composing systems:

[W]eakly emergent phenomena are ontologically dependent on and reducible to micro phenomena. (2002: 6)

[T]he macro is ontologically and causally reducible to the micro in principle. (2008: 445)

Notwithstanding these reductive assumptions, Bedau maintains that the autonomy of weakly emergent entities on his account is not just epistemological, but also properly metaphysical. He offers two reasons for thinking this, but as I'll now argue, neither establishes the claim.

The first is that the incompressibility of an algorithm or explanation is an objective metaphysical (if broadly formal) fact:

The modal terms in this definition are metaphysical, not epistemological. For P to be weakly emergent, what matters is that there is a derivation of P from D and S's external conditions and any such derivation is a simulation. [...] Underivability without simulation is a purely formal notion concerning the existence and nonexistence of certain kinds of derivations of macrostates from a system's underlying dynamic. (1997: 379)

But such facts about explanatory incompressibility, though objective and hence in some broad sense 'metaphysical', are not suited to ground the metaphysical autonomy of emergent entities. What is needed for such autonomy is not just some or other metaphysical

---

[14] The Game of Life takes place on a two-dimensional grid of cells, which may be either 'alive' or 'dead'. At each step in time, cells are updated as per the following rules: (1) any live cell with fewer than two live neighbours dies; (2) any live cell with two or three live neighbours stays alive; (3) any live cell with more than three live neighbours dies; (4) any dead cell with exactly three live neighbours becomes alive.

distinction between macro- and micro- goings-on, but moreover one which plausibly serves as a basis for rendering weakly emergent features ontologically autonomous from—that is, *distinct* from—the lower-level features upon which they depend.

The second reason Bedau gives is somewhat more promising; namely, that weakly emergent features typically enter into macro-level patterns and laws. As Bedau says:

[T]here is a clear sense in which the behaviors of weak emergent phenomena are autonomous with respect to the underlying processes. The sciences of complexity are discovering simple, general macro-level patterns and laws involving weak emergent phenomena. [...] In general, we can formulate and investigate the basic principles of weak emergent phenomena only by empirically observing them at the macro-level. In this sense, then, weakly emergent phenomena have an autonomous life at the macro-level. (1997: 395)

As such, Bedau maintains, 'weak emergence is not just in the mind; it is real and objective in nature' (2008: 444). Attention to macro-level patterns sounds like a move in the right direction towards autonomy; but, two points. First, I don't see how Bedau can maintain that some weakly emergent goings-on are not 'merely epistemological' (Bedau 2008: 451) and rather reflect an 'autonomous and irreducible macro-level ontology', while also maintaining that all weakly emergent goings-on are metaphysically ontologically and causally reducible to the micro-level goings-on. Either the metaphysical autonomy or the metaphysical reducibility has to go.[15]

Second, it isn't enough to block the potential reducibility of composite features to features of the composing base system, merely to point to the fact that the composite features enter into nomological patterns that are in some sense more general than those into which the composing features enter. To see this, it is useful to recall a related dialectic in the physicalism debates. There, would-be non-reductive physicalists point to the fact that mental features are associated with functional roles (i.e. 'macro-level patterns') that can be multiply implemented, or realized, by lower-level physical features; but the reductionist's ready response is that the existence of functional or other comparatively general patterns can be accommodated, on their terms, by identifying a given mental feature with (to cite the most salient candidates) *a disjunction* of its first-order physical realizers or the second-order *existential* property of having one or other of its first-order physical realizers. The dialectic sometimes continues, with the non-reductive physicalist rejecting, e.g., the existence of disjunctive features on grounds that they are too gerrymandered, are not projectible, or otherwise suspect; but such considerations seem, from a reductionist perspective, either unprincipled or uncompelling. Similarly, in the case of *being a glider gun*, while something seems right about attending to the comparative generality of the patterns into which this feature enters, more needs to be said if reductionist accommodation of such macro-level patterns is to be blocked in a principled and compelling fashion.

---

[15] My impression is that the tension here reflects Bedau's assumption that if a higher-level system is to be physically acceptable, then it must be ultimately ontologically reducible to some lower-level system. This is incorrect, as I will discuss in Section 3.1.

Bedau does not say more along these lines, however, and the upshot is that this strategy, like the previous, fails to establish that features of nonlinear systems are even weakly metaphysically emergent.

2.3 Batterman's asymptotic emergence

Batterman has in recent years written a great deal concerning the status as emergent or reducible of special science entities (see his 2002, 2005, and elsewhere); but perhaps because his discussions have tended to engage primarily with theoretical/representational and explanatory issues, there has remained unclarity as regards whether he takes emergence to be a metaphysical phenomenon, and if so, of what strength. As I'll discuss, there is good reason to think that Batterman does not have even a weak account of metaphysical emergence in mind (much less the strong account some attribute to him). Still, no discussion of emergence as relevant to nonlinear phenomena should neglect Batterman's work on emergence in asymptotic regions of the sort associated with phase transitions, since these share key features with chaotic nonlinear systems; and whatever Batterman's view of the matter, various features of systems in asymptotic regions are at least promising so far as indicating that weak metaphysical emergence is in place.

I'll start, then, by discussing some general features of Batterman's account of emergence as associated with asymptotic limits, and the specific application of his account to the case of systems undergoing phase transitions. I'll identify three related characteristics of such systems, each of which generally applies to chaotic nonlinear systems and might be thought promising as regards characterizing weak metaphysical emergence; namely, *eliminations in micro-level degrees of freedom (DOF)*, *asymptotic universality*, and *stability under permutation*. I'll say why it's fairly clear that Batterman does not see these features as tracking a genuinely metaphysical form of emergence. I'll then consider whether the latter two features, which are the primary running themes in Batterman's work (see his 1998, 2000, 2002, 2005), might nonetheless serve as sufficient criteria for weak emergence, and I'll argue that they cannot do so, since here again the having of these features is compatible with ontological reducibility. In the next section I turn to my preferred, explicitly metaphysical DOF-based account of weak emergence, which, I'll argue, is up to the task of guaranteeing ontological autonomy.

Let's summarize the basics of Batterman's account of asymptotic emergence.[16] An asymptote in mathematics is a limiting value of a function that is approached indefinitely closely, but never reached. So, for example, as $x \to 0$ the function $1/x$ goes to infinity; in this case (though not all, of course) the asymptote is associated with a discontinuity. Interestingly, many 'near-neighbour' scientific theories involve asymptotes: special relativity asymptotically approaches Newtonian mechanics in the limit as $v/c \to 0$, wave optics $\to$ ray optics as $1/\lambda$ approaches 0, (quantum mechanics) $\to$ Newtonian mechanics as Planck's constant $\to 0$, statistical mechanics $\to$ thermodynamics in the 'thermodynamic

---

[16] My discussion here leans heavily on Hooker's (2004) admirably clear summary of the view expressed in Batterman (2002).

limit', where particle number N and volume V→infinity. Now, in some of these cases—in particular, the latter three—the asymptotic limits at issue are associated with discontinuities in the regions near the asymptote. In such cases of 'singular' asymptotic limits, Batterman suggests, we have reason to take various objects or features associated with the asymptotic region (or associated theory) as emergent. In particular, to cut to the case which concerns us, Batterman suggests that various features of systems undergoing phase transitions, including those associated with certain critical exponents, are emergent features of such systems. Why so, and in what sense?

Batterman's most explicit stated considerations concern broadly explanatory factors. Again focusing on the case which concerns us, one explanatory concern reflects a kind of theoretical mismatch between the near-neighbour theories at issue, insofar as the discontinuities associated with taking the thermodynamic limit, and which are commonly supposed to be needed to accommodate the associated asymptotic phenomena, find no representational mirror in the analytic functions of statistical-mechanics.[17] Even if there were no problem with deriving specific instances of asymptotic features from the micro-theory, however, Batterman's second explanatory concern would remain; namely, that the characteristic *universality* of asymptotic phenomena cannot be properly explained by reference just to lower-level 'causal-mechanical' explanations. As above, the behaviour of systems undergoing phase transitions is characterized by a small set of dimensionless numbers called 'critical exponents'. As Batterman (1998) says:

> What is truly remarkable about these numbers is their universality [...] the critical behavior of systems whose components and interactions are radically different is virtually identical. Hence, such behavior must be largely independent of the details of the microstructures of the various systems. This is known in the literature as the 'universality of critical phenomena'. Surely one would like to account for this universality. (198)

Lower-level causal-mechanical explanations, even if available, cannot account for universality, for these 'will be infinitely various in detail and this will block any reconstruction of what is universal about them' (2004: 442).

By way of contrast, Batterman argues, various methods for modelling asymptotic phenomena—most notably, the Renormalization Group (RG) method—*do* provide an explanation of the universal features of systems undergoing phase transitions. The applicability here primarily reflects that near critical points, the systems at issue cease to have any characteristic length scale, and are 'self-similar' in that the laws governing the systems take the same form at all length scales. Accordingly, the RG method—which takes a system's governing laws (e.g. its Hamiltonian) and iteratively transforms these into laws having a similar form but (reflecting moves to increasingly 'larger' scales) fewer parameters—can be applied. In the limit, the resulting Hamiltonian describes the behaviour of a single 'block', corresponding to the macroscopic system. As Batterman (1998) puts it:

---

[17] See Callender and Menon (in progress) and Wilson (in progress) for discussion.

One introduces a transformation on this space that maps an initial physical Hamiltonian describing a real system to another Hamiltonian in the space. The transformation preserves, to some extent, the form of the original physical Hamiltonian so that when the interaction terms are properly adjusted (renormalized), the new renormalized Hamiltonian describes a system exhibiting the same or similar thermodynamical behavior. Most importantly, however, the transformation effects a reduction in the number of coupled components or degrees of freedom within the correlation length. Thus, the new renormalized Hamiltonian describes a system which presents a more tractable problem. It is to be hoped that by repeated application of this renormalization group transformation the problem becomes more and more tractable until one can solve the problem by relatively simple methods. In effect, the renormalization group transformation eliminates those degrees of freedom (those microscopic details) which are inessential or irrelevant for characterizing the system's dominant behavior at criticality. (1998: 200)

(I quote this and the next passage at length, in order to make explicit, for future purposes, Batterman's appeal to certain features potentially relevant to emergence.) In particular, application of the RG method in this case enables calculation of the critical exponents associated with phase transitions, and hence provides an explanation of the universal behaviour of systems near critical points:

[I]f the initial Hamiltonian describes a system at criticality, then each renormalized Hamiltonian must also be at criticality. The sequence of Hamiltonians thus generated defines a trajectory in the abstract space that, in the limit as the number of transformations goes to infinity, ends at a fixed point. The behavior of trajectories in the neighborhood of the fixed point can be determined by an analysis of the stability properties of the fixed point. This analysis also allows for the calculation of the critical exponents characterizing the critical behavior of the system. It turns out that different physical Hamiltonians can flow to the same fixed point. Thus, their critical behaviors are characterized by the same critical exponents. This is the essence of the explanation for the universality of critical behavior: Hamiltonians describing different physical systems fall into the basin of attraction of the same renormalization group fixed point. This means that if one were to alter, even quite considerably, some of the basic features of a system (say from those of a fluid F to a fluid F' composed of a different kind of molecule and a different interaction potential), the resulting system (F') will exhibit the same critical behavior. This stability under perturbation demonstrates that certain facts about the microconstituents of the systems are individually largely irrelevant for the systems' behaviors at criticality. (1998: 201)

Batterman's account of asymptotic emergence, especially as relevant to phase transitions, looks very promising, so far as vindicating the emergence of nonlinear systems is concerned. To start, there are three features associated with this account having at least *prima facie* promise for characterizing a form of weak metaphysical emergence, in particular:

(1) elimination of micro-level degrees of freedom (DOF);
(2) universality of certain features or behaviour;
(3) stability of certain behaviour under perturbation.

Moreover, these common features of systems undergoing phase transitions are more generally features of chaotic nonlinear systems, as Hooker (2004) implies:

In every case of so-called 'critical phenomena', e.g. near the 'critical point' beyond which there is no vapour phase between liquid and gas, the asymptotic domain shows a universally self-similar spectrum of fluctuations. [...] This is indicative of chaos and occurs when behaviours are super-complexly, but still systematically, interrelated [...]. (2004: 440)

Indeed, the core similarities between critical phenomena in statistical mechanics and chaotic nonlinear phenomena, including period doubling and intermittency routes to chaos of the sort displayed by the logistic map, have led to an active area of investigation in which 'the logistic map is [...] becoming a prototypical system [...] for the assessment of the validity and understanding of the reasons for applicability of the nonextensive generalization of [...] Boltzmann–Gibbs statistical mechanics' (Mayoral and Robledo 2006: 339). If we can understand the features entering into Batterman's account of emergence in metaphysical terms, we would have a nice result as regards the bearing of nonlinearity and metaphysical emergence.

To be sure, there is good reason to believe that Batterman does *not* intend his discussion to be interpreted as offering either an account of or a case of metaphysical emergence. As above, his discussion is squarely focused on the question of what is required if the critical behaviours of the systems in question are to be explained, with the general idea being that, in the case of such systems, neither theoretical derivations nor causal–mechanical considerations can do the trick. Hence Morrison (2012) reads Batterman as offering an 'explanatory' account of emergence:

I characterize Batterman's account [of emergence] as explanatory insofar as the main argument centers on how asymptotic methods (via the RG) allow us to explain features of universal phenomena that are not explainable using either intertheoretic reduction or traditional causal mechanical accounts [...]. (2012: 143)

I think Morrison's reading is correct,[18] but one might wonder if it is undermined by Batterman's seeming to suggest, especially in some passages in his (2002) book, that he sees metaphysical emergence as following from explanatory emergence, as when he says, 'It seems reasonable to consider these asymptotically emergent structures [as constituting] the ontology of an explanatory "theory"' (Batterman 2002: 96). For another

---

[18] In context, it is worth registering that Morrison (2012) makes this observation en route to offering her own account of metaphysical emergence, as inspired by cases of spontaneous symmetry breaking in superconducting fluids. I do not enter into the details of Morrison's account here, mainly because it is not completely clear to me whether Morrison's account is a variety of strong or of weak emergence, and a full investigation into this issue would take us too far afield. Morrison herself supposes that 'When one is dealing with emergence in physics, physicalism is not an issue. No one denies that condensed matter phenomena such as superconductivity, phenomena often described as emergent, [...] are physical in nature' (141–2). Still, on her account (which in certain respects follows Batterman's and my own in attending to the relative independence of weakly emergent phenomena from micro-physical details), 'the characteristics that define the superconducting state are not explained or predicted from those processes'—due, in particular, to the advent of spontaneous symmetry breaking and the introduction of a new order parameter—which to my mind opens the door to the possibility that the phenomena at issue are strongly, not weakly, emergent. This and other issues are explored in Wilson (forthcoming).

example, in discussing the asymptotic domain between wave and ray optics, Batterman first argues that rainbows cannot be explained without referring to 'caustics'—ray tangent curves associated with the higher-level, but not lower-level theory, then suggests that we are ontologically committed to such optical objects:

[I]f I'm right and there is a genuine, distinct, third theory (catastrophe optics) of the asymptotic borderland between wave and ray theories—a theory that of necessity makes reference to both ray theoretic and wave theoretic structures in characterising its 'ontology'—then, since it is this ontology that we take to be emergent, those phenomena are not predictable from the wave theory. They are 'contained' in the wave theory but aren't predictable from it. (2002: 119)

These suggestive passages are misleading, however, since Batterman has explicitly denied that the emergence at issue here carries ontological weight:

I do not believe that there is any new ontology in the asymptotic catastrophe optics. The wave theory has replaced the ray theory and there simply are no caustics (as characterized by the ray theory). Asymptotic analysis of the wave equation yields terms (think syntax here) which require for their interpretation (semantics) that we make reference to ray theoretic structures. In effect, it is the understanding/interpretation of these terms in the asymptotic expansions that requires 'appeal' or reference to structures that 'exist' only in the ray theory. (p.c. with Hooker, discussed in Hooker 2004: 448)

Hooker concludes that 'the status claimed for caustics based on essential reference is not after all that of ontological commitment but one of ineliminable semantic role, without ontological commitment' (2004: 448). Similar remarks would presumably go for the 'emergent' phenomena at issue in phase transitions or chaotic nonlinear systems, more generally. Strictly speaking, Batterman's account of asymptotic emergence is an account of theoretical/representational or epistemological, not metaphysical, emergence.

That said, nothing prevents the more metaphysically inclined from considering whether any of the aforementioned features—elimination in micro-level DOF, universality, and/or stability under perturbation—might serve as sufficient indicators of metaphysical emergence. With an eye to sticking somewhat closely to Batterman's work, we might look especially to the latter two features, since these features have been consistent themes in his work, which he has discussed as attaching to a variety of special science entities to which the RG approach and its associated strategy for eliminating DOF does not apply.[19]

Universality and stability under perturbations are really two sides of the same coin; as Batterman says, 'most broadly construed, universality concerns similarities in the behavior of diverse systems' (2000: 120). The suggestion that weak emergence might be a matter of universality or of stability under micro-level perturbations is common enough;

---

[19] Hence, for example, Batterman (2000) argues that certain considerations showing that universal features of systems undergoing phase transitions are emergent (in whatever sense) readily extend to pendulums and other special science entities, and he says that 'there is really no difference between the example of the pendulum and some of the more interesting cases' (121).

indeed, we have already seen a version of this claim in Bedau's suggestion that the fact that certain features of nonlinear automata (e.g. glider guns) enter into 'macro-level patterns' might support such features' being metaphysically autonomous. It is unsurprising, then, that the same concerns with Bedau's suggestion, which again echo the debate over the import of multiple realizability in the metaphysics of mind, also attach to attempts to locate metaphysical emergence in universal or stable features of composite entities; namely, that reductionists have various strategies for accommodating such features, and that the standard anti-reductivist responses (rejecting disjunctive properties, denying that these track genuine natural kinds, and the like) are not compelling. What is needed, if these features are to be seen as tracking the ontological autonomy (distinctness) of composite entities, is a better response to the usual reductivist strategies; but Batterman does not provide such a response—arguably because his concern is ultimately with whether an appropriately explanatory account of universal or multiply realized features is available, and not with whether such features are (or are not) ontologically reducible.[20]

Let's sum up the results of this section. I've considered a representative survey of accounts of weak, or physically acceptable, emergence intended to apply to nonlinear systems of one or the other variety, but in each case the occurrence of the feature at issue (epistemic indiscernibility, algorithmic or explanatory incompressibility, presence in a macro-pattern, universality or stability under perturbation) has turned out to be, at least for all that proponents of these accounts have shown, compatible with ontological reduction of the systems at issue. So far, then, it has not been established that any nonlinear systems are even weakly metaphysically emergent. I turn now to considering the somewhat better prospects, as regards both viability and potential application to nonlinear systems is concerned, of weak emergence understood as involving an *elimination in degrees of freedom* (DOF).

3 Nonlinearity and eliminations in DOF

In Wilson (2010) I proposed an account of weak emergence on which weakly emergent systems are both physically acceptable and ontologically autonomous from (that is, distinct from) the systems from which they emerge.[21] In this section I'll motivate and present this account, discuss how it accommodates both physical acceptability and autonomy, then argue that chaotic nonlinear systems satisfy the conditions of the account, hence are weakly metaphysically emergent.

---

[20] See especially the introductory remarks in his 2000: 115–16, where he expresses his desire to explore the nature of multiple realizability rather than enter into 'the reductionism debate'.

[21] Following contemporary concern with physicalism, I characterize the dependence condition in terms of physical acceptability, but the account more generally suffices to guarantee 'nothing over and aboveness' (in recently fashionable terms: 'grounding') of weakly emergent entities vis-à-vis whatever type of base entities might be at issue.

3.1 A DOF-based account of weak metaphysical emergence

My account is based in the notion of a degree of freedom (DOF). Call states upon which the law-governed (i.e. nomologically possible) properties and behaviour of an entity *E* functionally depend the 'characteristic states' of *E*. A DOF is then, roughly, a parameter in a minimal set needed to describe an entity as being in a characteristic state. Given an entity and characteristic state, the associated DOF are relativized to choice of coordinates, reflecting that different sets of parameters may be used to describe an entity as being in the state.[22] More precisely, the operative notion of DOF is as follows:

Degrees of Freedom (DOF): For an entity *E*, characteristic state *S*, and set of coordinates *C*, the associated DOF are parameters in a minimal set, expressed in coordinates *C*, needed to characterize *E* as being in *S*.

I'll sometimes speak for short of 'characterizing an entity', with state and coordinates assumed.

Some common characteristic states, and DOF needed to characterize certain systems as being in those states, are as follows:

The configuration state: tracks position. Specifying this state for a free point particle requires three parameters (e.g. *x*, *y*, and *z*; or *r*, ρ, and θ); hence a free point particle has 3 configuration DOF, and a system of *N* free point particles has 3*N* configuration DOF.

The kinematic state: tracks velocities (or momenta). Specifying this state for a free point particle requires six parameters: one for each configuration coordinate, and one for the velocity along that coordinate; hence a free point particle has 6 kinematic DOF, and a system of *N* free point particles has 6*N* kinematic DOF.

The dynamic state: tracks energies determining the motion. Specifying this state typically requires at least one dynamic DOF per configuration coordinate, tracking the kinetic energy associated with that coordinate; other dynamic DOF may track internal/external contributions to the potential energy.

Why attend to DOF in thinking about emergence? To start, as above, different systems, treated by different sciences, may be functionally dependent on the same characteristic state (e.g. the configuration state). Moreover, as above, the DOF needed to characterize intuitively different systems as being in these states typically vary. Following these observations, I take the main cash value of attention to DOF to lie in the fact that DOF track the *details* of a system's functional dependence on a given characteristic state in a more fine-grained way than the mere fact that the system is in the state does. Driving my account is the idea that the fine-grained details concerning functional dependence that are encoded in the DOF needed to characterize a given entity/system serve as a plausible ontological basis for the individuation of broadly scientific entities/systems.

---

[22] This relativization won't matter in what follows, since the relations between (sets of) DOF at issue in the ensuing account will be in place whatever the choice of coordinates.

I start by observing an important tripartite distinction (again, see Wilson 2010) relevant to such functional dependence, reflecting that the DOF needed to characterize an entity may be *reduced*, *restricted*, or *eliminated* in certain circumstances (typically associated with the imposition of certain constraints or more generally, the presence of certain energetic interactions), compared to those needed to characterize a (possibly distinct) entity, when such circumstances are not in place. To prefigure: eliminations in DOF, in particular, will enter into the upcoming account of weak metaphysical emergence. Let's get acquainted with these different relations and note an example of each.

First, constraints may *reduce* the DOF needed to characterize an entity as being in a given state. So, for example, a point particle constrained to move in a plane has 2 configuration DOF, rather than the 3 configuration DOF needed to characterize a free point particle. In cases where a given DOF is given a fixed value, the laws governing an entity so constrained are still functionally dependent on the (now constant) value of the DOF; hence such constraints do not eliminate the DOF, but rather reduce it to a constant value. By way of example: rigid bodies treated in classical mechanics have such a reduced set of DOF relative to the unconstrained system of their composing entities.

Second, constraints may also *restrict* DOF needed to characterize an entity. A point particle may be constrained, not to the plane, but to some region including and above the plane. Characterizing such a particle still requires 3 configuration DOF, but the values of one of these DOF will be restricted to only certain of the values needed to characterize the unconstrained particle. Cases of restriction in DOF are more like cases of reduction than elimination of DOF, in that, again, the entity's governing laws remain functionally dependent on specific values of the DOF. By way of example: molecules, whose bonds are like springs, have a restricted set of DOF relative to the unconstrained system of their composing entities.

Third, sometimes the imposition of constraints *eliminates* DOF. So, for example, N free point particles, having $3N$ configuration DOF, might come to compose an entity whose properties and behaviour can be characterized using fewer configuration DOF, not because certain of the DOF needed to characterize the unconstrained system are given a fixed value, but because the properties and behaviour of the composed entity are *functionally independent* of these DOF. By way of example: a spherical conductor of the sort treated in electrostatics has DOF that are eliminated relative to the system of its composing entities, since while the E-field due to free particles depends on all charged particles, the E-field due to the spherical conductor depends only on the charges of particles on its surface. Certain quantum DOF are also eliminated in the classical (macroscopic) limit. So, for example, spin is a DOF of quantum entities; entities of the sort treated by classical mechanics are ultimately composed of quantum entities; but the characteristic states of composed classical–mechanical entities do not functionally depend on the spins of their quantum components.[23]

---

[23] Recall that the characteristic states of an entity are those upon which its law-governed properties and behaviour functionally depend; for classical entities it is the laws of classical mechanics that are at issue. Hence notwithstanding that the values of quantum parameters may lead to macroscopic differences, it remains the case that quantum DOF such as spin are eliminated from those needed to characterize entities of the sort treated by classical mechanics.

Two features of the illustrative special science case studies are important for what follows. First is that the holding of the constraints relevant to reducing, restricting, or eliminating DOF occurs as a matter entirely of physical or physically acceptable processes. Such processes suffice to explain why sufficiently proximate atoms form certain atomic bonds, why atoms or molecules engage in the energetic interactions associated with SM ensembles, and so on. More generally, for each of the aforementioned special science entities E, the constraints on the e_i associated with their composing E are explicable using resources of the theory treating the e_i (or resources of some more fundamental theory, treating the constituents of the e_i). Call such constraints 'e_i-level constraints'. A second important feature of these special science entities E is that all of their properties and behaviour are completely determined by the properties and behaviour of their composing e_i, when these stand in the relations relevant to their composing E.[24] People disagree about the metaphysical ground for this determination, but all parties agree that the determination is in place.

These preliminaries in hand, the DOF-based account of weak metaphysical emergence is as follows:

DOF-based weak metaphysical emergence: An entity E is weakly metaphysically emergent from some entities e_i if:

(1) E is composed by the e_i, as a result of imposing some constraint(s) on the e_i.
(2) For some characteristic state S of E: at least one of the DOF required to characterize the system of unconstrained e_i as being in S is eliminated from the DOF required to characterize E as being in S.
(3) For every characteristic state S of E: every reduction, restriction, or elimination in the DOF needed to characterize E as being in S is associated with e_i-level constraints.
(4) The law-governed features of E are completely determined by the law-governed features of the e_i, when the e_i stand in the relations relevant to their composing E.

Systems that are emergent by lights of the above account are physically acceptable, given that the unconstrained system of composing entities is physically acceptable. In my (2010) I argue for this, but due to considerations of space, here I'll just observe that this result is to be expected, given that the constraints relevant to composing a weakly emergent entity E, as well as all of E's law-governed features, are physically acceptable.

I also argue in my (2010) that entities satisfying DOF-based weak metaphysical emergence plausibly satisfy *Non-reduction*. Since the possibility of ontologically irreducibility is, as above, the main sticking point so far as accounts of weak metaphysical emergence is concerned, it's important to present this for the reader's perusal; but in order to keep the presentation flowing, I've put

---

[24] Note that this feature does not in itself follow from E's being composed by e_i as a result of imposing e_i-level constraints: the British Emergentists agreed that the composition of base systems was a matter of lower-level processes, but maintained that some of the properties or behaviours of composite systems were not fully determined by lower-level processes.

my main argument for this claim in an appendix to this paper (in Section 4). In brief: the argument is an argument by cases, where I consider each of the lower-level entities that are candidates for being identical with a weakly emergent composite entity E; for each case I show that the candidate reductive base entity has *as many* DOF as the unconstrained system of E's composing entities, and so (given that E is weakly emergent, and so has strictly *fewer* DOF than the unconstrained system) cannot, by Leibniz's Law, be identical with E. Unlike all other accounts of weak emergence on the market, a DOF-based account provides the basis for an *argument* that a weakly emergent entity is ontologically autonomous from—that is, distinct from—the system of composing entities upon which the weakly emergent entity depends.

3.2 DOF-based weak emergence and chaotic nonlinear systems

Let's return now to cases of nonlinear systems, and consider whether they can be understood as weakly metaphysically emergent. Given Batterman's work on the Renormalization Group (RG) method, and my results concerning the sufficiency of eliminations of DOF (along with certain other suppositions which are here in place, concerning e_i constraints and e_i determination), we can be comparatively brief.

As previously noted, the RG method applies to systems undergoing phase transitions, which are relevantly similar to and indeed can be understood as chaotic nonlinear systems; and that the RG applies to a given system provides as good indication as we are likely to get that the system has DOF that are not just reduced or restricted, but *eliminated* as compared to the unconstrained system of its composing entities (that is, as compared to the system of composing entities when not energetically interacting in the way associated with phase transitions, or more generally, with chaotic behaviour). We can thus argue as follows:

(1) Systems that can be modelled by the RG have eliminated DOF (Batterman 1998 and elsewhere).
(2) Chaotic nonlinear systems are modelled by the RG.
(3) Therefore, chaotic nonlinear systems have eliminated DOF.
(4) Systems with eliminated DOF are weakly metaphysically emergent (Wilson 2010).
(5) Therefore, chaotic nonlinear systems are weakly metaphysically emergent.

As confirmation of the fact that chaotic nonlinear systems have eliminated DOF, it is worth noting that one of the puzzles that Batterman raises for thermodynamic systems carries over to nonlinear chaotic systems, and is answered in just the same way. The puzzle he raises concerns how thermodynamic systems can be a viable object of study. Such systems—e.g. an isolated gas E—are composed of massively large numbers of particles or molecules e_i. Since the composite entity E in this case is (boundary restrictions aside) effectively unstructured, shouldn't it have the same DOF as the system of unconstrained e_i? Supposing so, however, the success of SM is mysterious, since obviously we can't track $\sim 10^{26}$ DOF. As Batterman (1998) puts it:

One wants to know why the method of equilibrium SM-the Gibbs' phase averaging method is so broadly applicable; why, that is, do systems governed by completely different forces and composed of completely different types of molecules succumb to the same method for the calculation of their equilibrium properties? (1998: 185)

The answer reflects that while the e_i are not bonded, they are interacting via exchanges of energy, and such interactions may not only restrict or reduce, but eliminate DOF, which is indicated by the fact that the renormalization group method is appropriately applied to such systems. This, then, is the answer to the puzzle: such systems are tractable since the modes of interaction of their composing entities result in their having DOF that are massively *eliminated* compared to the unconstrained system of composing entities. Again:

[T]he renormalization group transformation eliminates those degrees of freedom (those microscopic details) which are inessential or irrelevant for characterizing the system's dominant behavior at criticality. (1998: 200)

A similar puzzle applies to chaotic nonlinear systems. Recall that chaotic nonlinear systems are characterized by their extreme sensitivity to initial conditions. If nonlinear systems are so sensitive and their resulting trajectories so 'chaotic', how is it that they can be, as they are, a viable object of scientific study? The answer, I take it, is effectively the same: the composing entities, though not bonded, are energetically interacting, in ways that, as application of the RG method reveals, massively eliminate the DOF needed to characterize the composite system. Here we have a solution to the puzzle, and more to the present point, a decisive, empirically supported case for taking the important class of chaotic nonlinear systems to be weakly metaphysically emergent.[25]

4 Appendix: the irreducibility of weakly emergent entities

The main objection to the claim that an entity can be both physically acceptable and metaphysically irreducible is the objection from theoretical deducibility, as follows.

To start, laws governing weakly metaphysically emergent entities are (I am granting) deducible consequences of the laws of the more fundamental theory. But in that case, the objector asks, why doesn't such deducibility indicate that weakly metaphysically emergent entities E are ontologically reducible to their composing e_i? Indeed, that theoretical deducibility entails ontological reducibility seems initially plausible, and has been commonly endorsed (Nagel 1961; Klee 1984).

---

[25] Might an equally good case be made for taking non-chaotic nonlinear systems to be weakly emergent, by lights of a DOF-based account? I am inclined to think that a case *can* be made, though perhaps not one as good, based in certain patterns of difference-making and counterfactual dependence (see Wilson (in progress)).

The concern can also be presented as a dilemma. As above, the constraints entering into the composition of our target special science entities are plausibly e_i-level constraints, and as indicated, this feature is crucial to establishing the physical acceptability of the target entities. But if the constraints are e_i-level, why can't the associated e_i-level relations enter, one way or another, into an ontological as well as a theoretical reduction of E to its composing e_i? This line of thought is, I think, at the heart of suspicions that there is no way for entities to be weakly metaphysically emergent.

To see how attention to DOF provides a way of avoiding the dilemma, let's first get clear on what would count as an ontological reduction of E to the e_i. Traditionally and reasonably, the candidate reducing entities include all the lower-level entities, properties and relations, plus any ontologically 'lightweight' constructions—lower-level relational, Boolean (conjunctive or disjunctive), or mereological—out of these. Hence if E is to be ontologically reducible to the e_i, then E must be identical to either:

(i)   a system consisting of the jointly existing e_i;
(ii) a relational entity consisting of the e_i standing in e_i-level relations; or
(iii) a relational entity consisting in a Boolean or mereological combination of the entities at issue in (i) and (ii).

Since E is weakly metaphysically emergent, there is some state S such that characterizing E as being in this state requires fewer DOF than are required to characterize the unconstrained system of E's composing e_i as being in S. Hence a necessary condition on E's being identical with an entity of the type of (i)–(iii) is that the DOF required to characterize the candidate reducing entity as being in S are similarly eliminated, relative to the unconstrained system. I'll now argue that this condition isn't met for any of the entities of type (i)–(iii).

First, consider the e_i understood as (merely) jointly existing, as per (i). Such a system of e_i is not subject to any constraints; hence for any state, characterizing this system will require the same DOF as are required to characterize the system of unconstrained e_i.

So E is not identical to the system consisting of (merely) jointly existing e_i.

Second, consider the relational entity e_r consisting of the e_i standing in certain e_i-level relations, as per (ii). Though e_r realizes a constrained entity (namely, E), e_r is not itself appropriately seen as constrained—even throwing the holding of the constraints into the mix of e_i-level relations at issue in e_r. Why not? Because the laws governing entities (such as e_r) consisting of the e_i standing in e_i-level relations are, unlike the laws governing E, compatible with the constraints *not* being in place. Hence characterizing e_r as entering into these laws, hence as capable of evolving into states (of, perhaps other e_i level entities) where the constraints are not in place, requires all the DOF associated with the unconstrained system of e_i. So E is not identical to e_r.

Third, consider a Boolean (disjunctive or conjunctive) or mereological combination of entities of the previous varieties (or the closure of any such entity). To start, consider a relational entity consisting in a disjunctive combination of entities of the sort at issue in (i) or (ii). The occurrence of a disjunctive entity consists in one of its disjunct entity's occurring. Hence for any state, characterizing a disjunctive entity as being in that state will require all the DOF required to characterize any of its disjunct entities as being in that state. Such disjunct entities, being of type (i) or (ii), will require all the DOF required to characterize the system of unconstrained e_i, for any state. So characterizing a disjunctive relational entity will require all the DOF required to characterize the system of unconstrained e_i, for any state. The same goes for conjunctive entities. So E isn't identical to a disjunctive or conjunctive relational entity. Finally, consider a relational entity consisting in a mereological combination of entities of the sort at issue in (i) or (ii). Mereological wholes are identified with the mere joint holding of their parts; hence characterizing the whole will require all the DOF required to characterize each of the parts. Such parts, being of type (i) or (ii), will require all the DOF required to characterize the system of unconstrained e_i, for any state. So characterizing a mereological relational entity will require all the DOF required to characterize the system of unconstrained e_i, for any state. So E isn't identical to a mereological relational entity.

That exhausts the available candidates to which weakly metaphysically emergent entities might be ontologically reduced. In each case a weakly emergent entity has fewer DOF than the candidate reducing entity, so by Leibniz's Law the former is not identical to the latter. Attention to the metaphysical implications of the eliminations of DOF at issue in weak metaphysical emergence indicates that theoretical deducibility is compatible with ontological irreducibility. So physical acceptability is compatible with ontological autonomy, as weak metaphysical emergence supposes.

References

Albert, D. (2000) *Time and Chance*, Cambridge MA: Harvard University Press.

Alexander, S. (1920) *Space, Time, and Deity*, Macmillan & Co: London.

Angel, R. (1980) *Relativity: The Theory and its Philosophy*, Oxford: Pergamon.

Aristotle *Metaphysics (Book θ)*, Makin, S. (trans. and commentary), Clarendon Aristotle Series, Oxford: Oxford University Press, 2006.

Armstrong, D. M. (1978) *Universals and Scientific Realism*, Cambridge: Cambridge University Press.

—— (1983) *What is a Law of Nature?* Cambridge: Cambridge University Press.

—— (1997) *A World of States of Affairs*, Cambridge: Cambridge University Press.

—— (1999) 'The Causal Theory of Properties: Properties According to Shoemaker, Ellis and Others', *Philosophical Topics*, 26: 25–37.

Augustine *The Literal Meaning of Genesis*, vol. 1, trans. J. Hammond Taylor, New York: Newman Press, 1982.

Ausloos, M. and Dirickx, M. (2006) *The Logistic Map and the Route to Chaos: From the Beginnings to Modern Applications*, New York: Springer-Verlag.

Ayer, A. J. (1936) *Language, Truth and Logic*, London: Victor Gollancz.

Bais, S. (2007) *Very Special Relativity*, Cambridge: Harvard University Press.

Balashov, Y. and Janssen, M. (2003) 'Critical Notice: Presentism and Relativity', *British Journal for the Philosophy of Science*, 54: 327–46.

Barbour, J. (1989) *Absolute or Relative Motion? Volume 1: The Discovery of Dynamics*, Oxford: Oxford University Press.

—— and Tipler, F. (1986) *The Anthropic Cosmological Principle*, Oxford: Clarendon.

Barton, G. (1999) *Introduction to the Relativity Principle*, Chichester: Wiley.

Batterman, R. W. (1998) 'Why Equilibrium Statistical Mechanics Works: Universality and the Renormalization Group', *Philosophy of Science*, 65: 183–208.

—— (2000) 'Multiple Realizability and Universality', *British Journal for the Philosophy of Science*, 51: 115–45.

—— (2002) *The Devil in the Details: Asymptotic Reasoning in Explanation, Reduction, and Emergence*, Oxford: Oxford University Press.

—— (2005) 'Critical Phenomena and Breaking Drops: Infinite Idealizations in Physics', *Studies in History and Philosophy of Science*, Part B 36: 225–44.

Bedau, M. (1997) 'Weak Emergence', *Philosophical Perspectives*, 11: *Mind, Causation and World*: 375–99.

—— (2002) 'Downward Causation and the Autonomy of Weak Emergence', *Principia*, 6: 5–50.

—— (2008) 'Is Weak Emergence Just in the Mind?' *Minds and Machines*, 18: 443–59.

Beebee, H. (2002) 'Contingent Laws Rule: Reply to Bird', *Analysis*, 62: 252–5.

—— and Sabbarton-Leary, N. (eds) (2010a) *The Semantics and Metaphysics of Natural Kinds*, New York: Routledge.

—— and Sabbarton-Leary, N. (2010b) 'Introduction', in Beebee and Sabbarton-Leary 2010a: 1–24.

—— and Sabbarton-Leary, N. (2010c) 'On the Abuse of the Necessary *A Posteriori*', in Beebee and Sabbarton-Leary, 2010a: 159–78.

Bennett, J. (2003) *A Philosophical Guide to Conditionals*, Oxford: Oxford University Press.

Bergmann, P. G. (1962) 'The Special Theory of Relativity', in S. Flügge (ed.), *Encyclopedia of Physics*, vol. 4, Berlin: Springer-Verlag, pp. 109–202.

Berzi, V. and Gorini, V. (1969) 'Reciprocity Principle and Lorentz Transformations', *Journal of Mathematical Physics*, 10: 1518–24.

Bird, A. (2001) 'Necessarily, Salt Dissolves in Water', *Analysis*, 61: 267–74.

—— (2007a) *Nature's Metaphysics: Laws and Properties*, Oxford: Oxford University Press.

—— (2007b) 'The Regress of Pure Powers?', *The Philosophical Quarterly*, 57: 513–34.

—— (2009) 'Essences and Natural Kinds', in R. Le Poidevin, P. Simons, A. McGonigal, and R. Cameron (eds), *Routledge Companion to Metaphysics*, Abingdon: Routledge, pp. 497–506.

—— (2010) 'Discovering the Essences of Natural Kinds', in H. Beebee and N. Sabbarton-Leary (eds), *The Semantics and Metaphysics of Natural Kinds*, New York: Routledge, pp. 125–36.

—— and Tobin, E. (2010) 'Natural Kinds', in E. N. Zalta (ed.), *Stanford Encyclopedia of Philosophy*, <http://plato.stanford.edu/archives/sum2010/entries/natural-kinds/>.

Bohm, A. (1986) *Quantum Mechanics: Foundations and Applications*, New York: Springer-Verlag.

Boyd, R. (1991) 'Realism, Anti-Foundationalism and the Enthusiasm for Natural Kinds', *Philosophical Studies*, 61: 127–48.

—— (1999a) 'Homeostasis, Species, and Higher Taxa', in R. Wilson (ed.), *Species: New Interdisciplinary Essays*, Cambridge MA: MIT Press, pp. 141–86.

—— (1999b) 'Kinds, Complexity and Multiple Realization', *Philosophical Studies*, 95: 67–98.

Braddon-Mitchell, D. and Jackson, F. (1996) *Philosophy of Mind and Cognition*, Oxford: Blackwell.

Broad, C. D. (1925) *Mind and Its Place in Nature*, Cambridge: Kegan Paul.

Brown, H. (2005) *Physical Relativity*, Oxford: Clarendon.

—— and Pooley, O. (2006) 'Minkowski Space-Time: A Glorious Non-Entity', in D. Dieks (ed.), *The Ontology of Spacetime*, Amsterdam: Elsevier, pp. 67–89.

Brown, R. and Ladyman, J. (2009) 'Physicalism, Supervenience and the Fundamental Level', *Philosophical Quarterly*, 59: 20–38.

Cacciatori, S., Gorini, V., and Kamenshchik, A. (2008) 'Special Relativity in the 21st Century', *Annalen der Physik*, 17: 728–68.

Callender, C. (2004) 'Measures, Explanation, and the Past: Should Special Initial Conditions be Explained?', *British Journal for the Philosophy of Science*, 55: 195–217.

—— and Menon, Turn (forthcoming) 'Turn and Face the Strange…Ch-ch-changes: Philosophical Questions Raised by Phase Transitions', in *Oxford Handbook of Philosophy of Physics*, edited by Robert Batterman, New York: Oxford University Press.

Carnap, R. (1935) *Philosophy and Logical Syntax*, London: Kegan Paul.

Carroll, J. (1994) *Laws of Nature*, Cambridge: Cambridge University Press.

Cartwright, N. (1979) 'Causal Laws and Effective Strategies', *Noûs*, 13: 419–37.

—— (1983) *How the Laws of Physics Lie*, Oxford: Oxford University Press.

—— (1999) *The Dappled World*, Cambridge: Cambridge University Press.

—— (2009) 'Causal Laws, Policy Predictionism and the Need for Genuine Powers', in T. Handfield (ed.), *Dispositions and Causes*, Oxford: Oxford University Press, pp. 127–57.

Collins, J., Hall, N., and Paul, L. (2004) 'Counterfactuals and Causation: History, Problems, and Prospects', in *Causation and Counterfactuals*, Cambridge MA: MIT Press, pp. 1–57.

Colyvan, M. (1998) 'Can the Eleatic Principle be Justified?', *Canadian Journal of Philosophy*, 28: 313–36.

Corry, L. (1997) 'Hermann Minkowski and the Postulate of Relativity', *Archive for History of Exact Sciences*, 51: 273–314.

Corry, R. (2009) 'How is Scientific Analysis Possible?', in T. Handfield (ed.), *Dispositions and Causes*, Oxford: Oxford University Press, pp. 158–88.

Craver, C. (2009) 'Mechanisms and Natural Kinds', *Philosophical Psychology*, 22.5: 575–94.

Crisp, T. (2008) 'Presentism, Eternalism and Relativity Physics', in W. Lane Craig and Q. Smith (eds), *Einstein, Relativity and Absolute Simultaneity*, London: Routledge, pp. 262–78.

Devitt, M. (1983) 'Realism and the Renegade Putnam: A Critical Study of *Meaning and the Moral Sciences*', *Noûs*, 17: 291–301.

—— and Sterelny, K. (1999) *Language and Reality: An Introduction to the Philosophy of Language* (2nd edn), Cambridge MA: MIT Press.

Dieks, D. (1981) *Studies in the Foundations of Physics*, PhD-thesis, Utrecht.

DiSalle, R. (2006) *Understanding Space-time*, Cambridge: Cambridge University Press.

Dorato, M. (2007) 'Relativity Theory Between Structural and Dynamical Explanations', *International Studies in the Philosophy of Science*, 21: 95–102.

Dowe, P. (2009) 'Causal Process Theories', in H. Beebee, C. Hitchcock, and P. Menzies (eds), *The Oxford Handbook of Causation*, Oxford: Oxford University Press, pp. 213–33.

Dumsday, T. (2010) 'Natural Kinds and the Problem of Complex Essences', *Australasian Journal of Philosophy*, 88: 619–34.

Dupré, J. (1993) *The Disorder of Things: Metaphysical Foundations of the Disunity of Science*, Cambridge MA: Harvard University Press.

—— (2004) 'Review of Natural Kinds and Conceptual Change', *Notre Dame Philosophical Reviews*, <http://ndpr.nd.edu/review.cfm?id=1439>.

Earman, J. (1989) *World Enough and Space-Time*, Cambridge MA: MIT Press.

—— and Roberts, J. (2005) 'Contact with the Nomic: A Challenge for Deniers of Humean Supervenience about Laws of Nature Part 11: The Epistemological Argument for Humean Supervenience', *Philosophy and Phenomenological Research*, 71: 253–86.

Ehrenfest, P. (1917) 'In What Way Does It Become Manifest in the Fundamental Laws of Physics that Space has Three Dimensions?', *Proceedings of the Amsterdam Academy*, 20: 200–9.

Einstein, A. (1905) 'On the Electrodynamics of Moving Bodies', in *The Collected Papers of Albert Einstein: Volume 2*, trans. A. Beck, Princeton: Princeton University Press, 1989, pp. 140–71.

—— (1911) ' "Discussion" following lecture version of "The Theory of Relativity" ', in *The Collected Papers of Albert Einstein: Volume 3*, trans. A. Beck, Princeton: Princeton University Press, 1993, pp. 351–8.

—— (1919) 'What is the Theory of Relativity?', *The Times (London)*, 28 November 1919, repr. in *Ideas and Opinions*, New York: Bonanza, 1954, pp. 27–32.

—— (1935) 'Elementary Derivation of the Equivalence of Mass and Energy', *Bulletin of the American Mathematical Society*, 41: 223–30.

—— (1955) Letter to Carl Seelig (2/19/55), repr. in M. Born, *Physics in My Generation*, London and New York: Pergamon Press, 1956, p. 194.

Elgin, C. (1995) 'Unnatural Science', *Journal of Philosophy*, 92: 289–30.

Ellis, B. (2001) *Scientific Essentialism*, Cambridge: Cambridge University Press.

—— (2009) *The Metaphysics of Scientific Realism*, Durham: Acumen.

Feyerabend, P. (1975) *Against Method*, London: Verso Books.

Feynman, R. (1967) *The Character of Physical Law*, Cambridge MA: MIT Press.

Field, H. (2003) 'Causation in a Physical World', in M. Loux and D. Zimmerman (eds), *The Oxford Handbook of Metaphysics*, Oxford: Oxford University Press, pp. 435–60.

Fine, K. (1975) Review of David Lewis's *Counterfactuals*, *Mind*, 84: 451–8.

—— (1994) 'Essence and Modality', *Philosophical Perspectives*, 8: 1–16.

Frege, G. (1892) 'On Sense and Reference', in P. Geach and M. Black (eds), *Translations from the Philosophical Writings of Gottlob Frege*, Oxford: Blackwell, 1952.

Friedman, M. (2002) 'Geometry as a Branch of Physics', in D. Malament (ed.), *Reading Natural Philosophy*, Chicago: Open Court, pp. 193–229.

Gannett, J. (2007) 'Nothing But Relativity, Redux', *European Journal of Physics*, 28: 1145–50.

Gell-Mann, M. (1994) *The Quark and the Jaguar: Adventures in the Simple and the Complex*, New York: Henry Holt & Co.

Geroch, R. (1978) *General Relativity from A to B*, Chicago: University of Chicago Press.

Ghiselin, M. T. (1974) 'A Radical Solution to the Species Problem', *Systematic Zoology*, 23: 536–44.

Gillett, C. (2002) 'The Dimensions of Realization: A Critique of the Standard View', *Analysis*, 62: 316–23.

Goodman, N. (1983) *Fact, Fiction, and Forecast*, 4th edn, Cambridge MA: Harvard University Press.

Grandy, R. E. (2007) 'Sortals', in E. N. Zalta (ed.), *Stanford Encyclopedia of Philosophy*, <http://plato.stanford.edu/entries/sortals/>.

Griffiths, P. (1999) 'Squaring the Circle: Natural Kinds with Historical Essences', in R. Wilson (ed.), *Species: New Interdisciplinary Essays*, Cambridge MA: MIT Press, pp. 219–28.

Gross, D. (1996) 'The Role of Symmetry in Fundamental Physics', *Proceedings of the National Academy of Sciences USA*, 93: 14256–9.

Haavelmo, T. (1944) 'The Probability Approach in Econometrics', *Econometrica*, 12 (Supplement), 1–118.

Hacking, I. (2007) 'Natural Kinds, Rosy Dawn, Scholastic Twilight', *Royal Institute of Philosophy Supplement*, 82: 203–39.

Hall, N. (2004) 'Two Concepts of Causation', in J. Collins, N. Hall, and L. Paul (eds), *Causation and Counterfactuals*, Cambridge MA: MIT Press, pp. 225–76.

—— (forthcoming) 'Humean Reductionism About Laws of Nature', <http://philpapers.org/rec/HALHRA>.

Handfield, T. (2009) 'The Metaphysics of Dispositions and Causes', in T. Handfield (ed.), *Dispositions and Causes*, Oxford: Oxford University Press, pp. 1–30.

Harré, R. and Madden, E. H. (1975) *Causal Powers: A Theory of Natural Necessity*, Oxford: Blackwell.

Hart, H. L. and Honoré, A. M. (1959) *Causation in the Law*, 2nd edn, 1985, Oxford: Oxford University Press.

Hausman, D. and Woodward, J. (1999) 'Independence, Invariance and the Causal Markov Condition', *British Journal for the Philosophy of Science*, 50: 521–83.

Hawley, K. and Bird, A. (2011) 'What are Natural Kinds?', *Philosophical Perspectives*, 25: 205–21.

Heil, J. (2003) *From an Ontological Point of View*, Oxford: Oxford University Press.

—— (2005) 'Dispositions', *Synthese*, 144: 343–56.

Hempel, C. (1965) *Aspects of Scientific Explanation*, New York: Free Press.

Hendry, R. (2006) 'Element, Compounds and Other Chemical Kinds', *Philosophy of Science*, 73: 864–75.

—— (2010) 'The Elements and Conceptual Change', in Beebee and Sabbarton-Leary (eds), *The Semantics and Metaphysics of Natural Kinds*, New York: Routledge, pp. 137–58.

Hitchcock, C. (2007) 'What Russell Got Right', in H. Price and R. Corry (eds), *Causation, Physics and the Constitution of Reality*, Oxford: Oxford University Press, pp. 45–65.

—— (2011) 'Probabilistic Causation', in E. N. Zalta (ed.), *Stanford Encyclopedia of Philosophy*, <http://plato.stanford.edu/archives/win2011/entries/causation-probabilistic/>.

Hooker, C. A. (2004) 'Asymptotics, Reduction, and Emergence', *British Journal for the Philosophy of Science*, 55: 435–79.

Horgan, T. E. (1993) 'From Supervenience to Superdupervenience: Meeting the Demands of a Material World', *Mind*, 102: 555–86.

Hughes R. I. G. (1989) *The Structure and Interpretation of Quantum Mechanic*, Cambridge MA: Harvard University Press.

Hull, D. L. (1965) 'The Effect of Essentialism on Taxonomy: 2,000 Years of Stasis', *British Journal for the Philosophy of Science*, 15: 314–26.

Humphreys, P. (1997) 'How Properties Emerge', *Philosophy of Science*, 64: 1–17.

Hüttemann, A. (1998) 'Laws and Dispositions', *Philosophy of Science*, 65: 121–35.

—— (2004) *What's Wrong with Microphysicalism?* London: Routledge.

—— (2005) 'Explanation, Emergence and Quantum-entanglement', *Philosophy of Science*, 72: 114–27.

—— (2009) 'Dispositions in Physics', in G. Damschen, R. Schnepf, and K. R. Stuber (eds), *Debating Dispositions: Issues in Metaphysics, Epistemology and Philosophy of Mind*, Berlin: Walter de Gruyter, pp. 223–37.

—— (unpublished) 'The Elimination of Causal Vocabulary from Physics'.

Jackson, F. (1992) 'Critical Notice of Susan Hurley's *Natural Reason*', *The Australasian Journal of Philosophy*, 70: 475–87.

—— (1998) *From Metaphysics to Ethics*, Oxford: Oxford University Press.

—— and Pettit, P. (1995) 'Moral Functionalism and Moral Motivation', *The Philosophical Quarterly*, 45: 20–39.

—— and Pettit, P. (1996) 'Moral Functionalism, Supervenience and Reductionism', *The Philosophical Quarterly*, 46: 82–6.

Janssen, M. (2009) 'Drawing the Line between Kinematics and Dynamics in Special Relativity', *Studies in History and Philosophy of Modern Physics*, 40: 26–52.

Kekes, J. (1966) 'Physicalism, the Identity Theory, and the Concept of Emergence', *Philosophy of Science*, 33: 360–75.

Khalidi, M. A. (1998) 'Natural Kinds and Crosscutting Categories', *Journal of Philosophy*, 95: 33–50.

Kim, J. (1976) 'Events as Property Exemplifications', in M. Brand and D. Walton (eds), *Action Theory*, Dordrecht: Reidel, pp. 159–77.

Kirchhoff, G. (1874) *Vorlesungen über Mathematische Physik. 1. Mechanik*, Leipzig: Trubner.

Kitcher, P. (1984) 'Species', *Philosophy of Science*, 51: 308–33.

Kittel, C., Knight, W. P., and Ruderman, M. A. (1973) *Mechanics: Berkeley Physics Course, Volume 1*, New York: McGraw-Hill.

Klee, Robert L. (1984) 'Microdeterminism and Concepts of Emergence', *Philosophy of Science*, 51: 44–63.

Kripke, S. (1971) 'Identity and Necessity', in M. K. Munitz (ed.), *Identity and Individuation*, New York: New York University Press, pp. 135–64.

—— (1972) 'Naming and Necessity', in G. Harman and D. Davidson (eds), *Semantics of Natural Language*, Dordrecht: Reidel, pp. 253–355.

—— (1980) *Naming and Necessity*, Oxford: Basil Blackwell.

Kuhn, T. (1970) *The Structure of Scientific Revolutions*, 2nd edn, Chicago: Chicago University Press.

—— (1990) 'The Road since *Structure*', *Proceedings of the Biennial Meeting of the Philosophy of Science Association*, II: 3–13.

Ladyman, J. and Ross, D. (2007) *Every Thing Must Go: Metaphysics Naturalized*, Oxford: Oxford University Press.

Lakatos, I. (1978) The *Methodology* of Scientific Research Programmes: Philosophical Papers Volume 1, J. Worrall and G. Currie (eds), Cambridge: Cambridge University Press.

Lange, M. (2005) 'Laws and Their Stability', *Synthese*, 144: 415–32.

—— (2007) 'Laws and Meta-Laws of Nature: Conservation Laws and Symmetries', *Studies in History and Philosophy of Modern Physics*, 38: 457–81.

—— (2009) *Laws and Lawmakers*, Oxford: Oxford University Press.

LaPorte, J. (2004) *Natural Kinds and Conceptual Change*, Cambridge: Cambridge University Press.

—— (2010) 'Theoretical Identity Statements, their Truth, and their Discovery', in H. Beebee and N. Sabbarton-Leary (eds), *The Semantics and Metaphysics of Natural Kinds.* New York: Routledge, pp. 104–24.

Lee, A. R. and Kalotas, T. M. (1975) 'Lorentz Transformations from the First Postulate', *American Journal of Physics*, 43: 434–7.

Lévy-Leblond, J.-M. (1976) 'One More Derivation of the Lorentz Transformations', *American Journal of Physics*, 44: 271–7.

Lewes, G. H. (1875) *Problems of Life and Mind*, London: Kegan Paul, Trench, Turbner & Co.

Lewis, D. (1970) 'How to Define Theoretical Terms', repr. in D. Lewis 1986b, pp. 78–95.

—— (1973) 'Causation', in D. Lewis 1986b, pp. 159–72.

—— (1979) 'Counterfactual Dependence and Time's Arrow', *Noûs*, 13: 455–76.

—— (1983a) 'New Work for a Theory of Universals', *The Australasian Journal of Philosophy*, 61, 343–77.

—— (1983b) 'Postscripts to "Counterpart Theory and Quantified Modal Logic"', *Philosophical Papers*, vol. I, Oxford: Blackwell.

—— (1984) 'Putnam's Paradox', *The Australasian Journal of Philosophy*, 62, 221–36.

—— (1986a) *On the Plurality of Worlds*, Oxford: Blackwell.

—— (1986b) *Philosophical Papers*, vol. II, Oxford: Oxford University Press.

—— (1997) 'Naming the Colours', *The Australasian Journal of Philosophy*, 75, 325–42.

—— (1999) *Papers in Metaphysics and Epistemology*, Cambridge: Cambridge University Press.

Lipton, P. (2004) 'What Good is an Explanation?', in J. Cornwell (ed.), *Explanations: Styles of Explanation in Science*, Oxford: Oxford University Press, pp. 1–21.

Loewer, B. (2007) 'Counterfactuals and the Second Law', in H. Price and R. Corry (eds), *Causation, Physics, and the Constitution of Reality*, Oxford: Oxford University Press.

Lowe, E. J. (1998) *The Possibility of Metaphysics: Substance, Identity, and Time*, Oxford: Oxford University Press.

—— (2006) *The Four-Category Ontology: A Metaphysical Foundation for Natural Science*, Oxford: Oxford University Press.

—— (2007) 'Sortals and the Individuation of Objects', *Mind and Language*, 22: 514–33.

Mach, E. (1883) *Die Mechanik*, Darmstadt: Wissenschaftliche Buchges, 1982.

—— (1896) *Principien der Wärmelehre*, 2nd edn, Leipzig: Barth, 1900.

—— (1905) *Erkenntnis und Irrtum*, Darmstadt: Wissenschaftliche Buchgesellschaft, 1980.

Machamer, P. K., Darden L., and Craver, C. F. (2000) 'Thinking about Mechanisms', *Philosophy of Science*, 67: 1–25.

Mackie, J. (1980) *The Cement of the Universe*, Oxford: Oxford University Press.

Martin, C. B. (1993) 'Power for Realists', in J. Bacon, K. Campbell, and L. Reinhardt (eds), *Ontology, Causality, and Mind*, Cambridge: Cambridge University Press, pp. 75–86.

—— (2008) *The Mind in Nature*, Oxford: Oxford University Press.

Maudlin, T. (2004) 'Causation, Counterfactuals and the Third Factor', in J. Collins, N. Hall, and L. Paul (eds), *Causation and Counterfactuals*, Cambridge MA: MIT Press, pp. 419–43.

Mayoral, E. and Robledo, A. (2006) 'A Recent Appreciation of the Singular Dynamics at the Edge of Chaos', in M. Ausloos and M. Dirickx, *The Logistic Map and the Route to Chaos: From the Beginnings to Modern Applications*, New York: Springer-Verlag, pp. 339–54.

McKitrick, J. (2009) 'Dispositions, Causes and Reduction', in T. Handfield (ed.), *Dispositions and Causes*, Oxford: Oxford University Press, pp. 31–64.

—— (2010) 'Manifestations as Effects', in A. Marmodoro (ed.), *The Metaphysics of Powers: Their Grounding and their Manifestations*, London: Routledge, pp. 73–83.

McLaughlin, B. (1992) 'The Rise and Fall of British Emergentism', in A. Beckermann, H. Flohr, and J. Kim (eds), *Emergence or Reduction?: Prospects for Nonreductive Physicalism*, Berlin: De Gruyter.

Melling, D. (1987) *Understanding Plato*, Oxford: Oxford University Press.

Mellor, D. H. (1991) *Matters of Metaphysics*, Cambridge: Cambridge University Press.

Menzies, P. (1999) 'Intrinsic Versus Extrinsic Conceptions of Causation', in H. Sankey (ed.), *Laws and Causation: Australasian Studies in the History and Philosophy of Science*, Dordrecht: Kluwer, 313–29.

—— (2007) 'Causation in Context', in H. Price and R. Corry (eds), *Causation, Physics and the Constitution of Reality*, Oxford: Oxford University Press, pp. 191–223.

Merrill, G. (1980) 'The Model-Theoretic Argument Against Realism', *Philosophy of Science*, 47: 69–81.

Mill, J. S. (1843) *A System of Logic*, Toronto: University of Toronto Press, 1973 (Vols II and III of *The Collected Works of John Stuart Mill*).

Minkowski, H. (1908) 'Space and Time', in H. A. Lorentz, A. Einstein, H. Minkowski, H. Weyl, and A. Sommerfield, *The Principle of Relativity*, New York: Dover, 1952, pp. 73–91.

Molnar, G. (2003) *Powers: A Study in Metaphysics*, S. Mumford (ed.), Oxford: Oxford University Press.

Morgan, C. Lloyd (1923) *Emergent Evolution*, London: Williams and Norgate.

Morrison, M. (2012) 'Emergent Physics and Micro-Ontology', *Philosophy of Science*, 79: 141–66.

Mumford, S. (2004) *Laws in Nature*, London: Routledge.

—— (2005) 'Kinds, Essences, Powers', *Ratio*, 18: 420–36.

—— (2009a) 'Passing Powers Around', *The Monist*, 92: 94–111.

—— (2009b) 'Causal Powers and Capacities', in H. Beebee, C. Hitchcock, and P. Menzies (eds), *The Oxford Handbook of Causation*, Oxford: Oxford University Press, pp. 265–78.

—— and Anjum, R. L. (2011) *Getting Causes from Powers*, Oxford: Oxford University Press.

Nagel, Ernest (1961) *The Structure of Science: Problems in the Logic of Scientific Explanation*, New York: Harcourt, Brace, & World.

Nerlich, G. (2006) Review of Brown's *Physical Relativity*, *Australasian Journal of Philosophy*, 84: 634–6.

Newman, D. (1996) 'Emergence and Strange Attractors', *Philosophy of Science*, 63: 245–61.

Newton, I. (1687) *The Principia: Mathematical Principles of Natural Philosophy*, I. B. Cohen and A. Whitman (trans.), Berkeley: University of California Press, 1999.

—— (1992) 'Philosophy of Space and Time', in M. Salmon, J. Earman, and C. Glymour (eds), *Introduction to the Philosophy of Science*, Englewood Cliffs: Prentice-Hall, pp. 171–231.

—— (2007) 'Causation as Folk Science', in H. Price and R. Corry (eds), *Causation, Physics and the Constitution of Reality*, Oxford: Oxford University Press, pp. 11–44.

Norton, J. (2008) 'Why Constructive Relativity Fails', *British Journal for the Philosophy of Science*, 59: 821–34.

Oderberg, D. (2007) *Real Essentialism*, London: Routledge.

Pais, A. (1986) *Inward Bound*, Oxford: Oxford University Press.

Pal, P. (2003) 'Nothing But Relativity', *European Journal of Physics*, 24: 315–19.

Pars, L. A. (1921) 'The Lorentz Transformation', *Philosophical Magazine*, 6th ser., 42: 249–58.

Paul, L. A. (2006) 'In Defense of Essentialism', *Philosophical Perspectives*, 20: 333–72.

Pauli, W. (1958) *Theory of Relativity*, New York: Pergamon.

Pauling, L. (1970) *General Chemistry: An Introduction to Descriptive Chemistry and Modern Chemical Theory*, 3rd edn, San Francisco: W. H. Freeman.

Penrose, R. (1987) 'Newton, Quantum Theory, and Reality', in S. Hawking and W. Israel (eds), *Three Hundred Years of Gravitation*, Cambridge: Cambridge University Press, pp. 17–49.

Poincaré H. (1905) 'On the Dynamics of the Electron', *Comptes Rendus*, 140: 1504–8, also in A. A. Logunov, *On the Articles by Henri Poincaré 'On the Dynamics of the Electron'*, trans. G. Pontecorvo, Dubna: Joint Institute for Nuclear Research, 2001.

Popper, K. (1957) 'Philosophy of Science: a Personal Report', in C. A. Mace (ed.), *British Philosophy in Mid-Century*, London: George Allen & Unwin, pp. 155–91.

—— and Eccles, J. (1977) *The Self and Its Brain: An Argument for Interactionism*, Dordrecht: Springer.

Psillos, S. (2002) 'Salt Does Dissolve in Water, but Not Necessarily', *Analysis*, 62: 255–7.

—— (2004) 'A Glimpse of the *Secret Connexion*: Harmonizing Mechanisms with Counterfactuals', *Perspectives on Science*, 12: 288–319.

Putnam, H. (1973) 'Meaning and Reference', *Journal of Philosophy*, 70: 699–711.

—— (1975) 'The Meaning of "Meaning"', in K. Gunderson (ed.), *Language, Mind and Knowledge*, Minnesota Studies in the Philosophy of Science VII, Minneapolis: Minnesota University Press, pp. 215–71. Also in H. Putnam, *Mind, Language and Reality: Philosophical Papers, vol. II*, Cambridge: Cambridge University Press, 1979, pp. 215–71.

—— (1977) 'Realism and Reason', *American Philosophical Association Proceedings and Addresses*, 50: 483–98.

—— (1980) 'Models and Reality', *Journal of Symbolic Logic*, 45: 464–82.

—— (1981) *Reason, Truth, and History*, Cambridge: Cambridge University Press.

Quine, W.V. (1951) 'The Two Dogmas of Empiricism', *The Philosophical Review*, 60: 20–43. Also in *From a Logical Point of View*, rev. edn, Cambridge MA: Harvard University Press, 1980.

—— (1953) 'Three Grades of Modal Involvement', in *The Ways of Paradox and Other Essays,* rev. edn, Cambridge MA: Harvard University Press, 1976, pp. 158–76.

—— (1960) *Word and Object*, Cambridge MA: MIT Press.

—— (1969) *Ontological Relativity and Other Essays*, New York: Columbia University Press.

Roberts, J.T. (2008) *The Law-Governed Universe*, Oxford: Oxford University Press.

Rueger, A. (2001) 'Physical Emergence, Diachronic and Synchronic', *Synthese*, 124: 297–322.

Russell, B. (1905) 'On Denoting', *Mind*, 14: 479–93, repr. in *Essays in Analysis*, London: Allen and Unwin, 1973: pp. 103–19.

—— (1912–13) 'On the Notion of Cause', *Proceedings of the Aristotelian Society*, 13: 1–26.

Salmon, N. (2005) *Reference and Essence,* 2nd edn, Amherst NY: Prometheus Books.

Salmon, W. (1989) 'Four Decades of Scientific Explanation', in P. Kitcher and W. Salmon (eds), *Scientific Explanation*, Minnesota Studies in the Philosophy of Science XIII, Minneapolis: University of Minnesota Press, pp. 3–219.

Schaffer, J. (2003) 'Is there a Fundamental Level?', *Noûs*, 37: 498–517.

—— (2004) 'Two Conceptions of Sparse Properties', *Pacific Philosophical Quarterly*, 85: 92–102.

Schlick, M. (1938) 'Form and Content: An Introduction to Philosophical Thinking', in *Collected Papers* 1, Dordrecht: Reidel.

Schrenk, M. (2010) 'On the Powerlessness of Necessity', *Noûs*, 44: 729–39.

Shoemaker, S. (1980) 'Causality and Properties', *Identity, Cause and Mind*, expanded edn, Oxford: Oxford University Press, 2003, pp. 206–33.

Sider, T. (2012) *Writing the Book of the World*, Oxford: Oxford University Press.

Silberstein, M. and McGeever, J. (1999) 'The Search for Ontological Emergence', *Philosophical Quarterly*, 50: 182–200.

Smith, M. (1994) *The Moral Problem*, Oxford: Blackwell Publishers.

Soames, S. (2007) 'What are Natural Kinds?', *Philosophical Topics*, 35: 329–42.

Sober, E. (1988) *Reconstructing the Past*, Cambridge MA: MIT Press.

Sosa, E. and Tooley, M. (1993) 'Introduction', in *Causation*, Oxford: Oxford University Press, pp. 1–32.

Spirtes, P., Glymour, C., and Scheines, R. (2001) *Causation, Prediction and Search*, Cambridge MA: MIT Press.

Stachel, J. (1995) 'History of Relativity', in L. Brown, A. Pais, and B. Pippard (eds), *Twentieth Century Physics* 1, New York: American Institute of Physics Press, pp. 249–356.

—— (2002) ' "What Song the Syrens Sang": How Did Einstein Discover Special Relativity?', in *Einstein from 'B' to 'Z': Einstein Studies* 9, Boston: Birkhäuser, pp. 157–70.

Strawson, P. (1997) *Entity and Identity*, Oxford: Oxford University Press.

Suppes, P. (1970) 'A Probabilistic Theory of Causality', *Acta Philosophica Fennica*, 24: 1–130.

Swinburne, R. (1980) 'Properties, Causation, and Projectibility: Reply to Shoemaker', in L. J. Cohen and M. Hesse (eds), *Applications of Inductive Logic*, Oxford: Oxford University Press, pp. 313–20.

Terletskii, Y. (1968) *Paradoxes in the Theory of Relativity*, New York: Plenum.

Thagard, P. (1978) 'Why Astrology is a Pseudoscience', in P. D. Asquith and I. Hacking (eds), *Philosophy of Science Association 1978* 1, East Lansing: Philosophy of Science Association.

Tobin, E. (2010) 'Crosscutting Natural Kinds and the Hierarchy Thesis', in H. Beebee and N. Sabbarton-Leary (eds), *The Semantics and Metaphysics of Natural Kinds*, New York: Routledge, pp. 179–91.

Unger, P. (1983) 'The Causal Theory of Reference', *Philosophical Studies*, 43: 1–45.

van Fraassen, B. (1989) *Laws and Symmetry*, Oxford: Oxford University Press.

—— (1995) 'Elgin on Lewis's "Putnam's Paradox" ', *Journal of Philosophy*, 92: 85–93.

—— (1997) 'Putnam's Paradox: Metaphysical Realism Revamped and Evaded', *Philosophical Perspectives*, 11: 17–42.

Vetter, B. (forthcoming) 'Dispositions without Conditionals', *Mind*.

Wiggins, D. (1980) *Sameness and Substance*, Cambridge MA: Harvard University Press.

—— (2001) *Sameness and Substance Renewed*, Cambridge: Cambridge University Press.

Wigner, E. (1972) 'Events, Laws of Nature, and Invariance Principles, in *Nobel Lectures: Physics 1963–1970*, Amsterdam: Elsevier, pp. 6–19.

—— (1979) *Symmetries and Reflections*, Woodbridge CT: Ox Bow Press.

—— (1985) 'Events, Laws of Nature, and Invariance Principles', in A. Zuchichi (ed.), *How Far Are We From the Gauge Forces*, New York and London: Plenum, pp. 699–708.

—— (1992) *Collected Papers of Eugene Paul Wigner* 3, Berlin: Springer.

Wilkerson, T. E. (1995) *Natural Kinds*, Aldershot: Avebury.

Williamson, J. (2009) 'Probabilistic Theories', in H. Beebee, C. Hitchcock, and P. Menzies (eds), *The Oxford Handbook of Causation*, Oxford: Oxford University Press, pp. 185–212.

Wilson, J. (2002) 'Causal Powers, Forces, and Superdupervenience', *Grazer Philosophische Studien*, 63: 53–77.

—— (2005) 'Supervenience-based Formulations of Physicalism', *Noûs*, 39: 426–59.

Wilson, Jessica M. (2007) 'Newtonian Forces', *British Journal for the Philosophy of Science*, 58: 173–205.

—— 'Non-Reductive Physicalism and Degrees of Freedom', *British Journal for Philosophy of Science*, 61: 279–311.

—— (forthcoming) *Metaphysical Emergence*.

Winnie, J. (1967) 'The Implicit Definition of Theoretical Terms', *British Journal of the Philosophy of Science*, 18: 223–9.

Woodward, J. (2003) *Making Things Happen: A Theory of Causal Explanation*, New York: Oxford University Press.

Worrall, J. (1989) 'Structural Realism: The Best of Both Worlds?', *Dialectica*, 43: 99–124.

Index

prominent policies in place to show that
you recognize the problems.

select Institutions — X — √. those institutions
where most poor
students go to.

Bkgd
cases - ego - consider how complete authority is
calif case
Affidavit   Rely on O'r drs - when t
purposed order   Sx's ~~and reasons~~, t your
                      responsible for care.

PAIN IS A sign, A Sx of what — try
to find some obj v. evidence of th caus

If ignored, or assigned a cause w/o
investigation, ~~that~~ does not fall under
the category of "scientific medical practice
"Art" is NOT drawing or doing painting — it
is the art of examing t acting on scientific
principles.

scientific
drgis supplied
available to
anyone the
practice.